Honor Your Anger

How Transforming Your Anger Style Can Change Your Life

Beverly Engel

JOHN WILEY & SONS, INC.

Published by John Wiley & Sons, Inc., Hoboken, New Jersey
Published simultaneously in Canada

For general information about our other products and services, please contact our Customer Care Department within the United States at (800) 762-2974, outside the United States at (317) 572-3993 or fax (317) 572-4002.

Wiley also publishes its books in a variety of electronic formats. Some content that appears in print may not be available in electronic books. For more information about Wiley products, visit our web site at www.wiley.com.

Library of Congress Cataloging-in-Publication Data:
Engel, Beverly.
    Honor your anger: how transforming your anger style can change your life / Beverly Engel.
        p. cm.
Includes bibliographical references and index.
ISBN 0-471-27316-3
    1. Anger. I. Title
        BF575.A5E54 2003
        152.4'7—dc21   2003005796

Printed in the United States of America

10   9   8   7   6   5   4

I dedicate this book to all the clients I've worked with who have struggled to find a way to honor their anger and at the same time to learn to express it in healthy ways.

Contents

Acknowledgments

My heartfelt appreciation goes to Tom Miller, my editor at John Wiley and Sons, for his continued support and expert editing. I feel so fortunate to have found such a talented editor and one who has such confidence in me. I am also continually grateful for my wonderful agents, Stedman Mays and Mary Tahan, whose talent, hard work, integrity, and enthusiasm continue to impress me.

I am indebted to all the anonymous people who shared their personal stories with me so that others could learn from their experience.

In the many years that I have studied anger I have learned from many people and many schools of thought. I owe the greatest debt of gratitude to the writings of Wilhelm Reich and Alexander Lowen, who taught me how anger affects the body and the mind, and the work of Chuck Kelly, Bioenergetics and the Radix Institute, who taught me to honor my anger. I also learned a great deal from the work of Dr. Lawrence LeShan, Manual J. Smith, and Robert E. Alberti. I have learned conflict resolution from many sources but particularly from the work of Arnold Mindell. I also wish to thank the Real Justice organization for their excellent Restorative Justice facilitator training.

I welcome your questions and feedback. You can e-mail me at: beverly@beverlyengel.com or write to: P. O. Box 6412, Los Osos, CA 93402.

Introduction

Everyone has issues and concerns about anger. Some people need help in managing anger that gets out of control; others need help in accessing buried anger. Some take anger that is meant for one person out on innocent people, while others take their anger out on themselves. Instead of confronting the people with whom they are angry, they become self-destructive in some way—by overeating or binge eating, smoking cigarettes, drinking alcohol or taking drugs, or relentlessly bombarding themselves with self-criticism. Others pretend they aren't angry but then get back at those who hurt or threaten them in indirect, often underhanded ways, such as gossiping, being sarcastic, or distancing themselves.

Unless you find healthy ways of owning and expressing your anger, it will find some outlet that might be inappropriate, unhealthy, or counterproductive. Anger can wreck havoc in your life and the lives of those around you unless you take charge of it.

You cannot avoid anger anymore than you can avoid conflict, yet many people believe that the ultimate indication of emotional health or enlightenment is to be anger-free. You won't hear any such message in this book. In *Honor Your Anger,* I will show you how to embrace anger. You will welcome it into your home and learn as much as you possibly can about it; for only by knowing your anger intimately can you gain control of it. For most of us, anger doesn't magically disappear just because we ignore it or decide we are not going to give it any credence. Instead, it either festers and grows stronger with each passing day or mutates into a distorted form of emotion that we can barely recognize.

Anger is a necessary and important emotion. It signals that something is wrong in a relationship, in your environment, or in yourself. When you ignore this signal, you cut yourself off from your other emotions. Unfortunately, even though we live in an age when we are far less repressed in many areas of life, including sexuality, we are no more tolerant of anger than our grandparents. In fact, although we may be freer to express passion, tenderness, or fear than our ancestors were, our tolerance of anger is actually declining.

Anger can create powerful changes in the world. It can be the catalyst for bringing atrocities to light, stamping out injustice, and creating new structures and systems to replace those that are corrupt or inadequate. Anger can empower those who have been tyrannized or victimized, imbuing them with the courage to stand up to their oppressors, to leave an abusive or tyrannical situation, and to stand on their own.

Anger can also create destruction. It can be the force behind war, long-term family feuds, and divorce. Words said in anger can sever the strongest of ties. Repressed anger from childhood can rear its ugly head and cause even the most loving parents to lash out at their precious children, continuing the cycle of abuse into a new generation. If you turn anger against yourself in the form of guilt and shame, it can eat away at your self-esteem to such an extent that it robs you of pride, motivation, and belief in yourself. Anger that has been held in and denied for years can fester until it bursts out unexpectedly—even causing someone to severely maim or kill another human being.

You would think that since anger has such potential for both good and bad, we would all know a great deal about it. From the time we are small children, we should all receive instruction on how to avoid unhealthy ways of releasing anger and suggestions and encouragement on how we can express anger in positive ways. Unfortunately, this isn't the case. We are discouraged from expressing our anger just as we are discouraged from showing the other so-called negative emotions such as fear, sorrow, guilt, and envy. Instead of being introduced to positive ways of coping with and expressing our anger and told about the positive ways that anger can be used to change our environment—and the world—we are given only half the story and told that anger is destructive and that we shouldn't feel it or express it. Like all children who try to mind their parents and their elders, we try to conform by repressing our anger. This only serves to turn healthy anger into unhealthy anger.

This book is about what happens when you aren't given permission to feel and express your anger. It is also about what occurs when you learn unhealthy ways of expressing your anger and how these unhealthy anger styles negatively affect your life and the lives of those around you.

Honor Your Anger is filled with innovative and practical tools that will empower those who act out their anger in negative ways to gain better control of their anger and their lives. But as aggression and violence in the family, in schools, and on the street continues, we must do more than learn anger management techniques. We need to explore the pain and shame underneath the anger and deal with an equally problematic part of the anger equation involving those who stand by while violence occurs. If you have submerged your anger out of fear or denial, *Honor Your Anger* will help to empower you so that you can begin to assert your anger in safe ways and to stand up for yourself and your children.

Underneath our anger, or our refusal to get angry, are core feelings that we need to unearth if we are to learn healthy ways of managing anger. *Honor Your Anger* will offer a program that will help readers who are stuck in anger and blame to go to a deeper level, uncover the reasons, and move past them.

In addition to learning how to handle anger in a healthier, more balanced way, we also need to learn how to put anger behind us. Instead of holding on to past resentments, ruminating on revenge fantasies, and distancing ourselves from others, we need to learn how to use anger to motivate and empower ourselves. In *Honor Your Anger,* readers will learn to communicate angry feelings in ways that will be heard and to resolve conflicts in ways that take into account each person's needs.

How *Honor Your Anger* Is Different from Other Anger Books

There are quite a few books available on anger, but most focus on helping those who are out of control or abusive learn to contain their anger or find healthy outlets for it. Although we certainly can't deny that those people create enormous problems for themselves, those close to them, and society at large, those who are unable to express their anger—either out of fear of consequences or because they are out of touch with themselves—pose an equal amount of problems. In this book, I will present the controversial thesis that those who withhold their anger can cause as many problems in relationships and in society as those who act out their anger inappropriately.

We all know there is a problem in our culture with violence in schools, work-related violence, gang violence, wife battering, child abuse, and violent crime, and that anger and rage lie at the core of these problems. Anger management has become a million-dollar industry, as have conflict resolution programs in schools and in the workplace. Companies pour millions of dollars into providing anger management courses for their employees. But few, if any, spend money on helping those who deny, suppress, or repress their anger. And while some books have pointed out to women that expressing their anger will help them to become more assertive and feel more confident, few make the point that women (and men) who submerge their anger actually *encourage* abuse and encourage others to act out their anger for them.

Honor Your Anger is not just another book on anger management. It is an in-depth look at how anger affects and even shapes our lives. It will encourage you to look deep inside to explore the roots of your anger. It will provide an opportunity for you to honestly evaluate what your anger says about you as an individual. And it will present alternatives to the old ways of thinking about anger and the customary methods of dealing with it.

Why I Wrote This Book

Anger has been of interest to me for a long time. For many years I've studied it, wrestled with it inside myself, and observed how my clients deal with it. I've noticed how anger is intricately tied in with other emotions—how it can mask feelings of vulnerability and pain, how some people need to express anger in order to get to the pain underneath, and how some need to express pain in order to get to the anger underneath. I've noticed how anger is often triggered by shame and how the way we express our anger can cause us shame. I've noticed how afraid many people are of their anger and how some seem to be oblivious to the fact that their anger frightens other people.

I've grown to know anger intimately not only through my practice as a psychotherapist but through my own personal work. When I first sought therapy in my mid-twenties, it was because I was deeply depressed. I would cry for hours and had difficulty leaving my home. I felt hopeless and helpless.

I knew that I had been sexually abused as a child, but I honestly thought I had put it behind me. In therapy I discovered that I was enraged at my abuser. I also discovered that I was enraged with my mother, who had been extremely emotionally abusive and neglectful of me. This rage felt so overwhelming and threatening that I was deathly afraid to touch it much less express it. Instead I chose to stuff my anger down with alcohol, food, and sex. And while I had allowed men to take advantage of me all my life, I had also taken my anger at my abuser and my mother out on these men by being overly demanding, distrustful, and accusatory.

It took many years of therapy with a supportive psychotherapist before I could own and honor my anger. Even then I was ashamed to express it in front of her. I tried going behind the couch where she couldn't see me to use the foam-covered bats that clients often use to express their anger in a safe way. But this didn't work either. Eventually

I began Neo-Reichian therapy (a body therapy with an emphasis on the physical release of emotions) to work past my fear and shame concerning my anger and to find ways to express my anger constructively. I found the support and the techniques that would help me tap into the deep pool of rage I had been carrying around most of my life. This work helped to empower me and to let go of what I came to realize was a victim mentality.

As so often happens, because I felt newly empowered and because I was determined never to be victimized again, I became the abuser in many of my relationships. I became extremely controlling because I still felt so out of control of myself. I still drank too much, and when I drank I became very critical of my partners, harassing them over and over with the same complaints. In essence, I had become my mother. It would take another round of therapy before I would be able to come to terms with my demons. This time the focus was on my shame and on my shadow, or dark side—that part of ourselves that we reject or deny in our attempts to be all good.

Throughout my life I have personally experienced every type of anger style I discuss in this book. I've expressed my anger directly and I've misdirected my anger. I've been both the victim and the abuser in my relationships. By focusing on my anger instead of hiding from it or running away from it, I've found that I have been able to develop an anger style that is assertive without being domineering or aggressive. I've learned when to express my anger and when to contain it. And I've learned to spot my anger in my projections, my depressions, and my conflicts with other people. In fact, the positive management of my anger has been one of my greatest accomplishments. Today I'm neither abusive with my anger nor do I allow others to abuse me with theirs. I become angry far less often, and when I do, I allow myself to feel and express the anger in appropriate ways. Most important, I learn from my anger. I learn what my anger is trying to tell me about myself, a situation, or another person. I learn what role I played in a conflict and how to avoid similar situations.

Overall, anger has served me well. It has motivated me to leave destructive relationships and it has been a guiding force behind my drive for success. It has helped me to fight some of my most difficult battles, including both my personal and professional battle against child sexual abuse. It has empowered me to take a stand on everything from child abuse to environmental issues.

I've also found that once I learned to channel my anger into creative endeavors, the misdirected anger that destroyed some of my relationships and the anger I turned on myself in the form of self-destructive behaviors was transformed into positive energy, inspiration, and insight. And I've learned that by having the courage to face how I have harmed other people with my anger, I've been able to let go of it and to forgive those who have harmed me. Because of this intensive personal work, the amount of studying I've done on anger, and the work I've done with my clients throughout the years, I believe I have a lot to share with you. I believe I have a unique perspective about anger and that I've even discovered some aspects of the subject that I've never read or heard about anywhere else.

In this book you will find that I do not talk down to anyone, even those who are guilty of abusive behavior. Instead I offer compassion and empathy and share accounts of my own struggles with my anger. This will give those of you who have been abusive with your anger permission to be as honest as possible about the negative effects your anger has had on others and will hopefully encourage you to continue struggling to overcome your destructive patterns, even when the going gets tough.

PART ONE

CHANGE YOUR ANGER STYLE, CHANGE YOUR LIFE

CHAPTER 1

One of the Most Important Changes You Will Ever Make

Laurie doesn't know why she explodes in anger so often. She'll be feeling perfectly fine when all of a sudden something or someone will trigger intense feelings of rage in her. Before she knows it, she's created havoc in her environment, upsetting everyone around her. The episode often lasts only minutes and her anger usually subsides for no apparent reason.

Rebecca never seems to get angry. Her family and friends marvel at how calm she remains, even when her husband, Carl, yells at her. But Rebecca has her own private ways of getting back at Carl for his abusiveness. She accidentally spills bleach on his favorite shirt, forgets to pick up his suit at the cleaners the afternoon of an important dinner party hosted by his boss, and often forgets to tell him when his mother calls.

Max often loses it with his children. He screams at them and shakes them really hard whenever they make a mistake, like spilling juice all over the new carpet. Max feels badly afterward, but he can't seem to control himself.

Rocky is supersensitive to criticism. If his wife says something to him that seems the slightest bit critical, he becomes enraged. How dare she insult him in this way! She needs to be punished! And that is what Rocky does. He sometimes rants and raves for hours, trying to make his wife feel as bad about herself as she made him feel with her comment. To anyone else it is clearly a case of overkill, but to Rocky his wife deserves to be brought to her knees.

Marcie is afraid of her own anger and she is always afraid others are going to get angry with her. Many of her conversations are prefaced with: "Don't get angry." "Don't get mad, but I'm going to be a few minutes late." "Please don't get angry, but I can't go with you like I said I would."

Tara doesn't know when she's angry. She's used food to avoid her feelings for so long that she's almost completely out of touch with what she is feeling at any given time.

Steven uses his anger to control others. Whenever things aren't going his way, he explodes and suddenly everyone gives in to him.

Janine is sweetness personified. She prides herself on the fact that she never gets angry and she seems to get along with everyone. But behind her constant smile and sweet words there is often a hint of sarcasm or contempt. Janine is angrier than she realizes.

Whenever something goes wrong in Roger's life, he immediately finds someone or something to blame. Instead of taking responsibility, he excuses his actions by saying that someone else "made him do it." Even when it is abundantly clear to everyone around him that he is responsible for the negative things in his life, Roger always feels like a victim.

Kate is a self-blamer. When someone gets angry with her, she tends to take on the blame instead of fighting back. She gets angry with herself for upsetting the other person and will often chastise herself mercilessly with negative self-talk.

Lily often assumes others are angry when they aren't, and her fear of others' anger sometimes creates the very situation she's trying to avoid. "Are you angry with me?" she'll ask if a friend or family member seems the least bit preoccupied or distant. Not trusting the answer, she'll sometimes press people again and again until they do get angry.

All of these people have unhealthy anger styles that are negatively affecting their life and the lives of those around them. While anger is a normal, healthy emotion, when you act out your anger in destructive or underhanded ways, or when you withhold anger and take in criticism or verbal abuse from others, then turn it against yourself, it can become a very negative emotion indeed.

When many people think of having a problem with their anger or having an unhealthy anger style, they think of having a bad temper or being unable to control their anger. But as you've seen from the examples above, there are many other unhealthy styles of anger. Some people express their anger too often or use their anger to control or manipulate those around them. Others don't express their anger often enough. Instead they harbor their anger, feeding it until it becomes a monster that contaminates their relationships. In this book, you'll learn that any extreme when it comes to anger can be problematic.

It is apparent that the misuse and abuse of anger has become a problem for people all over the world. The rate of child abuse continues to rise, there is an increase in cases of road rage, and sports violence is becoming more of a problem than ever, involving not only the fans of hockey and soccer games but now baseball as well. Clearly, many people need help when it comes to learning how to contain and control anger. But there are others who need help in learning how to express their anger—to let it out instead of allowing it to damage their health and their relationships or to distort their perceptions of others.

Anger can be a very complicated emotion. Those who appear to not have a problem with anger can actually be the ones who are in the most need of help. Essentially, you have a problem with your anger if

- You hurt others with your anger
- You hurt yourself with your anger
- You allow others to hurt you with their anger
- You are afraid to express your anger
- You never get angry
- You hold onto your anger and are unable to either forgive or forget
- You find sneaky ways of getting back at people instead of expressing your anger directly
- You are angry a great deal of the time
- You are out of control when it comes to your anger
- Your tendency to be negative, critical, or blaming is adversely affecting you, your family, your friends, or your coworkers
- Your way of expressing your anger leaves you feeling helpless and powerless
- Your way of expressing (or not expressing) your anger has jeopardized your job or damaged your career
- You don't know why you suddenly become angry
- You misdirect your anger (take your anger out on innocent people)
- Your anger is eating you up inside
- You continually get involved with angry, controlling, or abusive people
- You allow yourself to be emotionally or physically abused by someone else's anger
- You allow others to emotionally or physically abuse your children

If you are having any of these problems, this book will help you resolve them. You'll learn healthier ways of dealing with your anger and with the anger of others. You will learn how to create an anger style that is not only healthy but life-transforming. You will be encouraged to take on and practice an entirely different way of dealing with your anger than what is normal and automatic for you. This will initially feel like you are taking on an uncomfortable role. But we often need to step outside our comfort zone if we are to make real and lasting changes. The premise is that inside every critical, judgmental person is someone who is painfully afraid of being criticized or judged. Inside every passive, fearful person is someone who is incredibly angry. And inside every person who avoids anger is someone who is seething with anger inside.

How Your Anger Style Affects Your Life

Your anger style is the habitual way in which you handle your anger. While you may tend to manage your anger in different ways depending on the circumstances, most people develop certain patterns. From the way you express your anger toward your partner and children to the way you react to being cut off in traffic, your anger style affects literally every aspect of your life. The way you cope with and express your anger is one of the most telling things about you. It defines your personality, characterizes your relationships, affects your health, and can even influence your value system. Unfortunately, most people do not realize how much their lives are influenced and even shaped by their anger, nor do they realize just how powerful a force anger can be. Anger can motivate you to make needed changes in your life and the lives of others, or it can make you physically and emotionally ill. It can empower you and add vitality to your life, or it can sap your energy and poison your relationships. The way you handle your anger affects your physical and emotional health, self-esteem, motivation, and ability to defend yourself. Your anger style can affect your life in surprising yet profound ways. It not only determines how you react to stressful, painful, or anger-provoking situations but can influence your choice of partners, your interactions with loved ones, the way you raise your children, what you are willing to put up with in a relationship, and even how you express yourself sexually. Your anger style also affects your work performance and work relationships.

If you tend to act out your anger by blaming others, exploding in a rage, or venting your anger at those weaker than yourself, you may choose partners who deny their own anger or who tend to buy into the accusations of others and blame themselves. Conversely, if you deny your own anger or are afraid of your anger, you may be attracted to those who openly express theirs—even when that expression is abusive. It is as if your partners were acting out your repressed or suppressed anger for you.

Your anger style dictates how you react when your children disappoint you, make a mistake, or refuse to mind. Those with a controlling style of anger may punish their children in extremely harsh and insensitive ways, while those who have a more passive-aggressive style may turn a cold shoulder to their children, punishing them with silence or withdrawing love. Those who are afraid to express their anger in adult relationships may end up taking their anger out on their children either because they are less threatening or because a child's love tends to be unconditional.

Those who are controlling or explosive with their anger often create problems not only in their home life but in the work environment as well. They are often fired from jobs, passed over for promotions, or feared and hated by their employees. Those who are passive and fearful of anger often allow their coworkers or bosses to walk all over them. They become so afraid of making a mistake and angering others that they cannot perform at their peak. Others see them as inadequate or passive and don't trust them with important jobs. They are often made to be the scapegoats of coworkers who want to pass the buck and avoid taking responsibility for their own mistakes. And repressed and suppressed anger can thwart creativity and motivation.

Those who are aggressive or controlling with their anger can be insensitive to their mate's emotional needs. Some bulldoze their way in, insisting their partner have sex with them even if he or she is not in the mood or berating her if she doesn't give in. Some will even physically force a partner to have sex. Partners who deny their anger will often put up with such abusive behavior for years but begin to shut down sexually in the process. Few women, for example, feel like having sex after their partner has berated them for hours. Women tend to need to feel vulnerable and trusting in order to be ready for sex and few can feel that way after they have been verbally or physically attacked.

Men and women who are passive-aggressive often use sex as payback for real or imagined slights from their partner. Some feign a headache or other physical discomfort that keeps them from feeling sexual, and some develop various forms of sexual dysfunction, such as impotence or premature ejaculation in men and painful intercourse or an inability to have an orgasm in women.

EXERCISE: *How Is Your Anger Style Affecting Your Life?*

1. Even though you may not be clear at this point on what your specific anger style is, spend some time thinking about how the way you deal with your anger has affected your life.

2. Make a list of the negative physical, emotional, and behavioral consequences of the way you currently handle your anger.

Why We Need to Honor Our Anger

Like all our emotions, anger is a biological and psychological safeguard to ensure our survival. Biologically, anger is defined as a stress response to internal or external demands, threats, and pressures. Anger warns us that there is a problem or a potential threat. At the same time, it energizes us to face the problem or meet the threat and provides us with the power to overcome the obstacle. So, it is both a warning system and a survival mechanism.

Our first reaction to a perceived threat is fear. When we are faced with a threat to our survival, our nervous system prepares us to meet that threat by raising our defenses. This built-in defense mechanism is found in the sympathetic branch of the autonomic nervous system and is triggered by the release of the hormone adrenaline. Adrenaline helps by giving us an energetic boost, which in turn provides us with added strength and endurance to fight off our enemy or added speed in which to run from the enemy. This pattern of biological arousal is known as the *fight-or-flight response,* an involuntary mechanism shared with all other species.

Although it may not actually be a life or death struggle, we often feel threatened by the behavior or remarks of others; we experience a threat to our emotional well-being. When someone hurts or insults us (or someone we care about) by saying something inappropriate, disrespectful, or vicious, we become righteously angry.

Anger also helps us to defend our rights and therefore it often has a moral or ethical aspect to it. According to the *Random House Dictionary of the English Language: The Unabridged Edition*, anger is "a strong feeling of displeasure and belligerence aroused by real or supposed wrong." Those who are angry often have a strong sense of injustice, injury, and/or invasion.

Anger gets a bad rap because it is often erroneously associated with violence. But in reality, anger seems to be followed by aggression only about 10 percent of the time, according to Howard Kassinove, Ph.D., co-author of *Anger Management: The Complete Treatment Guide for Practice.* Used constructively, anger can help us restore our lost esteem, prestige, and sense of power and control over our life. It can help us to recover emotionally and restore our well-being.

The concept of constructive anger is gaining empirical support including evidence that it may have health benefits. Experts say that constructive anger can aid intimate relationships and improve work interactions and political expressions, including the public's response to the terrorist attacks on September 11, 2001. A study in *Psychological Science* by social psychologists Jennifer Lerner, Ph.D., Roxana Gonzalez, Deborah Small, and Baruch Fischoff, Ph.D., of Carnegie Mellon University, found that anger served an empowering function following the events of 9/11. The first part of the study, conducted nine days after the attacks, gathered baseline data on a representative sample of 1,786 people concerning their feelings about the attacks and their levels of anxiety, stress, and desire for vengence. The second part, conducted two months later, randomized 973 people from the original sample into a condition that primed fear and anger. People in the anger condition, for instance, elaborated on their feelings of anger following the attacks and viewed photos and listened to audio clips designed to provoke anger. Participants primed for anger gave more optimistic—and, as it turns out, realistic—risk assessments on twenty-five possible terrorist-related risks than those primed for fear. Anger is probably beneficial in this sort of context because it increases one's sense of control.

Your anger may signal that you are not addressing an important emotional issue in your life or in a relationship. It may be a message that your wants or needs are not being met, or it may warn you that you are giving too much or compromising too much of your values or beliefs in a relationship.

How We Turn Anger into a Negative Emotion

Anger is neither a positive nor a negative emotion. It is the way we handle our anger that makes it negative or positive. For example, when we use our anger to motivate us to make life changes or to make changes to dysfunctional systems, it becomes a very positive emotion. But when we express anger through aggressive or passive-aggressive ways (such as getting even or gossiping), it becomes a negative emotion. The following methods of dealing with anger cause the most problems both for the giver and the receiver.

Misplacing Anger

While anger can be a signal that something is wrong, often we do not take the time to discover exactly what the problem is. Instead we simply go with the anger and let it out on whoever is around us. Misplacing anger is when we take anger that is meant for one person out on another. We all misplace or misdirect our anger from time to time, sometimes consciously and sometimes unconsciously. Your boss bawls you out for being late again and you end up snapping at your coworkers; your husband criticizes the way you are managing money and you blow up at your teenage daughter for talking on the phone too long. We all need to curb our tendency to misdirect our anger in such ways and apologize to those we have hurt in the process. But when we misplace our anger on a regular basis, when we consistently avoid dealing with the people with whom we are really angry by discharging it on innocent people, it becomes a real problem.

Holding in Anger

It is also unhealthy when you take the anger that should be directed at someone else and turn it against yourself. Let's say someone criticizes you or falsely accuses you of something. What do you do? Do you remain quiet, believe what he or she is saying about you, and begin to feel bad about yourself? Or do you get angry and tell this person that you don't appreciate his criticism? If what he is saying isn't true, do you confront him with the truth or do you begin to doubt your own perceptions and believe his lies? In this case, anger held in can be very negative.

Becoming Abusive with Your Anger

Abusive anger is anger that is directed at someone else in an aggressive, hostile, or inappropriate way. For example, yelling at someone, name calling, throwing objects, and shoving or hitting someone are abusive ways of releasing anger. Verbal and emotional abuse (yelling, name calling, making demeaning or belittling comments, using sarcasm or making fun of someone) can be as damaging as physical abuse and often lead to physical abuse.

Many people don't know how to express their anger without attacking or belittling the other person. There is a big difference between verbal aggression ("You bastard," or "I'm going to knock the shit out of you!") and reporting your anger ("I'm so angry with you that I don't know what to do with myself").

Other forms of abusive anger include the "silent treatment"; dismissive, contemptuous looks; and threats of abandonment.

Holding on to Your Anger

Anger should be a temporary emotion that is relinquished once an issue has been addressed and resolved. Unfortunately, many people either choose to hold on to their anger, building up resentment or even hate toward the other person, or to continue to punish the other person for offending them in the first place. While a healthy person will communicate his or her anger in a way that others can understand, learning to let go and to forgive is also a sign of emotional health.

Using Anger to Avoid Other Feelings

In addition to anger being a signal that there is a problem, sometimes we become angry as a way of avoiding another feeling such as fear, sadness, guilt, or shame. Instead of allowing yourself to feel your sadness and grief over the loss of a relationship, you may choose to remain angry at the person who dumped you. Instead of feeling guilty for getting in a car accident while driving your friend's car, you may blame him for distracting you. Many people use anger as a defense against feeling afraid. They act tough so that they don't have to acknowledge their fear or so that others won't see just how vulnerable they really are.

Using Anger to Avoid Intimacy

Some people become angry or start a fight in order to create distance between themselves and another person. Let's say you and your partner have been spending a great deal of time together. You're beginning to feel a bit smothered. Instead of admitting this to yourself and explaining to your partner that you need a little space, you start a fight or get angry with him for some small thing he's done. That way you feel justified in walking out. When he calls later, you tell him you think it is better if you take a few days off from seeing each other since you aren't getting along. In reality, you wanted the space all along.

Getting Stuck in an Unhealthy Anger Style or Defense Strategy

While we all resort to some of the unhealthy ways of dealing with anger from time to time, many people get stuck in these anger styles to the point that they prevent the normal use of anger on a daily basis. Avoiders, for example, ignore the signal that something is wrong. Blamers can't let go of their resentments and aren't able to move on. Abusers won't or can't use their anger in moderation.

When you get stuck in an unhealthy anger style, you are unable to adapt to situations. Your rigidity forces you to respond the same way over and over again, even when your way of reacting gives negative results. Adaptive anger, on the other hand, enhances your ability not only to survive physically but to do so in a way that is harmonious with those around you.

Changing your anger style can be one of the most important changes you'll make in your life. In fact, it can literally change your life. This may sound like a rather grandiose claim, but I know it to be true in the lives of many of my clients throughout the years, as well as in my own life. Clients whose lives and the lives of their families were once nearly ruined by their inability to control their anger found ways to contain and control it and stop being abusive to their loved ones. And clients whose inability to express their anger assertively caused them to stay in abusive relationships were finally able to stand up for themselves and refuse to be abused again.

As I have shared in previous books and in the Introduction, I was emotionally and sexually abused as a child, so I grew up full of shame. This shame was so overwhelming that whenever I felt criticized, insulted, or rejected as an adult, I lashed out in a rage at those who triggered these feelings in me. I raved and ranted, sometimes for hours, trying to make the person who had hurt me feel as much shame as I was feeling. By learning that I could interrupt my rages by physically creating space between myself and the person with whom I was angry, I was able to stop this destructive behavior. I learned to take a time-out and walk off my anger, using the time and space away from the other person to connect with my feelings and discover what had triggered my anger. I could then return to the person and calmly discuss what had happened. Instead of carrying around more shame because of my inappropriate actions and experiencing one breakup after another, I eventually learned to talk about my shame with my partners, thus avoiding continual confrontations and outbursts. This is but one way that changing my anger style changed my life.

Instead of losing control and hurting those around you, you can learn to identify what triggers your anger and find appropriate ways of handling it. Instead of allowing others to dominate or abuse you with their anger, you can face your fear of anger and learn to defend yourself. You can learn to acknowledge your own anger and find assertive ways of speaking up for yourself—as opposed to pretending you aren't angry while quietly planning ways to get back at those who have hurt you, or taking too much criticism from others until you finally explode. Instead of controlling others with your anger you can find healthy ways of asking for what you need. Instead of taking your anger out on your spouse or children, you can begin to focus your anger where it belongs—whether it be on your boss, your parents, or a past relationship. You can learn to differentiate between the things you are responsible for and the things you are not and to push away the false accusations of others.

Changing your anger style can help you deal with the anger of your partner, your children, or your parents. Couples who read this book together will discover healthier ways of resolving conflicts and ways of expressing their anger that do not alienate them from one another. Parents will learn how to express anger and set limits without being controlling or abusive with their children and will be better equipped to handle both appropriate and inappropriate anger directed at them by their children. Those who have unresolved issues with their parents will learn how to stand up to controlling or abusive parents and to communicate their feelings and needs in such a way that their parents will be more inclined to hear them.

Once you are no longer a slave to your anger style, you'll find that you are free to express all your emotions in a healthier, more open way—including your feelings of love and joy. You'll feel better about yourself and your self-esteem will be higher. You'll find yourself less willing to put up with unacceptable behavior—whether it is from someone else or yourself. You'll also feel more energized and more creative. All the energy you once wasted by exploding against others and creating drama in your life can now be used in more positive ways. Those who once took in the anger of others and turned it into guilt and self-loathing will find themselves suddenly feeling lighter and far less depressed. And those who once denied their own anger may now find exciting outlets for it, including creative outlets such as painting, writing, or acting. Some may turn their righteous anger into political action. Those who have grown old prematurely by the heavy weight of their own unexpressed anger will feel younger and more vibrant as they rid themselves of anger from the past. And those who were locked in destructive or abusive relationships for years will be able to free themselves of this pattern and will find they are now attracted to healthier partners.

Changing your unhealthy anger styles into healthy ones can affect your physical health. For example, it has been well documented that there is a link between unhealthy anger expression (the use of obscenity, rudeness, or condescension) and cardiovascular disease in men, but recent research now indicates that the same holds true for women. Women who do not acknowledge anger or who are prone to high levels of anger are also vulnerable to headaches, stomachaches, asthma, arthritis, elevated blood pressure, insomnia, back pain, and obesity. Rates of diagnosed breast cancer are found to be higher in women who have openly expressed their anger only once or twice in their lives and in those who display frequent temper outbursts as compared to women who display less extreme expressions of their anger.

You would think that most of us would be aware of our negative anger styles and how they adversely affect us, but this is not the case. Anger styles are often habitual and unconscious, often taking root in early childhood experiences. What others may clearly see as a problem with your anger style may be invisible to you. And although we may be able to identify unhealthy anger styles in our partners, our parents, our children, and our friends, we often remain blind to our own. Throughout this book you will be provided with various questionnaires and exercises to help you determine your specific anger style. With this valuable information you will be better able to determine what changes you need to make to your anger style, which in turn will help you take charge of your anger and your life.

CHAPTER 2

The First Steps to Discovering Your Anger Style

Your overall anger style includes the way you tend to *experience, process, express*, and *communicate* your anger—in essence, how you feel and what you do when you get angry. In order to discover your particular anger style, you need to become more attuned to your anger, how your body responds to it, and how you cope with it once you feel it.

Let's start with how you experience anger. Some people experience anger physically as an overwhelming feeling that seems to take them over. Within seconds their body feels tight and hot and they feel that they will literally burst with emotion. Others don't feel much of anything. They are blinded by rage—they don't seem to feel their anger building up. Instead they immediately go into action by screaming, yelling, pushing, or hitting the person who angered them. Still others experience anger as an imaginary wall that comes up to protect them from someone who has hurt them.

And there are people who don't even know when they are angry. They are not able to identify the body signals that alert them to their anger. If you don't know you are getting angry, you don't have the opportunity to short-circuit your anger before it builds up to the point where you are out of control. If you don't know your body's anger signals, you may deny you are angry, even when others are keenly aware of it. When we become angry, we experience an increase in heart rate, blood pressure, and skin temperature, although the intensity and volatility differ from one person to the next. These bodily changes are usually imperceptible. How do you know when you are angry? What happens in your body? For example: Does your face become flushed? Does your jaw become tight? Do you tighten your shoulders? Do you get a splitting headache or does your stomach feel queasy?

In addition to physically experiencing anger, we experience it emotionally. Once you have become angry, you have an emotional reaction to your state of anger. You may feel empowered by it, afraid of it, or ashamed of it. For example, you may feel empowered by your anger because it overrides more vulnerable feelings such as fear or pain and allows you to stand up for yourself. You may be afraid of your anger because you believe that if you were to allow yourself to express your anger fully, you might bring harm to others or yourself. If you are ashamed of your anger, it is probably because you have already expressed it in inappropriate ways in the past or others have judged you harshly because of it. Some people actually feel angry at themselves for the way they deal with their anger—either because they aren't better able to stand up for themselves the way they know they should, or because they tend to lose control or make a fool out of themselves when they are angry.

We also experience anger mentally. For example, most people have rather strong feelings and opinions about whether anger is a positive or a negative emotion, so they judge themselves accordingly when they become angry.

EXERCISE: *How Do You Experience Your Anger Emotionally and Mentally?*

1. Take a few minutes to consider what you think about anger in general. Do you think anger is a good thing or a bad thing? Do you believe people have a right to become angry or do you think people should refrain from getting angry?

2. How do you feel about the way you tend to deal with your own anger? Do you feel afraid or ashamed of the way you have expressed your anger in the past? Do you feel angry at yourself for the way you express your anger, or because you haven't allowed yourself to get angry or stand up for yourself?

The way you process anger includes how rapidly you become angry, how long your anger lasts, and whether you honor your anger or turn it into another more "acceptable" emotion. (For example, women in general have not been given enough permission to get angry and so they often turn their anger into tears.) It also includes the way you monitor or don't monitor yourself when it comes to anger and the messages you tell yourself when you get angry, such as "I have a right to be angry. After all, he . . . ," "It's not okay to get angry no matter what she did to me," or "Don't show her you're angry—then she'll know she's getting to you."

QUESTIONNAIRE: *How Do You Process Your Anger?*

The following questions will help you to begin paying attention to how you process your anger. There are no right or wrong answers, just information that will help you define your anger style more clearly:

1. How quickly do you become angry? Does your anger build up slowly or does it come on suddenly?

2. Are you aware of your anger coming on?

3. How intense does your anger tend to be? If you were to rate it on a scale of 1 to 10, 10 being the highest, how would you rate the intensity of your anger?

4. Does your anger last long?

5. Do you allow yourself to become angry or do you try to talk yourself out of it?

6. Do you ever cry when you are really angry?

7. What messages do you tell yourself when you get angry?

The Many Ways of Expressing Anger

The way you express anger includes what you do with your anger energy once you begin to feel it or once you become aware of the fact that you are angry. When we generally think of the way people express their anger, we think of examples such as telling someone off, not speaking to someone, or perhaps punishing another person in some way. In the extreme, we think of pushing, shoving, hitting, or hurting someone else. We may get images of domestic violence, road rage, or teen violence. But there are many ways of expressing anger that are not so obvious. See if you can recognize any of these ways of expressing anger in yourself:

- Being critical of others

- Being impatient

- Gossiping about others

- Swearing a lot

- Assuming others are against you

- Seeing the worst in people

- Turning most of your conversations into debates

- Competing excessively in work or play

- Being a perfectionist

- Having difficulty getting along with people

- Giving condescending looks and comments

- Having difficulty relaxing

Men and women tend to express anger differently. In a survey of 1,300 people ages 18 to 90, Raymond DiGiuseppe, Ph.D., chair of the psychology department at St. John's University in New York, found that men scored higher on physical aggression and experiences of impulsivity dealing with their anger. They also more often had a revenge motive to their anger. Women, on the other hand, were found to be angry longer and be more resentful and less likely to express their anger compared with men. DiGiuseppe found that women used indirect aggression by "writing off" a higher number of people—intending to never speak to them again because of their anger.

Assignment. Spend a few moments thinking about the ways in which you generally express your anger. How does your anger style negatively affect your physical health, your relationships, and your work?

Anger-Out, Anger-In

Although it may seem overly simplistic for a complicated emotion such as anger, the truth is that when we feel anger we can basically do one of two things: we can either let it out (externalization) or keep it to ourselves (internalization). This concept is known as Anger-Out and Anger-In. Anger-Out is the external expression of anger and usually implies that anger is being used in a blaming or attacking way. Anger-In is when anger is experienced but not expressed. Accordingly, it has been my experience that very generally, there are basically two kinds of people: I call them Anger-Ins and Anger-Outs. While we may at times express our anger in both ways, most of us primarily operate out of one modality more than the other.

Ivan is the father of five children. To say that Ivan rules with an iron hand is an understatement. If his wife or one of his children makes a mistake, Ivan blows up. "What is wrong with you?" he'll yell, not caring where he is or who is listening. "How could you be so stupid?" He is the same at work. If one of his employees makes a mistake, he doesn't bother to discuss the problem or to explore ways to avoid making the mistake again. He just gets angry. And when he gets angry, he holds nothing back. He insults, yells, and humiliates the person who made him angry. Ivan is an Anger-Out.

Mary Ann is Ivan's wife. When Ivan explodes in anger, Mary Ann says nothing. She doesn't defend herself and she doesn't defend her children. She feels powerless to change the way Ivan is and she is afraid of him. So Mary Ann endures Ivan's blowups in silence. When he begins to barrage her with insults, she tightens her muscles and ducks her head as if she were enduring a storm. Mary Ann is an Anger-In.

The following questionnaire will help you decide if you are an Anger-In or an Anger-Out.

QUESTIONNAIRE: *Are You an Anger-In or an Anger-Out?*

1. Do you believe it is better to keep your anger to yourself?

2. Do you feel better after you've talked to someone else about what has angered you?

3. Do you normally try to talk yourself out of being angry?

4. Do you generally prefer to confront the person who angered you as soon as possible?

5. Do you think it is a sign of weakness to let someone know that he or she made you angry?

6. Do you often feel empowered by your anger?

7. Do you prefer to let bygones be bygones rather than confront someone who has hurt or offended you?

8. Are you unable to forgive and forget until you've expressed your anger toward the person who hurt you?

9. Would you describe yourself as someone who would do most anything to avoid an argument or fight?

10. Would you prefer to have it out with someone even if it involves an argument rather than having to sit on your feelings?

11. Do you tend to harbor bad feelings toward those who have hurt or angered you?

12. Do you get angry quickly but get over it just as quickly?

13. Do you often doubt whether you have a right to disagree or to be angry?

14. Do you feel you have a right to express your anger?

15. Do you sometimes get sick or depressed when there has been a disagreement between you and another person?

16. Have you found that physical exercise is a good way for you to blow off steam?

17. Would you rather just pretend to agree with someone rather than risk an argument?

18. Do you sometimes regret what you have said or done when you are angry?

19. Do you often refrain from getting angry because you are afraid of how the other person might react?

20. Do you tend to let off steam when you are angry without considering the possible consequences?

21. Do you believe some people think you are a pushover?

22. Do people tell you that you have a bad temper?

23. Are you afraid that if you were to begin to express your anger you might lose control?

24. Do you often feel out of control with your anger?

25. Do you find it difficult to find a way to release your anger?

26. Do you often raise your voice or scream when you are angry?

27. When someone has been critical of you, do you tend to believe the criticism and to berate yourself with it later on?

28. Do you feel that most people's accusations about you are false and that you need to defend yourself in order to protect your honor?

29. Do you tend to stay in relationships with angry, abusive people even though you would like to end them?

30. Have you ever ended a relationship when you were angry only to regret it later?

31. Are you afraid of physical anger or confrontations?

32. Have you ever gotten into trouble (at school, with the law, at work) because of your tendency to explode in anger?

33. Have you ever been physically abused by someone who was angry with you?

34. Have you ever become physically violent toward someone when you were angry?

If you answered yes to more than half of the odd-numbered questions, you are definitely an Anger-In. While there is nothing wrong with being an Anger-In, if you answered most of the odd-numbered questions in the affirmative you may need to strive for more balance. If you answered yes to many or most of the odd-numbered questions from number 15 on, your Anger-In style may be so extreme that it is causing you emotional and even physical harm.

If you answered yes to more than half of the even-numbered questions, you are almost certainly an Anger-Out. While there is nothing wrong with being an Anger-Out, if you answered most of the even-numbered questions in the affirmative you need to achieve more balance in your life concerning your anger. If you answered yes to many or most of the even-numbered questions starting with number 18, your Anger-Out style may be so extreme that it is causing problems in your life or causing you to endanger the safety of others.

Balance Is the Goal

How can you keep your anger from eating you up inside? On the other hand, how do you keep from spewing anger at everyone in your path and poisoning your relationships? Many people are uncertain about the way they should deal with their anger. Some overreact whenever they don't get their way; others suffer in silence. We are told it is better not to rock the boat and at the same time the squeaky wheel gets the grease. Some experts tell us to hold anger in, whereas others tell us to let it out. Who is right?

In addition to educating you about how your way of dealing with anger affects your life and the lives of those around you, another goal of this book is to encourage you to become more balanced by not going to extremes in either direction. Both extremes—Anger-In and Anger-Out—can create problems. Although neither Anger-Ins nor Anger-Outs are wrong in the way they deal with their anger, in the extreme anger externalized can turn into violence and anger internalized can cause depression, health problems, and communication difficulties. Anger-Ins and Anger-Outs can each benefit from observing how the other copes. Anger-Outs, especially those who tend to be abusive, can gain from learning to contain their anger instead of automatically striking back, and from learning to empathize with others and seek diplomatic resolutions to problems. Many Anger-Ins can benefit from acknowledging their anger and giving themselves permission to express it in appropriate ways instead of automatically talking themselves out of it, blaming themselves, or allowing others to blame them. Instead of always giving in to keep the peace, it would be far healthier for these people to stand up for their needs and beliefs.

Some of you may find that you are neither an Anger-In nor an Anger-Out but fall somewhere in between. This is good news. It is far healthier to be balanced in anger style than to be extreme in one direction or the other. Studies conducted by Catherine Stoney and her colleagues at Ohio State University show that when we examine people's anger expression on a continuum that ranges from people who always express their anger to those who always suppress their anger, those in the middle of the scale—called *flexible copers*—experience health benefits. For example, flexible copers might tone down their anger when having a conversation with their supervisors, but express their feelings more fully with their spouse. Compared with flexible copers, people who always vent or suppress their anger have significantly greater rises in blood pressure during a stressful event as well as higher cholesterol and higher levels of homocystine, an amino acid that's a risk factor for heart disease.

Part Two of this book contains a program that will help you modify your behavior, whether you tend to be an Anger-Out or an Anger-

In. If you tend to withhold your anger, you will learn specific ways to begin to release it safely and gradually. If you act out your anger, you will be instructed on how to begin to contain your anger and find other, more constructive ways of dealing with frustration, stress, fear, pain, and shame. Couples who represent both extremes are encouraged to learn from one another and to create a style of conflict resolution that takes into account each person's anger style and facilitates a more balanced style.

Assignment. Notice your Anger-In or Anger-Out style:

1.   For the next few days, notice each time you openly express your anger or hold your anger in. Don't make any judgments about it; just make a mental note each time you find yourself dealing with your anger in one of these two ways.

2.   Since some people vacillate between Anger-In and Anger-Out, depending on the situation, notice the circumstances in which you tend to express your anger directly and those in which you tend to withhold your anger.

Prescription for Change: Taking On the Opposite Style

In the introduction I wrote that one way of changing a troublesome anger style is to try expressing anger in the opposite way from the way you normally do. For example, if your natural tendency is to blow up over the slightest provocation, you need to learn how to contain your anger and discover what other emotions you might be feeling under the anger. If you normally hold in your anger due to the belief that you will alienate others if they were to know your true feelings, you need to take the risk of expressing how you honestly feel. If you tend to hold grudges or look for ways to exact revenge against those who anger you, you need to practice more direct ways of expressing your anger and ways to gain compassion for the mistakes and shortcomings of others. The following exercise will help you begin this process:

- If you normally hold your anger in, try letting it out. It may seem uncomfortable or even frightening, but try doing it a little at a time. If someone is inconsiderate or rude to you, risk telling him or her how it made you feel or that you didn't appreciate the way he or she treated you. If you tend to talk yourself out of your anger, telling yourself that you don't want to make waves, try telling yourself that it is okay to make waves sometimes and risk letting people know how you really feel.

- If, on the other hand, you tend to always let your anger out, try holding back and see what happens. It may feel like you are going to burst, but you won't. And you may find that your anger subsides on its own and that you avoided an argument or confrontation in the process.

- Pay attention to how you feel each time you practice this new way of dealing with your anger. Although it will undoubtedly be uncomfortable initially, notice what other feelings come up as you try on this new anger style. For example, Anger-Ins who practice letting their anger out often discover that they feel energized by the process or that they feel more confident and self-assured. On the other hand, some feel guilty about expressing their anger and feel worse about themselves. Anger-Outs who try containing their anger often feel frustrated initially since they are used to releasing tension and anxiety by blowing up at others. Others report feeling proud of themselves for avoiding an argument or for saying things they would regret later on.

- Keep a log or diary of each time you try on another anger style. In addition to recording the incident, record your feelings surrounding the incident and the end result.

- Even if it is uncomfortable, continue practicing your new style for at least a week. Take small risks at first, then venture to take even larger risks. For example, if you are an Anger-In, you may start by letting a rude stranger know you don't appreciate how he treated you. This may make you feel so empowered that you are willing to tell a co-worker that you don't want to be treated a certain way. By the end of the week, perhaps you will be ready to tell your husband when you are angry with him. If you are an Anger-Out, at first you may only be able to contain your anger when you experience a small offense. But as you continue to practice, you may discover that you are willing to let even a large offense go by in the interest of peace and feeling better about yourself.

CHAPTER 3

Discovering Your Primary Anger Style

Your Communication Style

Our communication style is an important aspect of the way in which we express our anger. In addition to having a primary way of expressing our anger energy (Anger-Out, Anger-In), we also have a primary way of communicating our feelings of anger to other people. Some people communicate their anger in a direct, forthright manner whereas others tend to couch their anger in sarcasm or jokes or by giving the silent treatment. Some communicate their anger in the moment whereas others tend to allow their anger to stew, letting it out later when the other person least expects it or not letting it out at all but allowing it to create distance in the relationship.

The way we choose to communicate (or not communicate) our feelings of anger to others is often closely related to the way we communicate in general—the way we express our needs, desires, and concern to others. Many years ago communication experts identified four communcation styles: passive, aggressive, passive-aggressive, and assertive.

Passive. People with this communication style avoid conflict or confrontation at all costs. Such individuals do not tend to express their needs and feelings. They have a difficult time saying no without feeling guilty and will avoid hurting others because it makes them feel guilty. They also avoid making others angry so that they can avoid feeling uncomfortable or fearful.

Aggressive. These individuals need to be in control—of themselves, other people, and situations. They do not take no for an answer and use hurt and anger to manipulate others into feeling guilty or backing down. Aggressive people use sarcasm, humiliation, put-downs, complaints, threats, and abuse to get what they want.

Passive-aggressive. These people want to get even and use trickery, seduction, and manipulation to get their way. Usually not as open as aggressive types, those who are passive-aggressive are often nice to your face and use behind-the-back techniques to get even. They attempt to gain control or get their way by using silent treatment, withdrawing affection and attention, gossiping, tattling, and refusing to cooperate. When asked what is wrong, they often say, "oh, nothing," even though their body language or their behavior is clearly stating that there is something wrong.

Assertive. These people state their needs in a direct, open, and honest way and don't wait for others to read their mind. At the same time, they take into account the needs and feelings of others. They are true to themselves and expect others to treat them with respect and dignity. They feel responsible for their own life and destiny and tend to take charge of a situation.

While working on this book it occurred to me that there was a communication style that was missing from all the materials I have read on communication and assertiveness. From my many years of working with clients I have identified a fifth communication style: projective-aggressive.

Projective-aggressive. Those with this communication style are seemingly passive individuals who get others to act out their anger for them. Like those with a passive-aggressive anger style, projective-aggressives are actually not passive at all. They are very angry, aggressive people who are afraid to own and express their anger. Instead they project their anger onto other people.

Which of these communication styles describes you the best? Everyone has components of each within their personality and your style of communicating may vary depending on the circumstances, but overall it is safe to say that most of us take on one communication style over the others.

How does your communication style connect with your anger style? The way we communicate our anger is one aspect of our overall communication style and vice versa—our communication style is one aspect of our anger style.

For years those in the communication business have touted the assertive style as the optimum, and for good reason. Assertive behavior is far superior to aggressive, passive, or passive-aggressive behavior. Stating our feelings and preferences directly, openly, and clearly instead of silently punishing others for hurting us or passively manipulating others into doing our bidding not only feels better to everyone concerned but produces better results. But when it comes to anger style—the way we cope with and communicate our angry feelings—assertiveness is not the only positive, constructive way of expressing ourselves. Assertiveness is an Anger-Out mode. Since Anger-Out is not inherently superior to Anger-In, what would be a positive Anger-In mode that would correspond to assertiveness?

> *Reflective.* When we are reflective, we allow ourselves to feel our initial anger at a situation or person but refrain from acting out our anger. We give ourselves time to calm down (however long that takes), then we think about why the situation occurred, what we can learn from it, and what steps we wish to take to prevent it from occurring again. This may or may not involve communicating our feelings and needs to others in an assertive way.

Assertiveness and reflectiveness are healthy anger styles that represent the optimum ways to cope with anger. When we are assertive, we let people know when we do not like something in a very direct way.

We do not blame; we do not whine; we simply state our grievance in a calm yet forceful manner. When we are reflective, we allow ourselves to feel our emotions but then thoughtfully analyze the situation to better learn from it. We don't rationalize or make excuses for the other person's behavior and we don't blame ourselves, but we look at the situation in a fair, open-minded way in order to see both sides of the situation more clearly. If there is something we need to communicate to the other person, we are in a much calmer frame of mind to do so.

While the terms *passive, aggressive, passive-aggressive,* and *assertive* have been used for years to describe specific communication styles, we are also going to use them to describe the primary anger styles. The terms *reflective* and *projective-aggressive* will be added to fill in the gaps in order to describe the full picture of how we experience, process, express, and communicate anger.

Later on we will explore ways of exchanging your present, less healthy anger styles for an assertive or reflective anger style. For now, let's focus on further identifying the unhealthy anger categories: aggressive, passive, passive-aggressive, and projective-aggressive.

The Aggressive Anger Style

If you operate mostly out of the aggressive anger style, you tend to express your anger in a direct but forceful way. You assume you have a right to be angry and to express your anger, and you tend to impose your anger on any situation or person without reservation. Your anger seems to take precedence over anything else that is happening and you don't seem to pay much attention to what anyone else is feeling at the time. If you are like most people who operate from this modality, you tend to insist that other people change or that other people take responsibility for making you feel angry. This is often done in a loud, blaming, attacking, or otherwise forceful way.

If your primary style of anger is aggressive, you tend to believe in getting what you want, even if it means that others get hurt in the process. No matter what the situation, you tend to react aggressively. You're not going to let anyone push you around—that's all there is to it.

To some people, Dana may seem to be a very assertive woman who is very much in control of herself. She is a popular middle school teacher who is active in the PTA and many other community organizations. She is a single parent with two teenage girls.

But Dana is far more aggressive than she is assertive. When things don't go her way, she demands to be heard and isn't satisfied until she feels she has gotten her point across. This often leaves those around her feeling exhausted and battered by her words. She is extremely sensitive to rejection, and when her daughters don't seem to appreciate what she has done for them, she feels unloved and becomes enraged. She accuses them of being selfish brats. She reminds them of all she does to help them. She threatens to take all their privileges away until they can learn to appreciate her. When it has blown over, she feels horrible and regretful, but this won't stop her from going on another rampage the next time she feels rejected or unappreciated.

The Passive or Avoidant Anger Style

The passive or avoidant anger style is the exact opposite of the aggressive style. If you operate mostly out of this style, you are bent on avoiding feeling angry. You may have cut off your angry feelings for so long that you no longer know when you are angry, or you may feel you don't have a right to be angry. You may be afraid of becoming angry out of fear of retribution, fear of losing control, or fear of alienating others. If you are like most people with this anger style, you tend to be overly concerned about what other people think and don't want people to think of you as an angry person.

In addition to wanting to avoid becoming angry, you may also want to circumvent conflict at all costs. Instead of stating an opposing opinion or standing your ground, you will pretend to agree, hold your tongue, or go along with things to which you are really opposed. Unfortunately, these strategies don't really work in the long run. Not speaking up for yourself eventually makes you angry at yourself. You begin to feel like a phony and grow to have contempt for yourself for being so dishonest.

You may become increasingly angry with others because you feel so controlled by them. Over time your unexpressed anger builds up, damaging your self-esteem and eventually causing you to blow up and say things that may irreparably damage your relationships. Horrified at your behavior, your belief about anger is now validated. It is bad to become angry. See what happens when you do?

Like many people with the passive anger style, Tara witnessed her parents fighting constantly and was made to endure the tirades and explosive episodes of an extremely abusive father. Because of this she vowed to never become like her father. The way she felt she could guarantee this was to never become angry. In one of our sessions she said, "I'm terrified of unleashing my anger and hurting someone. I become angry sometimes, but I hold it in. I have nightmares about blowing up and hurting people."

The Passive-Aggressive Anger Style

You have no doubt heard the phrase *passive-aggressive* before. It is a psychological term used to describe a defense mechanism involving indirect resistance to authority, responsibility, and obligations. Associated symptoms include complaining, irritability when faced with demands, and general discontent.

Many people mistakenly believe that someone who is passive-aggressive swings from one extreme to the other. But if you are passive-aggressive, you aren't passive one day and aggressive the next. Rather, you are simultaneously passive and aggressive. In spite of this duality, you will deny your aggressiveness—even to yourself. You may be completely convinced that you seldom become angry in spite of the fact that others experience you as a hostile person. You may see yourself as a nice person who is passive, agreeable, and cooperative, yet others, especially your partner, will experience you as difficult and resistant.

If you are passive-aggressive, you shy away from direct confrontation because you fear the challenge or the loss of support that may result. You don't believe you can handle an attack from the other person, so denial and avoidance seem to be the only alternative.

You pretend to be passive when you aren't that way at all. Underneath your apparent passivity lies aggression, which often arouses anger from others. Unlike the person with a passive anger style who poses no challenge and rarely elicits aggression in others, passive-aggressive people constantly irritate and provoke others because they give off little hints of their hostility.

Anger and hostility are at the core of passive-aggressiveness, even though they are usually denied, submerged, or labeled something else. If you have a passive-aggressive anger style, you usually express anger indirectly via resistance, delays, losing things, procrastinating, and sabotaging your own efforts or those of others. You may intentionally set out to irritate others or to oppose authority, in the manner similar to a rebellious teenager.

The passive-aggressive anger style is common with teenagers and people who are under the control of others. Women are often identified as using passive-aggressive forms of anger expression more than men, but there are as many men who feel dominated and controlled by others including their bosses at work or their female partners. The passive-aggressive individual is trying to achieve autonomy, albeit in an indirect way.

Even though passive-aggressors hate to be ordered around, it is common for them to become attracted to controlling people and vice versa. It is also common for them to get into serious conflicts with controlling people.

The passive-aggressive style of anger is most often expressed in intimate relationships and is frequently manifested by refusing to give a partner what he or she wants. For example, feeling pressured to perform sexually, a male partner may suffer from impotence. Or, if a woman is angry (unconsciously or consciously) with her partner for the way he acted at a party, she may become distant and aloof on the way home and remain that way for a few days. When a child is rude or acts out, instead of confronting or punishing him, an angry parent may tell the child no when he later asks for permission to go to a friend's house.

Genevieve is a passive-aggressive parent. She hates conflict and desperately wants her children to love her, so when they talk back to her or refuse to mind her, she just lets it go. Or at least it may appear this way on the surface. In reality, Genevieve gets back at her children for not minding her by forgetting to tell them when a friend calls, by subtly making comments to make them doubt themselves, or by changing her mind about taking them to an event. When her children confront her on her behavior she acts as if she doesn't have the vaguest idea what they are talking about and assures them that she is not the slightest bit angry with them.

The Projective-Aggressive Anger Style

If you have a projective-aggressive anger style, you are bent on avoiding, denying, or withholding your anger. The primary way that you accomplish this task is by projecting your anger onto other people. Projection is an unconscious defense mechanism employed to relieve feelings of anger, anxiety, pain, or shame. It is a way to deny your own unpleasant traits, behaviors, or feelings by attributing them to someone else.

If you believe that anger is an emotion that should be avoided at all costs, you may refuse to allow yourself to get angry or to acknowledge your anger. So what happens when you begin to feel anger? You must get rid of it as soon as possible. What better way than to put your anger off onto someone else? One of the most common ways this occurs is by accusing someone of being mad at you when it is actually you who is angry. Remember, this is usually an unconscious process, so you may not even be aware that you were angry in the first place. That's how defense mechanisms work.

This is the case with Tanya. She is unaware that she is angry with her husband. Instead she starts to think that he is angry with her. He seems to be acting distant and she feels criticized by a comment he made to her. She asks him if he is angry and he tells her he is not. But somehow she doesn't believe him. She asks him again. He once again says he isn't angry but sounds a bit impatient with her this time. When she accuses him of being angry because of his tone, he finally does get angry and tells her to leave him alone. This confirms to Tanya that she was right all along about her husband being angry with her.

Most often a projection of this kind comes entirely from the person's imagination. But sometimes a projection can be an exaggeration of something that has a basis in reality. So, for example, your partner may be a little irritated with you in the first place, but you accuse him of hating you.

Projection can also have another purpose. Many people fear that if their partner or other loved one finds out who they really are, they will be abandoned. They live in constant fear of being "found out." Projecting their so-called negative traits and feelings, such as anger, onto other people is a way to maintain the perfect image they've worked so hard to create.

Those with the projective-aggressive anger style are also good at getting others to act out their anger for them. Mary is feeling angry at her children because they are being loud and disruptive while she is trying to have a conversation with a friend who has come for a visit. She is embarrassed by how her children are acting in front of company. Mary quietly asks her children to calm down instead of firmly and assertively telling them to stop. The children don't stop but continue to interrupt, argue with one another, and make loud noises. Mary becomes increasingly angry but dares not show it or even acknowledge it to herself because she has a strong investment in being seen as a good parent. Instead she rolls her eyes, sighs, and looks around anxiously. Her friend, feeling Mary's unspoken anger and the tension in the room, finally speaks up: "Your mother and I are trying to have a conversation, but we can't hear ourselves think. You're being rude. Quiet down!"

The children, dumbfounded, quiet down immediately. Mary's youngest child begins to whimper. Mary comforts her and looks at her friend as if to say, "Look what you did." She makes some excuse for having to cut their visit short and thinks to herself that she's not so sure she wants to have her children exposed to such an angry, hostile person.

Like the person with a passive-aggressive anger style, those with a projective-aggressive style often elicit anger in others because their behavior can be very irritating. They can be maddeningly passive to the point that you want to shake them into making a decision or coming right out with what they are feeling instead of beating around the bush.

If you have the projective-aggressive style, you probably complain quite often to family and friends about someone who is mistreating you. Your friends and family will no doubt urge you to stand up for yourself, but you still can't seem to do it. Over time, friends and family will likely become angry at the person who is mistreating you, but surprisingly, you are still unable to get angry. In essence, you have gotten your friends and family to get angry for you.

If you are a projective-aggressor, you will not usually initiate an aggressive action against another person, but once someone becomes angry with you, it may activate the deep reservoir of anger that you carry around inside yourself. Once this reservoir is tapped, it may open the floodgates of rage. Not only will you release appropriate anger concerning the present situation but all the anger you have been storing up against other people and from other events will come forth. In some ways it may seem as if you were just waiting for an excuse to release your anger.

EXERCISE: *Scenarios*

Many of you have been able to identify your primary anger style from the descriptions I've given. But others may be having more difficulty. The following scenarios may help. Be as honest as you possibly can with yourself. You may know ahead of time that a particular choice may not be the most constructive way of dealing with the situation, but pick the way in which you would most likely react under the circumstances or the way you have reacted in the past.

Scenario 1

You are standing in line at the supermarket when someone cuts in front of you. How do you respond?

1. Push the person out of the way and step back in front of him or her.

2. Yell to the cashier, "Will you tell this creep to go to the end of the line?"

3. Do nothing out of fear of what the person might do if you were to say something.

4. Remove one of his items on the conveyer belt when he isn't looking and hide it on a shelf near the cashier.

5. Complain to the people in back of you until someone else gets mad and causes a scene.

6. Tell the person, "I was here first. Please get behind me."

- If you selected answer 1, you chose an aggressive way of dealing with the situation. Pushing the other person out of the way is obviously an aggressive act and really unnecessary. The same result could have been accomplished by choosing answer 6.

- If you picked answer 2, you also chose an aggressive style. By telling the person to get behind you in an assertive manner, you could have avoided insulting him or her in front of others and causing a scene.

- If you selected answer 3, you chose a passive way of dealing with the situation. By not speaking up for yourself, you allow other people to walk all over you, and you'll probably feel bad about yourself or angry with yourself for not saying something.

- If you opted for answer 4, you chose the passive-aggressive way of dealing with the person. Instead of standing up for yourself in an overt, assertive way, you passively and maliciously got back at him for cutting in line. You avoided a confrontation but chose the coward's way out.

- If you chose answer 5, you opted for a projective-aggressive way of dealing with the situation. By complaining to others and getting them to act out your anger for you, you may have avoided having to directly confront the person who cut in front of you, but the scene you caused would undoubtedly be upsetting to everyone, including yourself.

- If you picked answer 6, you chose the most assertive way of dealing with the situation. Sure, it required a risk on your part, but you stood up for yourself without insulting or embarrassing the other person and probably avoided a confrontation.

Scenario 2

Your friend is beginning to get on your nerves. She's very controlling. She always needs to have things her way and she seems to think that her way of doing things is always the right way. What do you do?

1. Stop calling her and stop returning her phone calls.

2. Tell her she's a control freak and you can't stand being around her anymore.

3. Accuse her of being mad at you.

4. Gossip about her to your other friends.

5. Tell her you'd like to have a serious conversation with her, then honestly share your feelings with her.

- If you selected answer 1, you chose a passive anger style. You avoided having to directly confront your friend, but you missed an opportunity to express your true feelings.

- If you selected answer 2, you opted for an aggressive anger style. Insulting your friend and ending the relationship is an extreme and hurtful way to handle the situation.

- If you chose answer 3, you selected a projective-aggressive anger style. By accusing her of being mad at you, you avoid having to face your own anger.

- If you opted for answer 4, you chose a passive-aggressive anger style instead of directly confronting your friend. Gossiping and starting rumors is a very hostile thing to do.

- If you chose answer 5, you selected an assertive anger style since you chose to directly confront the issue rather than blaming your friend or becoming aggressive.

Scenario 3

Your adolescent son is becoming a real smart aleck. He continuously mouths off to you, especially in front of his friends. Your feelings are hurt, but you're angry too. What do you do?

1. Threaten to bash his head in the next time he talks back to you.

2. The next time he mouths off to you in front of his friends, make fun of him in a way that you know will really hurt and embarrass him.

3. Tell him that you expect him to treat you with respect and that talking to you that way is unacceptable.

4. Keep quiet but roll your eyes and sigh a lot whenever you are around him.

5. Tell your spouse how hurt you are about your son's behavior even though your spouse has become emotionally or physically abusive with him in the past.

6. Keep quiet and blame yourself for not raising a son who respects you more.

- If you selected answer 1, you probably have an aggressive anger style, since even threats of violence are inappropriate and destructive.

- If you selected answer 2, you also chose an aggressive anger style. Mocking someone in front of others is emotionally abusive.

- If you opted for answer 3, you selected an assertive way of handling the situation. If this is generally the way you deal with situations, you probably have an assertive anger style.

- If you chose answer 4, you may have a passive-aggressive anger style since this type of behavior is particularly characteristic of this style.

- If you selected answer 5, you chose a projective-aggressive way of handling your anger. Instead of admitting your anger toward your son, you had your spouse act out your anger for you.

- If you opted for answer 6, you may have a passive anger style, which is characterized by holding in your anger and blaming yourself for someone else's behavior.

Scenario 4

Your husband (or wife) doesn't seem to appreciate anything you do for him. He seems to take it for granted that you'll go out of your way to do kind things for him and he hardly ever reciprocates. You're feeling taken for granted. What do you do?

1. Keep quiet about it because you know that it will only start an argument if you say something.

2. Tell him he's an ungrateful asshole who doesn't deserve a wife who cares about him.

3. Stop doing anything nice for him.

4. Complain about him to your mutual friends and family.

5. Tell him how you are feeling and how you are afraid it might permanently affect your feelings for him.

6. Start an argument about something else and try to push him into saying something horrible to you, or perhaps even push him into being physically aggressive with you. Then use his hurtful words or actions as a reason not to do anything nice for him again.

- If you chose answer 1, you may have a passive anger style, since you seem to want to avoid conflict and confrontations at all costs.

- If you opted for answer 2 or 3, you may have an aggressive anger style, since both of these choices are abusive, punishing actions.

- If you chose answer 4, you may have a passive-aggressive anger style, since bad-mouthing your partner to family and friends is an underhanded way of dealing with your anger.

- If you selected answer 5, you chose an assertive way of handling the situation. By honestly sharing your feelings and concerns with your partner instead of threatening or punishing him, you opened the door to positive communication.

- If you selected answer 6, you may have a projective-aggressive anger style. Instead of owning your anger, you pulled anger out of your partner, then used it to justify punishing him.

Your Anger Style Can Vary

You may find that your primary anger style changes depending on the situation or the person with whom you are interacting. You may have an aggressive style with one type of person and a passive style with another type. My client, Cheryl, explained her situation this way:

"I communicate my anger in a very assertive way with my friends and coworkers, but with my husband and my boss I become very passive. When either my husband or boss confront me about something, I take what they say to heart, even if I initially disagree with them. I feel more intimidated by them, and for some reason I seem to trust their judgment more than I do my friends and coworkers. Maybe it's an issue with authority figures—I don't know. If I respect someone and have them on a pedestal, I can't seem to get angry with them no matter how unfair or unreasonable they are."

It is quite common for people to practice an aggressive style with their mates and children and a passive or passive-aggressive style with everyone else. This is especially true of men who are abusive to their wives, as my client, Roger, will attest:

"When my boss complained about my work, I used to just swallow my anger and keep quiet. Then when I got home, I'd take my anger out on my wife. All she had to do was look at me wrong and I'd explode. I did it because I knew I could get away with it and because I hated myself for being such a coward at work."

Assignment. Describe how your anger style varies depending on the person and the situation.

Prescription for Change: Getting Feedback

Sometimes getting feedback from others will help you determine your basic anger style. We are often not objective about how we communicate or don't communicate our anger, but a trusted friend or partner can offer nonbiased feedback.

Assignment

- This week ask at least two people to describe to you how they see you dealing with and communicating your anger.

- Write down the feedback you receive from others so that you can refer to it later in case you conveniently forget what was said.

CHAPTER 4

Variations on a Theme: Discovering Your Secondary Anger Style

Everyone with a particular primary anger style does not act exactly the same. For example, although there are certainly many similarities among those with the aggressive anger style—namely that they tend to act out their anger versus holding it in and that they tend to express their anger in a rather aggressive manner—there are also some differences. The same is true for the other unhealthy anger styles—passive, passive-aggressive, and projective-aggressive. I have named these style variations according to their characteristic behaviors. For example, those whose primary anger style is aggressive tend to either be eruptors, ragers, blamers, controllers, or abusers. Those whose primary anger style is passive tend to be deniers, avoiders, stuffers, or self-blamers. Those with the primary anger style of passive-aggressive tend to be anger sneaks, escape artists, sulkers, or pretenders. And those with a projective-aggressive style tend to be ventriloquists, innocent victims, or anger magnets.

Variations on the Aggressive Anger Style

If you have determined that your primary anger style is aggressive, the following questionnaire will help you decide what variation on the aggressive anger style best describes you.

QUESTIONNAIRE: *What Is Your Secondary Anger Style?*

1. Do you often have outbursts of anger that catch you off-guard?

2. Do you often lose your temper and say or do things you regret later on?

3. Are you often totally unaware of the reasons for your anger?

4. Do you often become angry with your partner or your children for no apparent reason only to have your anger subside as mysteriously as it came upon you?

5. Have you ever been surprised at the fact that others have told you how frightened they were of you because of an angry outburst since you don't remember any such thing?

6. Have you tried to control your anger but have been unsuccessful?

7. Does anger seem to be an automatic response for you?

8. Are you extremely sensitive to criticism?

9. Do you feel so bad about yourself that you assume others must feel the same about you?

10. Do you tend to become extremely angry (enraged) when others make fun of you or point out your faults or shortcomings?

11. Do you have a difficult time letting go of your anger once it is activated?

12. Do you feel a need to make the person who criticized you feel horrible about himself or herself?

13. Do you sometimes get on a roll and continue berating someone for hours and hours?

14. Are you often disappointed in others because they don't meet your standards or expectations?

15. Do you often become angry with others when they make a mistake?

16. Do you feel you have the right to point out when someone is doing something wrong?

17. Are you willing to admit when you are wrong but find that you seldom have to do so?

18. Do you find yourself blaming others for mistakes you yourself have made?

19. Do you believe you have a right to make most of the decisions in a relationship?

20. Do you insist that people do as you say?

21. Do you often become angry when people don't do things your way or don't do as you ask?

22. Do you usually punish people in some way when they go against your wishes or don't do things your way?

23. Do you often become involved in arguments because people don't agree with you or don't understand your point of view?

24. Do you have a difficult time letting go of a subject or ending an argument until the other person has come around to your way of thinking?

25. Do you ever use intimidation or threats to control other people's behavior?

26. Have you ever threatened to hurt or destroy someone else's property?

27. Have you ever threatened to hurt someone?

28. Have you ever thrown or broken objects while in a rage or in an attempt to scare someone?

29. Have you ever refused to allow someone to leave a room?

30. Have you ever pushed, shoved, or hit someone in a fit of anger?

If you answered yes to the majority of question numbers 1–7, you are an Eruptor. If you answered yes to most of numbers 8–13, you are a Rager. If you answered yes to a majority of numbers 14–18, you are a Blamer. If you answered yes to most of questions 19–24, you are a Controller. If you answered in the affirmative to questions 25–30, you are an abuser.

In the following sections I describe in detail each of the subcategories of the aggressive style of anger. Read the category or categories that best define you based on your answers to the questionnaire. If you answered yes to the majority of questions in more than one category, read each section that applies. It is possible that you may have answered yes to all or to a majority of these questions. If this is the case, consider yourself an abuser. The abusive style of anger can have elements of erupting, blaming, and controlling, but your overall style would be considered abusive.

Eruptors

The eruptive style of anger is characterized by sudden outbursts, often without the least bit of warning. If you have an eruptive style, you are probably often described as having a bad temper or being a hothead. You probably get over your anger as quickly as you become angry. Unfortunately, it usually takes other people a lot longer to get over the things you say or do when you are angry.

"I NEVER KNOW WHEN I'M GOING TO BLOW UP"

Zack, a burly man in his mid-forties, came to see me because of his anger: "I never know when I'm going to blow up. Things can be going okay and all of a sudden one little thing will push me over the edge. I'll start screaming at whomever is around me. My wife and kids are afraid of me. This has been going on for years, but now I really want to do something about it. I'm afraid my wife will leave me or I'll end up doing something I can't take back."

If you are an Eruptor like Zack, you often don't see your anger coming. It catches you off-guard. Unlike most people, you often become angry without knowing what you are angry about. This is because you don't pay attention to the physical and emotional cues that warn you that your anger is building up.

Most people know they are becoming angry because they feel it. They may suddenly feel hot or sense pressure building up inside. They may notice that their voice has risen or that their breathing has become faster. They may notice an inner voice saying things like, "Who does he think he is? I'll show him." Or they may notice that when they become angry, they have a tendency to crack their knuckles, tap their foot, or clench their jaw. But Eruptors either don't notice these signs or they ignore them.

Some eruptors also tend to be unaware of the amount of stress and frustration that has been building up inside them. They may become extremely stressed or frustrated over a number of things until one comment or incident finally makes them blow up. This is often true of parents and those who have stressful or high-powered jobs. Just as they ignore signs of their anger, they ignore signs of stress. Instead of taking time off and learning ways of calming down and relaxing, they keep pushing themselves until they finally blow.

Other Eruptors simply can't handle frustration very well. If they have to wait too long in line at the grocery store, if the freeway is bumper to bumper, or if they don't get what they want when they want it, they explode.

Eruptors don't handle frustration well because they tend to be impatient. They want things now and it upsets them greatly when they don't get what they want when they want it. If you're like most eruptors, you take it personally if someone doesn't do something fast enough. A typical Eruptor tends to become very impatient with waitpersons, clerks in stores, and other service people, as well as with his or her children and spouse. This impatience often leads to an explosion.

Eruptors not only don't pay attention to the physical and emotional warning signs that anger is building up but don't recognize that anger itself is a messenger telling them that there is something wrong. They don't explode, then sit down calmly to discuss the problem. Instead, they see anger as the solution. Once they have blown up, they feel better. After all, they've released the built-up tension. They see no further need to discuss problems or to explore the cause of their anger.

But anger does not solve problems. In fact, it often causes more problems, especially for Eruptors. Not only do they never get to the source of their frustration or anger but they usually hurt or alienate other people with their eruptions. Although they may feel better in the moment, they usually feel worse in the long run once they come to recognize how childlike and out of control they must appear to others or once they must deal with the consequences of their actions.

Ragers

Ragers are overly sensitive to criticism or rejection. When someone says or does something that causes them to feel criticized, put down, or ignored, they retaliate with intense anger or rage. Their goal is to make the other person feel as badly as they feel. They may also want to send the message that they should not be criticized or disrespected again.

Ragers carry a great deal of shame–the painful feeling of being defective as a human being. Shame-based people feel worthless, unlovable, inadequate, and bad, usually because they were made to feel these things when they were growing up by their parents or other caretakers.

Ragers defend against their shame by becoming angry, or more accurately, by becoming enraged. Rage is by definition abusive. It is usually expressed by screaming, yelling, threats of violence, and physical expressions of violence, as well as sulking, manipulation, emotional blackmail, and silent smoldering. Raging gives the angry person a feeling of power that temporarily offsets feelings of shame and inadequacy.

AFRAID OF THE WATER

Shame-based anger, or rage, comes on fast, but unlike the anger of eruptors, it goes away very slowly. This is true for two reasons. First, ragers are usually attempting to rid themselves of the shame they experience when then feel criticized, insulted, rejected, or humiliated by dumping shame on others, which can take a long time. Most ragers have a storehouse full of shame that can be triggered at any time. They are not only feeling shamed by the new experience but by memories of past shaming.

Sally and her husband, Lawrence, recently had a dinner party for three other couples. One of the couples was a man from Lawrence's workplace and his wife. As the evening progressed, one of the guests invited everyone for a sailing weekend. Sally laughed and said, "Well, you better count us out. Lawrence is deathly afraid of the water. You'll never get him on a sailboat." The other guests laughed and started goading Lawrence, telling him that he should come anyway. Arnie, the man from work, teased him and said, "I didn't know you were such a wimp. Don't worry. We'll put a life vest on you so that you won't sink." Lawrence felt humiliated.

After their guests left, Lawrence laid into Sally: "How dare you humiliate me like that in front of other people. Arnie will tell everyone at work. I'll be the laughing stock of the office. Why didn't you just keep your big mouth shut?" Sally tried telling Lawrence that their guests didn't think less of him and that everyone has something they are afraid of, but it didn't help. No matter what she said or how much she tried to console him, he kept feeling worse and worse. The more humiliated he felt, the angrier he became. He continued to harass Sally all night, accusing her of deliberately trying to make him lose face in front of their guests, telling her that she was a horrible wife, even throwing the fact that she couldn't have children up in her face. By the time he finally stopped, it was almost dawn and Sally was so beaten down emotionally that she couldn't stop crying.

The other reason shame-based anger doesn't subside very quickly is that ragers usually feel worse about themselves after an outburst than they did before. In addition to the shame they felt at being criticized or insulted, they now feel ashamed about becoming enraged. For example, Lawrence knew he had gone off the deep end even while he continued to rage at Sally. He saw how tired his wife looked and how upset she was, but he just couldn't stop himself. At one point she curled up on the bed and started weeping. He felt a horrible pang of guilt and shame for causing her such distress, but this only fueled his anger.

Sally was unable to go to work the next morning. When Lawrence got home from work that evening, he felt horrible when he saw how upset she still was. His day had gone better than he'd expected since no one had teased him about his fear of the water. It seemed that Arnie had kept his mouth shut. He wished he could take back all the things he'd said to Sally the night before, but he couldn't.

Blamers

Blamers are seldom satisfied. They frequently complain about the behavior of others and seem to focus much more on the negative than the positive. For example, a mother who is a Blamer will focus on the one part of her child's room he forgot to clean instead of noticing and praising him for cleaning up the rest of the room.

Blamers also tend to focus on other people's behavior instead of attending to their own feelings and behavior. In this way they can avoid seeing their own mistakes or shortcomings. In fact, Blamers are often not very self-aware. They are fully capable of criticizing in others the very weaknesses and faults they themselves possess without realizing their hypocrisy.

If you are a Blamer, you are often angry. People usually fall short of your expectations and you blame others for your unhappiness. You are probably very verbal about your disappointment in others and tend to point out other people's mistakes or failures. Interestingly, you are often surprised when others become defensive or angry with you. After all, you were merely pointing out their mistakes. Why are they getting so angry?

"It's Always Someone Else's Fault"

Jessie, an adolescent client, was brought in by her mother because she refused to go to school. When she did go, she got into conflicts with her teachers and fights with other kids. When I asked Jessie why she didn't like school, she gave me a litany of reasons. Her teachers were stupid and they didn't understand her. The things they were teaching were a bunch of useless facts that she'd never use. Most of the kids in the school acted immature and she was bored with them.

After only a few sessions with Jessie, it became clear that she was suffering from more than typical adolescent rebellion. Jessie had already established a pattern of blaming others for her problems. Like most blamers, Jessie assumed she was right and others were wrong. She saw herself as innocent and others as guilty, herself as good and others as bad.

It was surprising to see someone as young as Jessie with such an extreme version of this attitude, and I was eager to know more about her family and her history. Her mother appeared to be a very empathetic, sweet person who genuinely cared about Jessie. But what about her father? As it turned out, Jessie's father had an even more extreme version of the blaming style than Jessie did. A successful lawyer, Mr. Adams accredited his success to the fact that he was absolutely certain he was right at all times. Jessie had grown up hearing her father rant and rave about how stupid, incompetent, and boring most people were. It became very clear that Jessie had taken on her father's anger style and that he encouraged her behavior by citing it as evidence of her intelligence.

If you are a Blamer like Jessie and her father, most people find that engaging in an argument with you is usually a waste of time. You have a difficult time admitting your part in creating a problem and you almost never take criticism well. You can dish it out, but you can't take it. In fact, you are likely to burst into anger when someone else points out your faults or criticizes you. This was the case with Jessie. Whenever her mother or a teacher tried to point out something she needed to work on, Jessie would lash out by listing all the things they had done wrong to cause her behavior.

Controllers

Controlling, domineering people behave in inflexible, even cruel ways, expecting everyone to bow down to them and do as they say. This is especially true of their family. Controllers demand that their children follow their rules without question and that they ask permission concerning even trivial matters. In the extreme, Controllers expect their spouses to get their approval before spending money, planning activities,

even before changing something about their persona
as getting a new hairstyle.

Controllers often explode in anger when som
tion their authority or acts independently. They try to g
who have offended them (usually for not doing as they say) and a
out their anger in abusive ways. Some pound their desks, some slam
doors, some put their fists through walls, and some attack those who
upset them. Others retaliate in less overt ways. They may give the
other person the silent treatment, withhold affection or sex, or stop
doing favors. The message is: "You do as I say or you will be sorry."

"Do As I Say"

Debbie is a Controller. She insists on having things her own way.
When her children go against her wishes, she becomes furious with
them. She storms around the house accusing them of not respecting
her and she punishes them by taking things away from them. For
example, if one of her children doesn't listen, she may cancel a promised shopping trip to the city. She explained her reasoning to me: "If
my kids don't respect me and do as I say, then they won't get any privileges. It's just that simple. Why should I be nice to them if they aren't
going to mind me?"

She has the same philosophy when it comes to her husband: "My
husband is the boss at work. I'm the boss at home. He likes the way I
cook and the way I keep the house nice and clean. But if he decides to
offer his two cents worth about the way I run the house or to oppose
me about something, then he'll have to pay the price. He'll have to eat
take-out for a few days and take his own clothes to the cleaners. Then
maybe he'll learn to appreciate me more and not to question my
authority."

Debbie is typical of most Controllers in that she believes she can
make people do what she wants by punishing, accusing, shaming,
yelling, shoving, throwing things, or hitting. She wants her children
and her husband to be afraid of her because then she knows she'll get
her way. Controllers rule by intimidation. They gain power by making
others afraid of them.

Unfortunately, Controllers like Debbie pay a heavy price for intimidating and domineering others. Most partners get tired of being controlled and end the relationship or act out their anger by having affairs, spending money, or retaliating in some way. Children who are controlled grow resentful and distant. Many become bullies, emotionally or physically abusing other children, or they get into trouble with the law due to their deep resentment toward authority figures. Most grow up severely damaged emotionally and either become involved with controlling, abusive partners or become Controllers themselves. Many Controllers get fired or passed over for promotions because they do not get along with their coworkers. Controllers who become violent often get in trouble with the law.

Abusers

While many people can become verbally, emotionally, or even physically abusive at certain times in their lives, those with an abusive anger style are consistently abusive to others. If you have this anger style, you insist on being respected by others while giving little or no respect in return. Your needs are paramount and you show a blatant disregard for the needs and feelings of others. The basic personality of Abusers is characterized by

- A tendency to be unreasonable and demanding

- A need to dominate and control others

- A tendency to blame others for all their problems and to take all their frustrations out on other people

- A tendency to misuse power, control, and authority

- A tendency to verbally abuse others

- Frequent emotional and sometimes physical outbursts, and an overwhelming need to retaliate and hurt others for real and imagined slights or affronts

- An inability to empathize with others

- A tendency to be overly jealous and possessive

- A tendency to be emotionally needy, often requiring constant attention, appreciation, or praise

The abusive anger style includes elements from all the other aggressive anger styles plus some additional characteristics such as lack of empathy, jealousy, and neediness. People with an abusive anger style also tend to exhibit a more extreme version of blaming, controlling, and erupting.

Many with an abusive anger style wreak havoc with the lives of nearly every person they come in contact with. They verbally abuse their coworkers or employees, they are insulting and obnoxious to service people, they are controlling and domineering toward their children, and they constantly blame others when things go wrong.

It will undoubtedly be extremely difficult for you to admit that you have an abusive style of anger or an abusive personality. But in order for you to change, you will need to be brutally honest with yourself. If you still doubt that your anger style is really abusive, answer the following questions as honestly as you can.

QUESTIONNAIRE: *Are You an Abuser?*

1. Do you become enraged when others don't listen to your advice or do as you say?

2. Do you deliberately point out others' weakness or vulnerability as a way of putting them in their place?

3. Do you often swear or curse at people when you are angry?

4. Do you often lose your temper and yell or scream at people?

5. Do you often slam doors or throw things when you are angry?

6. Have you ever threatened to hurt someone or destroy something of value owned by someone else?

7. Have you ever pushed or shoved someone in the heat of anger?

8. Do you sometimes allow yourself to behave inappropriately when you are angry because you want the release it will provide?

9. Have you ever abused someone verbally, emotionally, physically, or sexually in a fit of rage?

10. Has a partner ever left you or threatened to leave you because of your anger?

11. Have you ever lost a job or been passed over for a promotion because of your anger?

12. Have you ever lost a friend because of your anger?

13. Have you ever been arrested because of your anger?

If you answered yes to one or more of these questions, you likely have an abusive anger style. This doesn't mean you are a bad person. Most abusers were themselves abused as children or adults; they are unconsciously repeating the pattern and passing on the abuse to others. Most are unaware that they are actually being abusive and often feel as if they were actually the victim in the situation. What it does mean is that you need to work on changing this negative anger style into a more positive and constructive one.

LETTING OFF STEAM

Vince came to see me because his wife recently left him. "I want her back, and the only way this is going to happen is if I learn how to control my anger," he told me during our first session. "I'll admit it: I become abusive—mostly verbally, but sometimes I push her around and I know it scares her. I never hit her, but I came really close."

When I asked Vince if he knew why he became abusive, he explained, "I know it is wrong, but I do it anyway. I want the release. It feels so good to yell and scream and get things off my chest. At that moment I don't care how it makes my wife feel. I regret it afterward, but I guess the truth is that when I am doing it, I just don't care."

We can't change what we don't acknowledge. Vince has taken the first steps in admitting that he is abusive. He isn't blaming his wife for "making" him lose his temper and he isn't making any excuses.

Variations on the Passive Anger Style

If you have identified yourself as having a passive anger style, the following questions will help you determine which variation on this style best describes you.

QUESTIONNAIRE: *What Is Your Secondary Anger Style?*

1. Do you seldom if ever become angry?

2. Are you unable to identify when you are angry?

3. Are you unaware of how your body feels—what bodily sensations you experience—when you are angry?

4. Do others often accuse you of being angry when you don't feel it?

5. Do you often look back on a situation and realize you were angry even though you were completely unaware of it at the time?

6. Are you often surprised at the intensity of your anger when it does come out?

7. Do you think anger is a very negative, destructive emotion that should be avoided at all costs?

8. Are you afraid of becoming angry?

9. Do you try to never get angry?

10. Do you feel it is beneath you to become angry or let someone know you are angry?

11. When things begin to heat up in a conversation, will you often find an excuse to end it or opt out of the conversation in some way?

12. Do you consciously try to push your anger down?

13. When you do become angry, do you try to talk yourself out of it or distract yourself from it?

14. Do you think you sometimes eat, drink alcohol, take drugs, shoplift, gamble, or have sex as a way of avoiding or coping with your anger?

15. Do you suspect that anger is at the root of your food, alcohol, drug, shoplifting, gambling, or sex addiction problem?

16. Instead of allowing yourself to get angry at others, do you often blame yourself for their behavior or for causing their behavior?

17. Do you often believe people who say you are responsible for their anger?

18. Do you think you bring out the worst in others?

19. Do you have a tendency to get depressed?

20. Have you ever blamed yourself for the fact that someone else became emotionally, physically, or sexually abusive toward you?

If you answered yes to the majority of questions 1–6, you are a Denier. If you answered yes to most of questions 7–11, you are an Avoider. If you answered yes to the majority of questions 12–15, you are a Stuffer. If you answered yes to most of questions 16–20, you are a Self-blamer.

Deniers

Deniers have disowned their anger to such an extent that they are often unaware of feeling angry. They have an investment in not becoming angry either because they are afraid of their anger, believing that anger leads to abuse, or because they are afraid of what others will do or say to them if they become angry. Some are able to subvert their anger to such a degree that no one knows they are angry. Others show signs of anger but are completely unaware of them even when someone points them out.

"I NEVER GET ANGRY"

"I never get angry," my client, Carrie, shared with me. "I feel hurt by what people sometimes do and I sometimes feel frustrated with a situation, but I just don't get angry." How can someone never feel angry? People who say they are never angry are in denial about their anger. Denial is an unconscious defense mechanism that helps us withstand great pain and survive even the most traumatic situations. If we did not use this defense mechanism, we couldn't tolerate life very well. But denial also causes us to avoid feelings we need to face if we are going to function in a healthy way. Sometimes people become so afraid of their anger that they deny its existence. They either repress (unconsciously deny) or suppress (consciously choose to avoid) their anger to such an extent that they become completely disconnected from it.

When Carrie was a child, she often witnessed her father becoming enraged. He would yell and scream, punch holes through the walls, and throw objects across the room. Once he only narrowly missed hitting Carrie in the head when he threw a vase. Carrie became deathly afraid of her father and equally afraid of anger.

Several weeks after working with me, Carrie was able to make the connection: "I couldn't afford to get angry at my father. It wasn't safe. So I convinced myself that I wasn't angry at all." Because it didn't feel safe to express or even acknowledge her anger toward her father, it didn't feel safe to be angry with other people either. After all, they might explode in anger the way her father did.

Avoiders

Unlike Deniers, Avoiders are usually conscious of their anger. They deliberately set out to avoid becoming angry in the first place, or they ignore or suppress their reactions when they do become angry. If you are an Avoider, you probably realize when you are angry but do not let other people know. You may be guarded about sharing your feelings with others or may deliberately refuse to let others know when you are angry as a power play. Some people with this anger style will stew in their anger for hours, days, or even weeks at a time, and many hold grudges and are unforgiving.

"Don't Let Them See You Sweat"

"You've heard the expression, 'Don't let them see you sweat,'" my client, Bruce, shared with me one day. "Well, I believe you shouldn't let them see you get angry. I try to avoid getting angry at all costs because I don't want anyone to know they can get to me. If you don't get angry, you can stay in control."

Unfortunately, Bruce wasn't able to express any of his other emotions either, which is why he entered counseling. His wife accused him of being cold and callous and was threatening to divorce him. "She wants me to exude emotion all over the place, but that's not who I am," Bruce explained to me. "I love her and don't want to lose her, but I can't be something I'm not."

I explored Bruce's history with him. His mother was a highly emotional woman who alternated between rages and deep depression. She'd sometimes cry for hours and she had tried to commit suicide twice. His mother's emotionality had frightened Bruce to the extent that he put a lid on his own feelings.

Stuffers

Stuffers are Deniers or Avoiders who use food or other substances to push down their anger. Instead of acknowledging, feeling, and expressing their anger, they overeat, smoke cigarettes, drink alcohol, or take drugs so that they can block out their anger or avoid having to confront someone who has treated them unfairly.

"Why Should I Even Speak to Her?"

Felicia wanted to understand why she ate compulsively. After a few sessions, she felt comfortable enough to share with me that she was very angry with her mother: "She was horrible to me when I was growing up and now she wants us to be friends. Why should I try to be close to her when she didn't have time for me when I was a kid? Why should I even speak to her?"

Because Felicia's mother was going out of her way to be nice, Felicia felt guilty for being so angry with her. Whenever her mother called, Felicia tried to be polite to her even though she was raging inside. But as soon as she got off the phone, she would go into the refrigerator and eat anything and everything she could put her hands on.

After several more sessions, Felicia made even more connections: "I guess I'm trying to push all my anger down with the food. But it only works for a short time. The very next time I talk to her, I'm angry all over again. I guess if I want to lose weight, I'm going to have to tell her how I really feel, even if she is being nice to me now."

Several studies have examined the link between overeating and emotions. An intensive study conducted by Russell and Shirk in 1993 with 535 subjects found eating to be a response to almost every emotion, with "injustice, resentment, discrimination and rejection" common factors that triggered eating. In her study of eating patterns and personality traits among twenty obese women, Woodman (1980) observed eating as a way of repressing anger to be present in all twenty subjects. Rage was rarely expressed among the obese women studied.

Purging among bulimics is interpreted as a self-punishing act. But the 1983 Mintz study suggests, "Vomiting has long been considered a symbolic expression of rage." The "physiological and tranquilizing" component of purging was reported by Valentis and Devane in 1994; they suggest that "purging is a protection against the self and its rage." The authors quote therapist Pam Killen's explanations that endorphins are released in vomiting that "soothe that rage and act as palliatives for murderous feelings."

The suppression of anger by using chemicals is considered to be socially acceptable and fairly common in our society. Seabrook found that high-risk drinkers showed a higher propensity to become angry, displayed more angry symptoms in their bodies such as headaches and shakiness, and tended to dwell on angry thoughts. These women were found to be less likely to engage in a discussion about their angry feelings in a healthy or productive way. Women with anger symptoms (e.g., having a headache when angry) were found to drink more alcohol and use prescription drugs.

Self-Blamers

Self-blamers avoid their anger at others by turning it on themselves. Instead of admitting they are angry with someone, or even admitting that they have a reason to be angry, they will blame themselves for the incident or justify the other person's behavior by claiming responsibility. For example, it is common for a self-blamer to say, "If I hadn't _____ [said the wrong thing, cooked his meal wrong, looked at her in the wrong way] he/she wouldn't have _____ [yelled at me, hit me, flirted with another man]."

Self-blamers are the polar opposite of blamers. Self-blamers tend to have too much empathy for other people and not enough empathy for themselves, whereas blamers have little empathy for others and tend to only focus on how something or someone affects them. Self-blamers and blamers are often attracted to one another and tend to create extremely dysfunctional if not abusive relationships.

THE PERFECT COMBINATION

Clark blamed Wendy for nearly everything that went wrong in his life. If he was late for work, it was because Wendy forgot to wake him up. If he didn't get a report completed on time, it was because he was too tired from having to entertain Wendy's parents when they visited. If he got a stomachache, it was because of Wendy's cooking. Wendy fed right into Clark's tendency to blame by believing she was responsible for everything that went wrong. She chastised herself mercilessly for not making sure Clark was awake before she left for work. She felt guilty about the fact that her parents had visited and took up Clark's time when he should have been working on his report. And she was fully convinced that she was a horrible cook. Each time Clark got angry with her, she'd promise herself she was going to do better, and she would try. But there was always something else she'd do wrong to make Clark angry. She just wasn't a very good partner.

Variations on the Passive-Aggressive Anger Style

If you have identified yourself as having the passive-aggressive anger style, this questionnaire will help you determine your particular version of this style:

QUESTIONNAIRE: *What Is Your Secondary Anger Style?*

1. Instead of communicating your angry feelings directly, do you tend to plot ways of getting back at the person who upset you?

2. Have you been guilty of getting back at people in sneaky ways such as stealing something of theirs, starting a nasty rumor, or contaminating their food?

3. Have you ever been accused of getting back at someone in an underhanded way?

4. Do you think revenge is sweet? Do you love movies or books that involve someone getting secret revenge against another person?

5. Do you frequently forget to do things you've said you'd do?

6. Do you frequently arrive late or accidentally break objects that belong to others, and have you ever suspected that it might be your way of getting back at others?

7. Do you often agree to do things for others but fail to follow through?

8. Do others frequently put pressure on you because you haven't completed a task?

9. Do you often feel pressured by others to complete tasks in a certain way or in a certain amount of time?

10. Do you often wonder why people are frequently angry with you for not getting something done? After all, you're working on it.

11. Instead of telling people you are angry with them, do you tend to sulk or pout?

12. Do you let people know you are unhappy or angry by rolling your eyes, making faces, or sighing?

13. Do you often punish others by withdrawing from them or giving them the silent treatment?

14. Do you withhold affection, sex, or money when your partner doesn't do as you wish?

15. Do you withhold approval, affection, or money when your children disappoint you or don't mind you?

16. Do you pride yourself on seldom or never showing others when you are angry?

17. Do you feel it is beneath you to get angry?

18. Do you think it is a sign of mental health or spiritual enlightenment to avoid getting angry?

19. Have you ever been surprised by someone accusing you of being angry or controlling when that is not how you see yourself at all?

20. Do you think that when you put your mind to it and put on a happy face you can will yourself to let go of your anger no matter how angry you really are?

If you answered yes to most of questions 1–4, you are an Anger Sneak. If you answered yes to the majority of questions 5–10, you are an Escape Artist. If most of your answers to questions 11–15 were yes, you are a Sulker. If you answered yes to the majority of questions 16–20, you are a Pretender.

Anger Sneaks

Anger sneaks find underhanded ways of getting back at those with whom they are angry. Instead of communicating their anger directly, they silently plan revenge. Although everyone who has a passive-aggressive style of anger expresses their anger in indirect ways, anger sneaks do it in a much more conscious manner.

Those who are being emotionally or physically abused by their partner and are afraid or unwilling to confront this person about his or her behavior or to leave the relationship will often get back at their abuser in a sneaky way. Victims have often told me about how they put urine, cigarette ashes, or even dog excrement in their partner's food.

"THAT'LL TEACH YOU"

Karen became very angry at her coworker, Robin, because she had presented Karen's idea to their boss, then took credit for it. But instead of taking Robin aside and confronting her about it, Karen remained silent. "I'll get you back, Just wait and see," she thought to herself.

About a week later, Karen got her chance. Robin had left an important report on her desk while she went to lunch. Karen took the report and hid it in a storage room. When Robin came back, Karen watched while Robin frantically searched her desk for the report that she was supposed to present at an important board meeting in five minutes. When Robin asked Karen if she'd seen the report, Karen said no and silently celebrated as she saw the panic on Robin's face. Robin had to go into the meeting empty-handed and explain to her boss that she'd misplaced it. Karen got her revenge.

Escape Artists

Like most of those with a passive-aggressive anger style, Escape Artists don't like being told what to do. But instead of standing up for themselves and simply saying they don't want to do something, they find manipulative ways of getting out of it. Some act helpless or play dumb in order to avoid having to do things. For example, your wife asks you to do the laundry while she's out of town for the weekend. You'd planned on an entire weekend with no one around demanding anything of you, so you're angry. But instead of telling her how you feel, you tell her you'd love to help out but don't know how to do laundry. "I'm afraid I'll ruin the clothes. I don't know which colors go where. It would be better to wait until you come back."

Not only do escape artists not like being told what to do but they even resent being asked to do something. Instead of taking the chance of creating a conflict, some will agree to do it even though they have no intention of following through. Instead they will conveniently forget to do it. When reminded, they'll become grumpy and insist that they don't need the reminder. Then they'll proceed to forget all over again.

"CALL ME IRRESPONSIBLE"

Although this tactic may discourage people from asking things of you, you soon develop a reputation for being irresponsible. And your irresponsibility might even end up harming you or someone else, as it almost did with a client of mine.

Jacob's wife, Marcie, expected him to maintain the car. She thought of it as a man's job, and since she didn't know anything about cars, she wanted him to take over the responsibility of making sure the car had frequent oil changes and other maintenance. Jacob didn't like to be told what to do and he was silently angry at his wife because he felt she tried to control him too much. So whenever Marcie asked Jacob if he had the oil changed, he'd become defensive and tell her to stop reminding him. After all, he'd say, "I'm a grown man. You don't have to talk to me like I'm a child." Marcie decided that perhaps he was right and left him alone. Then late one night when Marcie was driving home from visiting her parents the engine light went on in the car. She was miles from a service station, so she kept on driving. The car started smoking so Marcie stopped the car at the side of the road. She got out just before the entire front end of the car became engulfed in fire. The reason for the fire: Jacob had not had the oil changed in the car for over two years. He'd forgotten.

Many Escape Artists use procrastination as a way of silently communicating their displeasure at being asked to do something. These passive-aggressors feel pressured whenever someone expects something of them. For example, you may promise to do something but resent the imposition, so you put it off as long as you possibly can. When someone asks you when you're going to start the project, you mumble something about doing it soon or you may make excuses, such as saying you haven't had time.

You also resent being pushed in any way. In fact, the more someone pushes you to complete a task, the more resentful you become and the slower you may move. When someone complains that you are not getting the job done fast enough, you insist that you're going as fast as you can. You'll finally finish the job but only just before the absolute deadline. By that time the other person is totally exasperated with you and may vow to never ask you to do anything again or to never work with you again. That suits you just fine. Your delaying tactics send a strong yet indirect message: "Don't ask me to do anything. Don't expect anything of me."

Sulkers

Sulkers let people know they are angry in very indirect ways. Instead of raising their voice, exploding in anger, or coming clean about what is bothering them, these passive-aggressors sulk, pout, withdraw, punish with silence, or give dirty or pitiful looks. Deep sighs may be their preferred mode of communication and they will often refuse to participate until they get their way. When called on their behavior or attitude, they will probably deny they are angry and may accuse the other person of being the one who is really angry, of trying to start a fight, or of making a big deal out of nothing.

Sulkers also express their anger by withholding affection, money, or sex from their partners or by withholding affection, money, or favors from their children. In this way they are able to control others without taking the risk of expressing their anger directly.

If you are a Sulker, you aren't courageous enough to own up to your anger. But at the same time you want the other person to know how angry or displeased you really are so that he or she will stop doing whatever it is you don't like. You will contain your anger, but your message— "I'm angry and it's your fault"—comes through loud and clear.

"SURE, I'LL DO IT YOUR WAY, BUT I'LL MAKE YOU MISERABLE IN THE PROCESS"

Whenever Janine doesn't get her way, she makes her husband, Steve, miserable. For example, one afternoon she called him at work and told him she was craving Mexican food and that she wanted to go out to her favorite Mexican restaurant that night. Steve told her that he was just about to call her because they had been invited by a coworker to a new trendy restaurant that night. Janine didn't want to go and tried to persuade Steve to cancel with his friend so that just she and Steve could go out instead. But Steve said he didn't want to insult his coworker and he'd been wanting to check out the new restaurant anyway. Janine was angry that Steve didn't put her feelings first, but she didn't say anything.

On the way to the restaurant, Janine pouted in silence. When Steve asked her what was wrong, she said, "Oh, nothing," with a big sigh. She continued to suffer in silence throughout the entire evening. Usually cordial and talkative, Janine hardly spoke to Steve's coworker, making him very uncomfortable. Instead she sat looking off into space. Several times Steve asked Janine, "Are you feeling okay? Is there something wrong?" but she continued to insist everything was fine. This made Steve furious. On the way home, he snapped at her. "Well, I hope you're happy. You managed to ruin my evening and Todd's too with your pouting and sulking. I know you wanted Mexican food, but would it have been such a big deal for you to at least try to enjoy yourself?"

Pretenders

Pretenders couch their anger and resentment in sweet, loving words. Because of this they have an uncanny ability to make others angry.

When this happens, they are often mortified and confused. "What did I do?" they'll ask. "Why are you so angry with me?" Although they try to disguise it, their anger is never really concealed. In fact, they're experts at communicating hostility. See if you can identify with any of these tactics: You're angry at your partner for calling you at work, but instead of asking him not to call or telling him it is inconvenient for you to talk, you tell him you have another call and put him on hold for five minutes. You complain to friends about women who try to look young by wearing too much makeup and wearing short skirts in front of your wife who wears quite a bit of makeup and is wearing a short skirt. You tell your partner that your friends all thought he drank too much at the party last night and made a fool of himself. When he asks you if you agree, you say no; he may have gotten a little tipsy, but you thought it was cute.

SWEET ON THE OUTSIDE, ANGRY ON THE INSIDE

Lexi is a good example of this anger style. She's sweet and cooperative on the outside and angry and resistant on the inside. Lexi is a deeply spiritual person. In fact, she once lived in a spiritual community, devoting her life to her spiritual practice. She often appears to be very calm and centered, almost as if she were in a meditative state. She speaks with a low, melodious voice and often decorates her sentences with flowery words. But underneath Lexi's calm exterior lies a deeply angry, controlling person. Lexi has to have things her way. If she agrees with you, you are the recipient of all her loving support. If she disagrees, or if you cross her in any way, another Lexi will emerge. You may have to look closely, but behind her sweet smile there is just a hint of angry intensity. She gives it away by the rigidity of her body and the tightness in her jaw. If you don't observe carefully, you'll be fooled by her overly sugary words. She can find the nicest, most subtle way to put you down. She'll do it so artfully that you won't realize what hit you until later.

Sometimes Pretenders are conscious of their duality and other times they are not. Lexi was totally convinced that she was projecting only sweetness and light. When she was confronted by a member of her spiritual community, albeit in a gentle, loving way, she refused to believe the woman: "I really didn't know what Margaret meant when she said I was angry and controlling. I just don't see myself that way. In fact, I work hard letting go of any need I have for something to be a certain way. I believe you should come from a place of acceptance— that you should just let things be. I assumed she must be projecting her own issues onto me. After all, who is she to judge me?"

But Margaret was not the only person who experienced Lexi as angry and controlling. In time, several other members of her community came to her and told her they were put off by her need to control. Lexi was forced to take a closer look at herself: "It took some real soul-searching and more feedback from others, but I finally began to see what they were talking about. I have such a strong need to project only light that I submerged my darker emotions. Unfortunately, my darker side just kept getting bigger and bigger the more I tried to ignore it. Finally it began to seep out all over the place. My words and my conscious intention may have been to be cooperative and accepting, but my true intention was to subtly put down anyone who didn't agree with me. What an eye-opener!"

Variations on the Projective-Aggressive Anger Style

If you believe you have the projective-aggressive anger style, the following questions will help you determine your particular version of this style.

QUESTIONNAIRE: *What Is Your Secondary Anger Style?*

1. Do you often feel that others are angry with you or against you?

2. Do you continue to believe others are angry with you even though they deny it?

3. Do you tend to be suspicious and distrustful of other people?

4. Are you afraid of other people's anger?

5. When it becomes clear to you that someone is against you, does it give you permission to be angry with him or her?

6. Do you seldom if ever get angry but find you are often the victim of someone else's anger?

7. Are you afraid of your anger and the anger of others?

8. Do you believe it is wrong to get angry?

9. Do you often complain to those you are close to about the behavior of others, secretly hoping they will do something about the situation for you?

10. Do you prefer to let someone else handle conflicts with others rather than get involved yourself, even when the situation concerns you?

11. Have you ever been intimately involved with an abusive person?

12. Have you ever stayed in a relationship with someone who emotionally, physically, or sexually abused you or your children?

13. Are you often attracted to intense, angry, or aggressive people?

14. Are angry people often attracted to you?

15. Are you often surprised to discover that someone is an extremely angry person because that is not how you originally perceived him or her?

16. Do angry people single you out in a crowd?

17. Do you have a pattern of getting involved with angry or abusive people?

If you answered yes to the majority of questions 1–5, you are what I call a Ventriloquist. If you answered yes to most of questions 6–12, you are an Innocent Victim. If you answered yes to the majority of questions 13–17, you are an Anger Magnet.

Ventriloquists

Just like professional ventriloquists throw their voice to make it look like their dummy is speaking, Ventriloquists throw their anger to make

eone else is the angry one. Like the Denier or Avoider,
. on avoiding their anger, but instead of burying their
..r, they avoid it in a more convoluted, albeit unconscious, way.
They project it onto other people. Projection is a defense mechanism
that allows you to deny characteristics or emotions within yourself of
which you don't approve. When you project your anger, you see anger
in other people that actually belongs to you. You're seeing your own
anger reflected back at yourself just as you would if you were looking
in a mirror.

Ventriloquists were often raised in environments where the
expression of anger was not allowed or where any display of anger
was severely punished. Some grew up in homes where one or both
parents were extremely abusive. In both situations, these people came
to believe that anger was a very negative emotion to be avoided at all
costs, and they learned at an early age to repress or suppress their
anger. Unfortunately, repressed anger does not just magically go
away. It goes underground waiting for a way to express itself. For
Ventriloquists, it expresses itself in a form of almost paranoia-like
distrust of others.

Many Ventriloquists feel that the world is an unsafe place and that
they must be extremely careful and not trust anyone, causing them to
be excessively suspicious of others. They often feel certain that others
are trying to hurt them even when there is no clear evidence that this
is true. Some Ventriloquists are able to trust a few people, but they are
always waiting for the other shoe to drop.

Like all those with the projective-aggressive anger style, if you
are a Ventriloquist you do not know how angry you are. Instead, you
often think others are angry with you. Robert is a case in point.

"What Did I Ever Do to Him?"

Robert is furious with his neighbor for cutting down a beautiful tree
that provided a lot of shade in his backyard in the summer. He's so
furious he'd like to walk over to his neighbor's house and punch him in
the mouth. But Robert was raised in a strongly religious home where
he was taught that anger is not only an unacceptable emotion but an

evil one. Whenever he got angry as a child, he was punished severely. So Robert tries to push his anger out of his mind. He's pretty successful too. He pushes his anger out of his mind and right into his neighbor's. Robert becomes convinced that his neighbor is actually angry with him. In fact, he begins to think that his neighbor cut down the tree deliberately to get back at him for some unknown act on his part.

"Boy, you should have seen the dirty look Oscar gave me when I drove into the driveway," Robert tells his wife the next day. "He's really got it in for me. What did I ever do to him? Do you think he could be angry with me for having that garage sale last weekend? Do you think he was bothered by the people parking in front of his house?"

Robert's wife doesn't think so. In fact, she reminds him that Oscar came over and bought some tools from him. But Robert is still convinced Oscar is angry with him. "Maybe I should go over there and have it out with him," he tells his wife. Flabbergasted, his wife asks him why in the world he would want to do such a thing when he isn't even sure Oscar is angry with him. She tries to convince him to calm down, but Robert isn't having any of it. He goes over to Oscar's house unannounced and accuses him of cutting down the tree deliberately. "And I'm tired of all those dirty looks you're giving me too. Why don't you be a man and tell me what this is all about?" Oscar is dumbfounded. He doesn't have the faintest idea what Robert is talking about.

Robert truly believes he was defending himself against Oscar's anger when in reality he was actually defending himself from his own anger. By accusing Oscar of being out to get him, Robert is able to justify his own anger and avoid feeling guilty.

Many Ventriloquists also use the defense mechanism called projective identification—a process whereby you behave toward others in such a manner that elicits the very behavior that will confirm your own underlying beliefs. For example, Anita feels angry with herself for spending too much money shopping. She knows she has a problem with overspending and she has tried to watch herself, but she just can't seem to control her buying impulse. She is disgusted with herself for not having more self-control.

She knows her husband is going to hit the roof when he finds out how much she spent, so she sneaks the shopping bags into the house while he is in the shower. But she knows that he will eventually see the credit card bills. That night at dinner, her husband makes a comment about the fact that she made filet mignon for dinner. "Gosh, honey, what's the occasion?" is all he said. But Anita heard, "You spent too much money," so she answered, "I know you think I have no control and no consideration for the fact that you work hard for this family, but you don't have to get on me all the time about spending. I disgust you, don't I? You think I'm a failure, don't you?" Anita's husband wasn't thinking any such thing. It was how Anita felt about herself.

Innocent Victims

Innocent Victims are often seemingly passive people who seldom or never get angry but who often feel victimized by other people's aggression or anger. They tend to take on the victim role in relationships, allowing other more aggressive or dominant people to take charge of situations. This is often the case with battered women, women who allow their husbands to abuse their children, and men who allow themselves to be dominated by their partner. Although they don't actually cause someone to be abusive, their passive behavior can encourage abuse in others.

Innocent Victims often become involved with abusive partners. The partner who is playing the role of the Innocent Victim—remaining passive and seldom if ever getting angry—is likely to become involved with a partner who expresses himself in an overtly aggressive manner. The more she withholds her anger, the more her partner will experience and express more than his share.

The phenomenon of the Innocent Victim is also explained by the concept of the shadow or dark side in Jungian psychology. The theory says that the more you repress what you consider to be unacceptable or repulsive characteristics within yourself, the more you create a dark side of yourself called the shadow. The shadow concept also works in relationships. People are often attracted to partners who represent their shadow and who, in fact, act out their repressed emotions for them.

If you are an Innocent Victim, you are either afraid of your own anger or you have a strong belief that it is not okay to get angry. So instead of getting angry yourself, you get involved with angry, aggressive, or abusive people who act out your anger for you. Sometimes your passive behavior actually pulls anger out of others. You may or may not engage in behavior that antagonizes others, but your very passivity is so potent that it encourages aggression in others.

"You Do My Dirty Work for Me"

Virginia grew up in a household where men were valued much more than women. She and her sisters were required to cater to the men in the family, including her younger brothers. Both parents showed an obvious preference for the boys. Virginia's mother spent very little time with her daughters except when they were cleaning the house. Virginia's brothers were allowed far more privileges as they were growing up, and they were sent to college, whereas she and her sisters were told that college would be a waste of money.

Virginia got married just out of high school to a man who had a reputation for being a hothead. Because it was expected of her, Virginia had two children: one boy and one girl. Carrying on the family tradition, Virginia preferred her son over her daughter. Her husband was also misogynistic and practically ignored their daughter except to single her out for punishment. In fact, he was downright cruel to her. Instead of feeling a mother's natural sense of protectiveness toward her daughter, Virginia actually encouraged her husband's cruelty. She would often complain about her daughter even though she knew it would mean certain punishment for the girl. Eventually, Virginia's husband and her oldest son both began sexually abusing her daughter. But once again, instead of feeling protective, Virginia convinced herself that her daughter was asking for it.

Finally her daughter's sexual abuse was reported to the authorities by a concerned teacher. In order to regain custody of her daughter, Virginia was ordered by the court to attend counseling sessions. During these sessions, Virginia came to recognize how she was allowing her husband and older son to act out the anger she herself felt toward her daughter. In actuality, it was the anger she felt toward her own mother for ignoring her and favoring her brothers.

Anger Magnets

Anger Magnets attract angry people. Often this occurs because angry and abusive people are attracted to passive partners who will allow themselves to be dominated and controlled. But it is also because Anger Magnets are often so deadened to their own anger that they simply cannot spot anger in others. While everyone around them may realize that a potential partner is an extremely angry person, Anger Magnets are oblivious. This was the case with Roxy. When Terence first started asking her out, Roxy's friends warned her that there was something about him that didn't feel right. They told her that he seemed like a very angry person and they were afraid for her. Roxy just blew them off, saying they were being paranoid. Even after one friend reported to Roxy that she'd seen Terence blow up at a waitress for not bringing his coffee, Roxy made excuses for him, saying that everyone has a bad day.

Once Roxy got involved with Terence, her friends became even more concerned. He was extremely sarcastic toward her, even in front of her friends, and he frequently blew up over minor things and stormed off. But Roxy continued to make excuses for his behavior and refused to believe he was an angry, abusive person. It wasn't until he became physically abusive to her that she finally had to face the truth.

In addition to attracting angry people to them, Anger Magnets are also attracted to angry people. Those who tend to repress their anger are often attracted to those who express their anger freely. There is more going on here than merely opposites attracting. In many circumstances, people actually choose partners who will act out their (unconscious) anger for them.

"What Do You Mean He's Violent?"

Myrna had a history of attracting angry men. Her first boyfriend, Dan, was convicted of involuntary manslaughter after getting into a fight with another man at a bar. Witnesses testified that Dan became so enraged that he continued to hit the man even though the man had been knocked unconscious and he attacked anyone who tried to pull him away. Although several of his friends testified in court that Dan had a history of violence, Myrna stood by him and went to see him in jail for several months.

Then Myrna became involved with a man who became physically abusive toward her. This was a complete shock to Myrna, who saw him as a gentle, caring man who wouldn't hurt anyone. After he beat her up the first time, she still refused to believe he was an angry abuser. He told her that he had never hit a woman before. Two months later, he beat Myrna so badly that she had to go to the hospital.

When Myrna's friends confronted her about her tendency to get involved with violent men, Myrna refused to see a pattern. She swore it was just a coincidence.

In reality, Myrna was an intensely angry person herself. She was afraid of her own anger because her mother had been very volatile and abusive and Myrna was afraid of becoming like her.

PART TWO

CHANGING YOUR ANGER STYLE

CHAPTER 5

The First Steps to Change

In chapters 6 through 9, you'll learn specific strategies to help modify or transform each of the major unhealthy anger styles and their variations. This chapter presents a nine-step program to get you started in changing your anger style no matter what it is. These steps include

1. Learning what healthy anger looks like

2. Discovering the origins of your anger style

3. Writing your anger autobiography

4. Discovering the feelings underneath your unhealthy anger style

5. Learning effective communication and assertiveness skills

6. Learning stress reduction skills

7. Learning anger management skills

8. Taking care of your unfinished business

9. Reminding yourself why you wish to change your anger style and believing you can do it

Although you will no doubt be anxious to move on to the chapter or chapters specifically addressing your anger style, don't short change yourself by skipping these important steps. I also suggest you buy a notebook or journal to use specifically for your anger work. Some of my clients call this their *anger journal*. You can use your anger journal to keep track of your moods, help discover your particular anger triggers, and record your progress along the way. Later on, I will recommend several writing exercises and you'll also be making several lists along the way.

Step One:
Learn What Healthy Anger Looks Like

Anger is like an internal alarm system telling us that there is something wrong. Some people choose to ignore the alarm completely and go back to sleep. This is obviously not a healthy way of dealing with anger anymore than it would be if your smoke or burglar alarm went off in the middle of the night and you just turned over and went back to sleep as if nothing were wrong. When you have a healthy relationship with anger, you view your anger as a warning sign and take the time to look for the reason for it. Sometimes the reason may be obvious and other times it may take a little more investigating. When you do discover what is wrong in your environment, a relationship with someone else, or the relationship with yourself, you take action. This change may involve modifying something in your environment, communicating your feelings or difficulties with the other person, or addressing the feelings that triggered your anger in the first place.

If you have a healthy relationship with anger, you understand that anger, like all feelings, is a normal part of life. You know that becoming angry does not make you a bad person and that everyone becomes angry at times. You don't hide from your own anger or the anger of others because you recognize it is a signal that there is a problem that needs to be solved.

Often we become angry because there is a conflict of some kind (internal or external). For example, perhaps you want something from someone, but your needs are not being met. This impasse causes frustration, which in turn causes anger. In this case, the solution is for you to communicate in a very direct way what you feel, as well as what you want or need from the other person. For example, instead of using "you" messages (e.g., "You never think about my needs and feelings. You're so selfish"), it is best to use "I" messages that communicate what you are feeling without putting the other person down (e.g., "I would like you to pay more attention to me").

A person with a healthy relationship with anger is able to make a distinction between which situations warrant an angry response and which do not. We are all bombarded daily with situations that could cause us to become angry: the teller at the grocery store is slow; someone interrupts you in a conversation; someone cuts in front of you and takes your parking space; a friend is late for lunch. If we became angry at all these situations, we would end up being angry all the time. Healthy people recognize that in the interest of their mental and physical well-being they have to ignore some of the less important infractions. They must make a distinction between what is merely annoying and what is important to address—that is, they must choose their battles. Getting angry every time you get a slow teller at the grocery store is a waste of time and energy, so you need to take a deep breath and let it go. The same holds true of every time someone cuts you off on the freeway or takes the parking space you were waiting for. But telling a friend who keeps you waiting for forty-five minutes that you are angry may be a necessary move in order to maintain the relationship or to avoid having to wait for her in the future.

People who use anger well understand that the purpose of anger is to solve problems, not just to ventilate their feelings and certainly not to hurt other people. They understand they need to express their anger appropriately and in moderation as opposed to losing control and yelling, screaming, or belittling the other person. We need to take responsibility for what we say and do, even in the heat of anger, and not use our anger as an excuse to become abusive or behave in another inappropriate way. If someone takes the parking space you were waiting for, it is understandable if you get angry. Leaning out of your car window to say, "Hey, I was waiting for that parking space," may be appropriate. Getting out of your car, going over to the person, and screaming, "You asshole! You saw me waiting for that parking space!" is not appropriate, or for that matter, safe.

People with a healthy attitude concerning anger understand the difference between constructive and destructive anger. Anger is constructive when your anger expression affirms and acknowledges your integrity and boundaries without intending to threaten or violate another person's integrity or boundaries. Destructive anger is when your expression of anger is a defensive and rigid attempt to protect your vulnerability and boundaries by intending to threaten or violate another's integrity and boundaries (whether the intention is conscious or not). If you have a healthy relationship with anger, you have learned how to transform anger from a weapon that wounds others and yourself to a tool that promotes understanding and healthy change in relationships. Anger is most constructive when it is used to solve a problem, rather than merely to prove a point or vent your feelings.

Another way to differentiate between healthy and unhealthy anger is to determine whether your anger is appropriate to the situation or irrational and excessive. Although it may be important to tell your friend that you are angry she kept you waiting, it would be inappropriate for you to yell at her or tell her that she is an inconsiderate, selfish bitch who thinks only of herself. It would be excessive for you to make a scene in the restaurant or to get up and charge out of the room.

In general, anger becomes unhealthy whenever it is taken to extremes. This includes

- When you get angry too often. Getting angry too frequently is usually a sign that you are too controlling or too sensitive.

- When your anger is too intense. High degrees of intensity seldom produce positive results. In fact, intense anger is often frightening to people, causing them to close down emotionally and to stop listening to you.

- When your anger lasts too long. When you don't express your anger in a healthy way, your anger will tend to linger. When you find that your anger does not subside even after you have spoken your mind, it is usually an indication that your intent is to humiliate or control the other person. Also, when your anger does not subside, your body's systems are prevented from returning to normal levels, making you susceptible to further aggravation.

There are distinct disadvantages to excessive, irrational anger.

- Others usually react negatively to it.
- It frequently increases frustration rather than releasing it.
- It causes you to lash out at others, including those you love.
- It can lead to antisocial acts.
- It can cause you to become obsessed with people and to become paralyzed with anger.
- It leads to more anger.

Another measure of having a healthy relationship with anger is the ability to let go of anger once it has served its purpose. Once you've recognized the problem and communicated your feelings and needs, it is time to let it go. Unfortunately, many of us have a difficult time letting go of our anger once it is activated. It's almost as if we want to punish the other person for causing us to become angry in the first place instead of recognizing our choice in becoming angry. This is especially true of those who view anger as a negative emotion and those who don't like losing control. But once the problem has been addressed and solved, it is time to move on, not to continue to wallow in anger. In summary, you have a healthy relationship with anger when you are able to

- Recognize that anger is a signal that there is a problem
- Discover what the problem is
- Act on the problem in an appropriate way (usually by communicating your feelings and needs)
- Let it go once you have expressed your feelings or the problem has been resolved.

Step Two:
Discover the Origins of Your Anger Style

Usually the key to your beliefs about anger and your anger style lie in your childhood. Most of us were raised to believe that anger is a negative emotion, and only a fortunate few grew up in families where it felt truly safe to express their angry feelings. We often take on our anger style because of parental or societal messages. Most of us didn't have positive role models when it came to discovering healthy ways to deal with our anger and we often repeat the ways our parents interacted with one another or the ways they treated us. The following set of questionnaires and exercises will help you identify patterns you may have established based on parental messages and your parents' behavior.

QUESTIONNAIRE: *Parental and Cultural Messages*

The following questions have no right or wrong answers and there is no scoring. They are intended to help you discover the origins of your anger style. I suggest you spend as much time as necessary answering them because they may provide insights into your behavior that you may not find anywhere else.

1. What was your mother's anger style? What about your father?

2. Which style of anger did you and do you identify with the most—your mother's or your father's?

3. Do you remember thinking to yourself that you never wanted to express anger the way one or both of your parents did?

4. Which way of expressing anger were you most comfortable with when you were a child—Anger-In or Anger-Out?

5. What was the most acceptable way to express anger in your family?

6. What was the most acceptable way to express anger in the culture (ethnic, religious background) in which you were raised—Anger-In or Anger-Out?

7. What were the messages you received from your family about expressing anger? For example, was it acceptable or unacceptable to confront someone when you were angry?

8. Were you ever punished for expressing your anger?

9. Were you ever rewarded for not expressing your anger?

10. Were males in your family given more permission to be Anger-Outs than females? How about in the larger community—at school, in the neighborhood, in your culture or religion?

QUESTIONNAIRE: *How Did Your Parents Interact When They Were Angry?*

1. Did your parents discuss problems rationally or did they tend to blow up at one another?

2. Did they express emotions easily or did they hold in their feelings?

3. Did your parents tend to blame one another for their problems?

4. Did your parents often argue?

5. Did your parents give one another the silent treatment?

6. Did your parents yell at one another?

7. Did your parents emotionally or verbally abuse one another?

The answers to these questions will help you begin to make the connection between how your parents interacted and the way you have chosen to interact with others. The following writing exercise will help you still further.

EXERCISE: *Your Anger Legacy*

1. Which of your parents do you feel handles anger the best? List the ways this parent copes with his or her anger.

2. Which parent handles his or her anger the worst? List the negative ways this parent expresses his or her anger.

3. Which one of your parents are you most like when it comes to expressing your own anger? List the ways you are like this parent in terms of anger expression.

4. Which of your parents are you most like when it comes to dealing with other people's anger?

These questionnaires and the exercise may have unearthed some painful truths for you. As much as we often try hard not to be like our parents, especially a parent who was explosive, abusive, or who put up with the abuse of others, we often become more like them than we care to admit. If you have found this to be true, don't get discouraged. Now that you are aware of the similarities, you can make changes.

In addition to the role of parents and other caretakers in shaping your anger style, painful or traumatic events can also help shape your anger style. The following exercise will help you make the connection between these events and your decision about which anger style to take on.

EXERCISE: *Your Anger Decisions*

1. Close your eyes and remember the worst experience you ever had of either witnessing or experiencing someone else's anger.

2. How did this experience make you feel about yourself? About the person expressing anger?

3. Did you make any conscious decisions about anger or about the way anger should or should not be expressed based on this experience? If so, write these decisions down on a sheet of paper or in your journal.

4. Close your eyes and remember the last time you became extremely angry. How did you feel about the fact that you were so angry (i.e., Were you embarrassed? Afraid? Ashamed?). What sensations did you experience in your body?

5. Based on how you felt, did you make any conscious decisions about allowing yourself to become extremely angry in the future? If so, write them down.

6. Go back to the last time you experienced anger in an intense way. Did you express your anger outwardly in any way? If so, were there any consequences? How did others react to your expression of anger?

7. How did you feel about the way you expressed your anger? How did you feel about others' reactions?

8. Based on this experience, did you make any decisions about the way you would express your anger in the future? If so, be sure to write them down.

Changing your negative anger beliefs and negative anger patterns will be an ongoing process. You have taken an important first step by identifying your beliefs and patterns, recognizing their origins, and acknowledging the decisions you have made about anger.

Assignment. Keep an ongoing list of the messages you remember receiving from your parents (and other caretakers and authority figures) about anger. Include both verbal and nonverbal messages (e.g., facial expressions when you got angry). Also include the messages you received about anger from watching your parents interact with one another and from the way they dealt with their anger toward you.

We will return to the subject of your anger beliefs later on in this chapter. For now, let's go on to Step Three, where you will get an even clearer picture of where your anger beliefs and decisions originated.

Step Three:
Write Your Anger Autobiography

Throughout your life, you may change your anger style from passive to aggressive, from aggressive to passive, from passive to passive-aggressive, from projective-aggressive to aggressive, and every other variation. You may have started out as an assertive child only to learn that it wasn't safe to express your anger in an open and honest way. You may have learned by observing the adults around you that it is better to mask your anger by presenting a false front of congeniality or to get even with the person in an underhanded way. Or, you may have learned early on to deny your anger or to turn your anger against yourself. Later on in your life, your repressed anger may have burst out of you, causing you to become abusive to your spouse, children, or aging parents.

We all have an anger story. It is a chronology of how we developed our anger style, how our anger has changed through time, and how our anger style varies from one situation to the next. Writing down your anger story will help you become more clear about the origins of your anger style and why you react in one way with some people and a different way with others. Most important, writing down your anger story will provide you with clarity so that you can begin to make healthy changes. The following questions and suggestions will aid you in getting started and in deciding what to write about:

1.   Study childhood pictures of yourself, starting when you were about six months old and continuing all the way up through high school. Pay attention to any significant changes you see in your facial expression and posture, especially during times of change or crisis (the birth of a sibling, a move to a new city, the death of a close relative or parent, your parents' divorce, an incident of sexual abuse).

2.   When was the first time you remember being angry?

3.   Remember the ways you coped with anger as a child. Can you remember any significant incidences regarding the way you acted out your anger (e.g., getting into trouble at home for hitting your siblings, being expelled from school for fighting, bullying other children, or vandalizing other people's property)?

4.   Remember any incidences where you were bullied by other children or abused by your parents or other authority figures. How did you express your anger at having been violated in this way?

5. Ask your parents and/or siblings about the way you expressed (or didn't express) anger when you were a child and adolescent.

6. Do you remember a time when you changed your anger style (e.g., from passive to assertive after you took karate lessons, from aggressive to passive-aggressive after your father beat you for hitting your sister)?

7. Do you feel that anger has been an asset or a liability in your life?

My Anger Story

I share my anger story with you as a way of modeling one way of writing yours.

A happy, sweet-looking little baby with a wide open, trusting face and big smile—that's what I see when I look at my baby picture at six months old. A sullen, angry child with the kind of defiant look you find in the eyes of juvenile delinquents or adult criminals—that's what I see when I look at the next professional picture taken of me at four years old. What happened in those three and a half years to change me so much? I have no memory of much of what happened during that time, but I do know a few things. The sweet little baby my mother adored had grown into an inquisitive, independent child who didn't hesitate to speak her mind or question the reasons why she should do something. This was unacceptable to my mother, who was raised to never question authority, to be a "nice" little girl, and to subvert her anger. She had to break me—meaning she had to let me know who was boss and take away any vestiges of defiance from me—much like people do with horses so that they can ride them. This was a common practice of parents during the 1950s, especially those from the South. Unfortunately, breaking a child of any tendency to be defiant also tends to break their spirit.

In many ways my mother did break my spirit—in the sense that I lost some of my exuberance and spontaneity and my self-esteem was lowered. Mostly she made me even more defiant. As often happens with men in our culture who are tyrannized by their fathers, I became so overwhelmed with shame and my self-esteem was so damaged by my mother's harshness and criticism that I had to create a false self in order to cover up my true self, who was far too vulnerable to survive.

Whereas my nature had originally been very gregarious and outgoing, I took on a quality of "niceness" when I was around my mother and a quality of defiance when I was out of her sight. I nearly flunked kindergarten because I wouldn't mind my teacher when she tried to make me stop talking so much to my two friends. When my third-grade teacher, Mrs. Haight, scolded me for writing too small when we were studying penmanship, I wrote in huge letters outside her room, "I HATE MRS. HAIGHT." My assertive style of expressing my anger had become more aggressive.

Then I was sexually molested when I was nine years old. This experience added to the shame I already felt from my mother's tyranny and her unreasonable expectations that I be a perfect little girl. The sexual abuse merely confirmed what I already knew—I was a bad seed, an evil person who deserved any bad treatment that came my way. I acted out my shame and anger by introducing other children to sex—essentially passing on the abuse that had been acted out against me. I compensated for this by trying extra hard to be good when I was at home—never arguing with my mother, no matter how unreasonable she was.

Around this time I also started stuffing my anger and sadness by overeating. When kids at school made fun of me or rejected me because I didn't have nice clothes to wear, I came home and comforted myself by overeating. When my mother was unreasonable or went to bed leaving me by myself for the evening, I sneaked into the kitchen and ate myself into oblivion.

By the time I was twelve, all vestiges of my good girl act were gone. I began acting out my anger in more overt ways. We moved to a new neighborhood where the kids were much more streetwise than the kids I had been raised around. I started smoking, drinking, and sneaking out of the house to have dates with boys who were in their twenties. Although I stopped short of having sex with them, I would make out with them for hours. After I was raped by one man, I took my anger out on society by shoplifting every weekend for months until I was finally caught. Shamed by the experience of being brought home in a police car and humiliated by my mother beating me with a switch from an apricot tree in front of the neighbors, I turned myself around in high school and once again became a good girl, submerging any anger I felt.

We moved to a new neighborhood and I got a fresh start at a new school. I still stuffed my anger down with food, but there was no more acting out. I'd been scared straight. But even though I had turned a new leaf, my mother didn't trust me and constantly accused me of lying. I felt like I couldn't win and started arguing with her. It seemed that the more independent I became the more she wanted to control me. Meanwhile, my mother's drinking, which was on a nightly basis, crossed the line into alcoholism. After a few drinks her personality changed and she would become argumentative. I lost whatever respect for her I still had and began talking back to her. At times our arguments escalated into knock-down, drag-out fights.

As you can see I changed my anger style several times. By the time I reached four years old I had changed from an assertive anger style to an aggressive one. But I'd also learned that I couldn't be aggressive with my mother, so with her I was passive-aggressive, quietly going along with whatever she wanted but sneaking behind her back to do whatever I wanted. I also took on the passive anger style of stuffing my anger whenever I couldn't afford to express my aggression (with the kids who taunted me) and as a way of punishing myself. By late adolescence, I was able to stand up for myself with my mother but in a very aggressive way.

Assignment. Now it is your turn to write your anger story. Take as much time as you need. You may want to write it in segments, as I have done, writing about your childhood, then your early twenties, and so forth.

Step Four: Discover the Feelings underneath Your Unhealthy Anger Style

In order to manage your anger in a healthy way, you will need to discover the emotions that lie underneath your anger. For example, if you tend to stuff your anger, you may be coming from a place of fear. If you tend to blame yourself when things go wrong, you may be stuck in shame.

Fear

Some believe that fear and anger are, in many ways, variations of the same emotion. This is based on the fight-or-flight response discussed earlier. Situational factors (How big is the threatening person in front of me? Does he have a gun? Do I remember karate?) can determine whether the emotion will be experienced as fear or anger.

It may seem preferable to choose the fight response over flight, but some people are unrealistic about their ability to fight off would-be attackers, choosing to fight even if outmuscled or outsmarted. Others believe that fear is always underneath anger. Some people are so used to responding with anger to threatening situations that they become oblivious to feelings of fear. For example, children who grow up in alcoholic or otherwise dysfunctional families learn at an early age that no one is there to protect them and that they must grow up fast in order to protect themselves. These children become "pseudoadults," acting far older and more mature than they really are. Some assume the responsibility of taking care of younger siblings and some even take care of a weak, sick, or inadequate parent. Because these children have so much adult responsibility, they simply can't afford to allow themselves to feel afraid. Instead they cover up their fear with a mask of bravado and learn to fight their way through life.

Unfortunately, because they are out of touch with their fear and vulnerability, as adults they have difficulty experiencing true intimacy with a partner and they may become deadened to softer emotions. They may also become dependent or even addicted to stimulants such as coffee or stimulant-type drugs, and they often become addicted to drama or risk-taking behavior. In order to heal from these tendencies, a fear-avoidant person will need to look under his or her anger to discover the fear underneath.

Sadness

Many of us were raised to believe that it is a weakness to cry or feel sadness. For example, when Cameron was growing up, his father always told him that big boys don't cry. If he fell down, scraped his knee, and started crying, his father would make fun of him and call him a crybaby. If he came home crying because another kid beat him up, his father would scold him and tell him: "As long as you cry and carry on like that, every bully at school is going to come after you. You've got to toughen up. You've got to become a man."

And that's exactly what Cameron did. He not only doesn't cry but he doesn't allow himself to feel sadness or pain. Instead he covers it up with anger. If people hurt his feelings, he puts them down. If he feels rejected by a woman, he calls her horrible names and tells her she wasn't worth his time. When his dog became sick and he had to put him to sleep, Cameron didn't cry, even though he loved his dog deeply. Instead he raved and ranted at the vet, blaming him for not diagnosing his dog properly.

If you continually cover up your sadness with anger, you risk seriously affecting your ability to experience true intimacy with others. Your tough exterior may hide your pain, but it also keeps others away. Eventually you won't be able to open up emotionally, even if it is safe to do so. In order to tear down the defensive wall that separates you from others and from your true self, you need to allow yourself to grieve. You need to cry all the tears you weren't allowed to cry before.

Guilt

We often defend against feelings of guilt with anger. For example, parents can't help feeling guilty when harm comes to their child. It's a natural reaction even when a parent is not responsible for the incident. But instead of facing their guilt over not being able to protect their child better, many parents cover it up with anger. Some take their anger out on their child, blaming her for causing her own accident, for not minding them, and so on. Others blame teachers, police officers or other authorities, and some even blame the law. Although anger is sometimes warranted, in many cases it is just a way to defend against guilt feelings, especially when there actually was something that could have been done to prevent harm.

Some people know in their heart that they didn't try hard enough to save a relationship. When the relationship ends, they are initially overwhelmed with guilt, but instead of facing their true feelings and taking responsibility, they blame their partner.

Why should you allow yourself to feel the guilt under your anger? Feeling guilt over an act or a failure on your part helps you to feel empathy for others. It motivates you to take responsibility for your actions by confessing, apologizing, making amends, or repairing the harm that you caused. By defending against your guilt with anger, you enable yourself to continue harming others (and yourself) by repeating unacceptable behavior. You don't learn from your mistakes but instead blame others for them.

Shame

For many people, especially those who are Ragers, Blamers, or Self-blamers, shame is the emotion that most often motivates their anger. Shame activates a wish to hide, shrink, or disappear that can become so overwhelming that we have to distance ourselves from others because of it. We usually do this by blaming or attacking others or by projecting onto others.

Shame is often confused with guilt, but it is not the same emotion. When you feel guilt, you feel badly about something you did or neglected to do. When you feel shame, you feel badly about who you are. When you feel guilty, you need to learn that it is okay to make mistakes. When you feel shame, you need to learn that it is okay to be who you are.

The initial sense of shame often fosters a subsequent anger—a humiliated fury—as an attempt to provide temporary relief from the debilitating experience and effects of shame. In fact, experts such as

Donald Nathanson, the author of *Shame and Pride,* suggest that "the most prominent stimulus to anger is humiliation." As shame typically involves a real or imagined disapproving other, this fury is easily directed toward others.

Anger is most commonly used to defend against shame in shame-based people who suffer from low self-esteem, feelings of worthlessness, and self-hatred and who feel inferior, bad, unacceptable, and different from others. Shame-based people were often taught that they were worthless or bad by hearing adults say things like, "You are in my way," "I wish you were never born," or "You'll never amount to anything."

Shame is also the result of severe physical discipline, emotional abuse, neglect, and abandonment, which all send the message that the child is worthless, unacceptable, and bad. These acts also convey that adults will treat children any way they want to because children are a worthless commodity. Children feel humiliated for their so-called bad behavior and the consequences (i.e., being chastised or beaten in front of others, being told, "What's wrong with you?" or "What would your precious teacher think of you if she knew who you *really* are"). Last but not least, shame comes from having to endure shame-inducing traumas like child sexual abuse.

By discovering the emotions underneath your anger, you will be better able to define the problem clearly, affording you a better chance of solving it. The following assignment will help you in this endeavor.

Assignment. Identify your underlying emotions. For one week, make a note in your journal of each and every time you become even slightly angry. For each incident, describe what happened and try to identify your underlying emotions (i.e., fear, shame, guilt, frustration, disappointment). Then write about this underlying emotion. For example: "I'm afraid Mark's going to leave me now that he knows who I really am. I guess that's why I started the argument. I wanted to push him away before he had a chance to reject me."

Step Five: Learn Effective Communication and Assertiveness Skills

Learning how to communicate your angry feelings in a direct and con-structive way is one of the most important steps in transforming your anger into a positive force. When should you take the risk of commu-nicating your angry feelings? Research shows that the direct expres-sion of anger at the time that it occurs and toward the immediate cause is the healthiest and most satisfying way of releasing tension.

How do you know whether it will be constructive to express your angry feelings directly to the person with whom you are upset? There are at least four constructive expressions of anger. Before you choose to confront someone with your anger, ask yourself if you are moti-vated by a desire for at least one of the following:

1. To communicate feelings of hurt

2. To change the hurtful situation

3. To prevent a recurrence of the same hurt

4. To improve the relationship and increase communication

The most effective way of communicating your anger is to trans-late it into clear, nonblaming statements that establish boundaries. This is commonly referred to as being assertive. Many people associ-ate being angry with yelling and being out of control, but expressing anger can become a positive thing when done with a firm, controlled tone of voice, good eye contact, and a confident posture that's neither aggressive nor robotic. With assertive confrontation, you need to take responsibility for your emotions and clarify your expectations and limits. Unlike aggression, assertive behavior does not push others around, deny their rights, or run over people. Instead assertiveness reflects genuine concern for everyone's rights since it is grounded in the belief that every human being is of equal value.

No matter what your anger style, learning assertiveness will help you communicate your feelings and needs more effectively. Those with an aggressive anger style often become frustrated because they lack good communication skills and feel like others can talk circles around them. Those with a passive anger style are usually afraid to communicate their feelings directly and firmly, so others tend to speak over them or outshout them. Those with a passive-aggressive anger style mask their anger in judgments, criticisms, condescending sarcasm, or underhanded retaliation not only because they are afraid of rejection or retaliation but because they lack the assertiveness skills to communicate their anger directly. Assertiveness will benefit those with a projective-aggressive anger style by offering them the permission and tools they need to own their own anger instead of projecting it onto others.

Assertive Statements

What you say and the way you say it makes all the difference between being heard and being ignored or dismissed. It is not necessary to put the other person down (aggressive) to express your feelings (assertive). It is important to express yourself and take responsibility for your feelings, not to blame the other person for how you feel. An assertive statement to communicate anger needs to contain two thoughts:

1. The fact that you are angry and the reason why you are angry

2. What you want the other person to do or how you want the situation to change

A simple form for such a statement is: "I feel angry because _____. I want you to _____. Every situation is different, of course, so the words may differ. Be sure to follow these simple rules:

- Avoid using "you" messages, which not only put the person receiving the message on the defensive but can reinforce feelings of helplessness in the person sending the message.

- Always use "I" statements in order to take responsibility for your reactions. "I" statements give information about you as opposed to making judgments about others.

- Avoid name calling, insults, or sarcasm.

- Avoid using the words *never* and *always,* which tend to shame the other person and make him or her feel hopeless and misunderstood.

- Always express why you are angry and what you think could improve the situation.

Important Aspects of Assertive Behavior

These rules can help you to be more assertive, but there are also other aspects of behavior that can contribute to the success of an assertive exchange. In order for an interaction to be effective, follow these guidelines:

1. *Have good eye contact.* When you look directly at the person as you speak, it helps to communicate your sincerity and to improve the directness of your message. If you look down or away most of the time (as those who have a passive anger style tend to do), you present a lack of confidence. But if you stare too intently (as those with an aggressive anger style tend to do), the other person may feel uncomfortable.

2. *Notice your body posture.* An active and erect posture while facing the other person directly will lend additional impact to your message. In some situations in which you are called upon to stand up for yourself, it may be helpful to do just that. Standing up will undoubtedly give you additional courage and will encourage the other person to take you more seriously and pay closer attention to what you are saying.

3. *Notice your distance and physical contact.* Distance from another person has a considerable effect on communication. Standing or sitting very closely to another person, or touching another person, suggests intimacy in a relationship (unless you happen to be in a crowd or in a very cramped space). This can put the other person at ease, assuring him or her that while your words may be confrontational, you still feel close to him or her. Sitting close can also be intimidat-

ing. Coming too close to another person may offend her or make her defensive. If you are unsure as to whether you are encroaching on another person's space, check it out with her.

4. *Pay attention to your facial expressions.* In order to communicate effectively and assertively, your facial expression needs to be congruent with your message and your intention. An angry message is clearest when delivered with a straight, nonsmiling facial expression as opposed to a weak, smiling expression. (Those with a passive anger style often deliver their messages in this weak manner because they want to soft-pedal what they are saying.) A friendly communication should not be delivered with a dark frown, which can be intimidating. (Those with an aggressive anger style often look angry even when they are not.) Let your face say the same things that your words are saying.

5. *Pay attention to your gestures.* Accentuating your message with appropriate gestures can add emphasis, openness, and warmth. On the other hand, intense, abrupt, or threatening gestures such as finger-pointing, table-pounding, and fist-making can be intimidating or frightening.

6. *Notice your voice, tone, volume, and inflection.* The same words spoken through clenched teeth in anger offer an entirely different message than when they are whispered in fear. If you can control and use your voice effectively, you can acquire a powerful tool for self-expression. Practice speaking into a tape recorder, trying out different styles until you achieve a style you like.

Step Six: Learn Stress Reduction Techniques

Researchers have discovered that higher stress is associated with higher anger levels. It has also been found that stress-related anger is more likely to find expression in physical symptoms or vented outwardly in blaming statements rather than being suppressed or discussed in constructive ways.

As mentioned earlier, the fight-or-flight response serves an important function in emergency situations that require quick physical responses. Unlike our ancestors, whose lives were constantly threatened by wild animals or enemies who wished to kill them or take their property, most of us do not encounter physical threats very often. This doesn't mean we don't still feel threatened, however. We may often feel afraid that someone will take our property, threaten our job, or hurt our child. Those who live in crime-ridden cities feel threatened on a daily basis. Even though we may feel like defending ourselves or running away, we seldom do. We've learned that it is usually unwarranted except in extreme circumstances when we or someone close to us is actually being physically threatened. But our bodies still sense danger and still prepare us to fight or flee. For example, the body can respond to stress in the following ways:

- Hormones and adrenaline are released to increase energy to ensure faster response.

- Muscle tension increases for readiness to run or fight.

- Breathing becomes rapid to send more oxygen to the brain.

- Increased heart rate and blood pressure ensure that cells have sufficient blood supply.

- The digestive process shuts down to divert the blood flow to the muscles and brain.

- Pupils dilate to let more light enter the eye.

In other words, our bodies are on alert. So what do we do with that adrenaline? What do we do with our muscle tension and hyperalertness? Some people go into an exaggerated sense of fear or even panic. But most of us end up turning this stress into anger, and we take our anger out on those around us, most especially our loved ones. We blow up at our partner or our kids after an especially stressful day. We overreact when someone says something that hurts our feelings and end up yelling. We snap at the waitress who forgets to bring the water. Our anger isn't always proportionate to the offense.

Not all stress is caused by emergencies. There are many other kinds of stress-inducing events that occur all the time, ranging from small short-term stressors like being late for work to long-duration stressors like serious illness, financial problems, or legal battles. It is the buildup of stress that causes us problems. Over time stress can create depression, anxiety, pessimism, and dissatisfaction. It can make you difficult to live with because people under stress are often irritable, irrational, and hostile. And stress can lead to many physical problems such as insomnia and breathing problems, fatigue, headaches, chest pain, aches and pains, heart palpitations and dizziness, and digestive problems and loss of appetite or compulsive eating. It can raise blood cholesterol levels, thereby increasing a person's risk for cardiovascular disease and heart disease. Stress can contribute to weakening the body's immune system, which may result in increased susceptibility to infection. For all these reasons it is imperative that stress-reduction methods be used to reduce stress levels in general and stress-related anger levels in particular.

The Relaxation Response

Relaxation is the primary antidote to stress. According to Herbert Benson, a Harvard physician and noted stress researcher, each of us possesses an innate protective mechanism from overstress—the relaxation response. By developing this relaxation response, you can counteract the increased sympathetic nervous system activity that accompanies the arousal of the fight-or-flight response (i.e., anger arousal) and restore your body to its normal balance. Relaxation can be intentionally induced by activities that decrease sympathetic nervous system activity by programming the hypothalamus to trigger lower blood pressure and a reduced heart rate. The relaxation response decreases oxygen consumption and carbon dioxide elimination. The heart and breathing rates simultaneously slow and blood flow to the muscles is stabilized. A quiet, restful, relaxation state results.

There are numerous techniques that you can use to develop your relaxation response, such as meditation, yoga, progressive relaxation, self-hypnosis, autogenic training, and biofeedback. Before I describe some relaxation techniques, it is important to know that there are four components necessary no matter which method you use:

1. *A quiet environment.* Choose a quiet, calm environment without distractions.

2. *A mental device.* Having a mental device—a sound, word, image, statement, fixed gaze—helps you shift your mind from being externally oriented to being internally oriented. This is important because it enables you to feel what is going on in your body and to overcome your tendency to let your mind wander. Use the same image, word, or sound each time you practice your relaxation response, since consistency will strengthen the association between your thoughts and the desired level of physiological arousal.

3. *A passive attitude.* This is probably the most important component. Adapt a let-it-happen attitude instead of trying to force yourself to relax. When distracting thoughts occur, just return to your mental device.

4. *A comfortable position.* Remain in a comfortable position so that there is no undue muscular tension. When a position gets uncomfortable, it is a sign that tension is increasing. Switch to a position that makes you feel more comfortable.

Relaxation Response Exercises

1. *Deep breathing exercises.* Slow breathing from the diaphragm is one of the most effective ways of managing stress and can help release tension in a difficult situation.

    • Slowly inhale as you count to two, hold your breath for two counts, then exhale your breath for two counts.

    • Repeat this pattern twenty times. Notice how much more relaxed you are.

- Once you have become proficient in this technique, slow down your breathing even more by inhaling as you count to four, holding your breath for four counts, then exhaling to four counts.

2. *Relaxation exercises.* By following these instructions for only fifteen minutes a day, you can substantially lower your stress level and your tendency to erupt in frustration or anger.

   - Lie on your back on your bed or a mat.

   - Allow your feet to flop outward and your hands to rest by your sides (make sure your hands are not in a fist or otherwise tightened).

   - Close your eyes and sigh several times to release tension.

   - Begin to breathe slowly, pausing after each exhalation.

   - Relax your toes, feet, and legs. Allow all tension to drain.

   - Do the same with your fingertips, arms, and neck.

   - Ease the tension in your shoulders by lowering them.

   - Mentally smooth the muscles in your face.

   - Be aware of the relaxation in your muscles. When you are ready, slowly open your eyes and stretch. Bend your knees and roll on your side before getting up slowly.

3. *Mind/body techniques.* These powerful methods of stress control work for many people.

   - Meditation, which induces deep physical relaxation and mental awareness:

     Sit comfortably and upright, close your eyes, and relax.

     Focus your mind on an object, breathing out and in to the count of four, or look at an object such as a candle flame or flower.

     Repeat a word such as *peace* or *ohm* either out loud or silently. Continue for at least fifteen minutes.

- Visualization, which assists in calming you before or after a high-pressure event, situation, or conflict:

Either sit comfortably or lie down.

Relax your body and clear your mind by doing the breathing or relaxation exercises just described.

Imagine yourself in a peaceful, beautiful place, perhaps a serene garden, a quiet beach, or on top of a hill with a beautiful vista. Smell the scents and hear the sounds.

Now, as you take in a deep breath, imagine yourself being there and feeling comfortable, safe, and relaxed.

Continue taking slow, deep breaths, allowing yourself to enjoy the relaxation.

Repeat affirmation phrases such as "I feel peaceful" or "I am completely relaxed."

Remind yourself that this place is available to you whenever you feel stressed out. It is just a few slow, deep breaths away.

- Mindfulness or active meditation, which helps you stay in the moment instead of worrying or obsessing:

Focus all your attention on whatever you are doing. Observe shapes, colors, and textures. Focus on the movement of your body.

Stay in the present moment without worrying about the past or the future.

Further Tips for Stress Reduction

The following are more stress-reduction techniques and strategies. I'll provide more throughout the book:

- *Keep a stress diary.* You can add this information to your anger journal if you have been keeping one. Begin to keep track of situations that cause you stress. Describe situations and people with whom you have conflicts or circumstances that make you anxious. Ask yourself why a particular situation or person caused you to feel upset. How might you think or act differently in the future to help you cope more effectively?

- *Be active.* Exercise helps eliminate stress hormones from the bloodstream and stimulates the release of endorphins, which provide a feeling of well-being. Aim for at least thirty minutes of moderate activity a day.

- *Avoid stimulants.* Stimulants such as caffeine, nicotine, and alcohol stress out the body and can make you more irritable and impatient. Try herbal teas and drink lots of water.

- *Laugh more.* There has been considerable research on the healing benefits of laughter. Tell jokes, read humor books, and watch comedies. Cut out humorous cartoons and share them with a friend.

- *Add aromatherapy oils to your bath or shower.* Choose from basil, cedarwood, geranium, juniper, lavender, rose, and ylang-ylang. Use alone or combine two or three.

Step Seven:
Learn Anger Management Skills

The goal of anger management is to reduce both your emotional feelings and the physiological arousal that anger causes. Although those with an aggressive anger style are most in need of anger management skills, everyone can benefit from the following strategies:

1. *Learn to tune in to the true sources of your anger.* Ask yourself questions such as "What about the situation made me angry?" "Am I feeling hurt? Afraid? Threatened?"

2. *Learn what your purpose is in becoming angry.* Ask yourself what you want to accomplish by being angry. For example, "What are the things I will do or not do?" or "What specifically do I want to change?"

3. *Learn communication skills that will maximize your chances of being heard and that will facilitate the resolution of conflicts.* Blowing up or arguing can offer temporary relief, but it doesn't really change the situation. Follow the suggestions for assertive communication.

4. *Learn to calm down or take a time-out.* It is impossible to think clearly when your emotions are high. By calming down, stepping back, or taking a time-out, you can gain more clarity about the situation and better determine what role you played in the interaction.

5. *Learn that you cannot change another person.* You can only change yourself, the way you react to another person, or your circumstances.

6. *Learn from your anger.* Ask yourself what you can learn from the situation. For example, "What is the real issue here?" or "What role did I play in this?" or "What can I do differently next time?"

7. *Learn to self-observe and to change your part in negative relationship patterns.*

8. *Learn to identify your particular anger triggers.*

Step Eight:
Take Care of Your Unfinished Business

As discussed early in this chapter, we usually take on a particular anger style because of the way one or both of our parents dealt with anger. Often our fear of becoming like one of our parents causes us to take on the opposite anger style or to become so afraid of anger that we are unable to function properly in adult relationships. Some of us become so afraid that we will repeat one or both of our parents' ways of expressing anger that we avoid certain situations like getting married or having a child. For example, I was so afraid of becoming like my emotionally abusive mother that I chose not to have children. I was certain that I would belittle and berate my children as my mother had done to me, and I didn't want to be responsible for damaging a child in that way. Looking back, if I had had a child in my twenties or thirties, I'm certain that I would have been abusive. It wasn't until I had completed my unfinished business with my mother and my sexual perpetrator that I was free of the rage that had so controlled my life—and by that time I had reached forty.

If you find that you are afraid of repeating your parent's anger style, the key will be for you to complete your unfinished business with that parent and with your past. By releasing your unexpressed emotions concerning your parent and resolving your relationship, you can successfully individuate from your parent and thus create a separate identity. It is normal and healthy for you to feel angry at a parent who was a poor role model. One aspect of completing your unfinished business with your parents will be for you to name, own, and release this anger. The following exercise will help.

EXERCISE: *Your Anger toward Your Parents*

- Write your parent (or other caretaker) a letter expressing how you feel about the fact that he or she gave you such negative messages about anger or was such a poor role model concerning the expression of anger. Don't hold back and don't censor yourself. Your parent need never know anything about your anger or this letter.

- Include in your letter exactly how your parent's way of expressing and dealing with anger affected you and why (for example, you may wish to list specific incidents).

- Once you have completed the letter, you can choose to tear it up, keep it for your records, or actually send it to your parent.

Although our current anger may feel new, it is often old anger that has come back to haunt us. In fact, we often place the faces of people from our past onto those who are currently in our lives. Our current anger often reflects the same old unresolved issues that have evoked anger throughout much of our lives. Instead of reacting to a present-day situation, we may be reacting to another incident, often a traumatic one. Someone may remind us of a parent or other caretaker, or a particular situation may bring back unpleasant memories. In order to prevent this from happening on an ongoing basis, disrupting our lives and causing problems in our relationships, we need to work on our unfinished business from the past. The best way to do this is to examine why we got angry in a particular situation, then try to make connections with our past.

EXERCISE: *Taking Care of Unresolved Issues*

This exercise will help to clear up the backlog of hurtful, unresolved issues from your past.

1. Make a list of all the people who harmed you in the past. Go back as far as you can remember to include your parents and other caretakers, other family members, childhood friends, and past lovers and partners.

2. Go through your list and one by one write down all the reasons why you are angry with the person in question. Writing helps you get in touch with your true feelings. It brings to the surface emotions that have been buried deep inside that you have been afraid to acknowledge. And writing down your feelings helps with the confusion you may feel about exactly why you are angry.

3. Now write a letter to each person who wronged you, outlining all the reasons why you are angry and hurt. Don't censor yourself—say exactly what you feel. Explain in detail how the person's actions or inaction harmed you. You can decide at a later date whether you wish to actually send the letter. For now, the purpose of the letter is to help you get your anger and pain out.

This process will obviously take a great deal of time and energy, but it will be well worth it. Take your time and don't try to do too much in one sitting. Continue this process until you have addressed everyone on your list.

Step Nine:
Remind Yourself Why You Wish to Change Your Anger Style and Believe You Can Do It

Although your reaction to a threatening episode may initially appear to be instinctive and impulsive, this does not mean you can't change your anger style. Each episode of anger actually contains a series of split-second decisions. You may choose to bury your anger, cool the anger/ aggression, run it off, scrub the kitchen, paint a picture, or stuff it down by eating a forbidden food. You may yell at the object of your anger or tell him or her why you feel as you do. However you decide to deal with your anger, it is important to understand that it is under your control.

By learning what messages you received about anger, studying your anger history, learning effective communication and stress-reduction skills, and consciously monitoring your anger, you can successfully change your anger style. It helps to imagine and visualize how your life will be different once you have transformed your unhealthy anger style into a healthier one.

Prescription for Change: Let the Transformation Begin

1. Make a list of all the reasons why you want to change your anger style. Include the reasons why your current anger style is not working for you.

2. Make a list of how changing your anger style will positively affect your life or write about how you imagine your life will be different. Make sure you include such areas of your life as your intimate relationships, your relationships with your children, your work relationships, your self-image, your career, and your health. For example, write about how it will feel

when your spouse and children no longer have a reason to be afraid of you and when you no longer have to worry about exploding at work and jeopardizing your job.

3. Visualize how your life will change once you have transformed your anger style into a healthier, more effective one. Envision yourself coping with and expressing your anger in positive ways. For example, if you are an Avoider, visualize yourself being able to stand up to the people in your life who have taken you for granted or walked all over you. Hear yourself calmly but firmly insisting on being treated with respect. Feel the satisfaction and self-respect you deserve.

4. Whenever the going gets tough and you begin to question why you are putting in so much effort to change your anger style, take a look at your list or reread the narrative you wrote. Continue to visualize how your life will be transformed once you've accomplished your goal.

The next four chapters are devoted to changing each of the four unhealthy anger styles. You may identify with more than one anger style (i.e., passive and passive-aggressive, or passive and projective-aggressive) and so the advice given in both these chapters could apply to you. If you choose to read all four chapters, perhaps because you want to understand someone who is close to you, be aware that since the advice given is specifically designed for a particular anger style, it likely won't apply to you unless you have that anger style. For example, those with an aggressive style are encouraged to contain their anger and discouraged from venting it in certain physical ways, while those with a passive style are actually encouraged to vent their anger, sometimes in ways that would be inappropriate for someone with an aggressive anger style.

CHAPTER 6

Modifying or Transforming an Aggressive Style

I used to think the most powerful person was the one who yelled the loudest. Now I know it is the person who is able to stay centered and stay open—the person who is able to listen and communicate.

—SARA, AGE 45

Luther came to see me at the recommendation of his doctor. He had recently experienced a mild heart attack and his doctor was concerned that if he didn't change his lifestyle and his attitude he was a prime candidate for a major attack. When I saw Luther, he was scared: "I know I have to change. I'm angry all the time. I get angry over small things as much as I get angry over big things. The truth is, I get angry anytime things don't go my way. I push myself too hard and I push other people too hard. Instead of slowing down, I expect other people to keep up with me. I'm a perfectionist and I'm impatient. I've got to find a way to slow down and to control my emotions better, but I honestly don't know how. It feels like I've been acting this way most of my life and now it seems like a permanent part of who I am. Can you help me?"

Luther was like many of the men and women I see every day—people who have become so accustomed to responding to life's stresses with anger that they don't know any other way to react; people who are so aggressive, intense, emotional, and competitive that they endanger their own health and well-being, and who are so impatient, demanding, and concerned with perfectionism that they threaten the well-being of those around them.

I assured Luther that I could help him but that he would have to help himself as well by following the program I outlined for him. If you have determined that you have an aggressive anger style, I want to tell you the same thing. You don't have to spend the rest of your life struggling in vain to handle anger that has gotten out of control. It will take effort and patience on your part, but if you follow the recommendations I outline in this chapter, you will be able to successfully transform your anger style into one that is far more healthy and balanced.

Generally speaking, in order to transform your aggressive anger style into a healthier one, your task will involve the following steps:

1. Discovering ways to gain control over your aggressive impulses

2. Identifying your anger triggers

3. Identifying the beliefs that trigger your anger

4. Discovering the emotions underneath your anger

5. Finding ways to manage your anger

6. Finding ways to prevent anger from building up (stress reduction and relaxation)

7. Completing your unfinished business

Step One: Discover Ways to Gain Control over Your Aggressive Impulses

You've learned so far that anger is a normal and healthy emotion but that becoming angry too often and experiencing anger that is too intense is not healthy or normal. Those with an aggressive anger style are not just overly angry but tend to be hostile and overly aggressive. Normal, healthy anger is different from hostility and aggression. Anger is a signal that something is wrong either inside ourselves or in our environment. Hostility is a more pervasive and enduring antagonistic mental attitude. Hostile behavior is anger either previously unexpressed or anger that has been expressed and has failed to effect a desired change. Aggression is behavior directed toward another person (or a person's property) with the intent to do harm, even if the aggressor was unsuccessful. An easier way of making the distinction between anger, hostility, and aggression is that healthy anger is simply an emotion, hostility is an attitude of ill will, and aggression refers to behavior that is meant to harm.

We all have aggressive impulses when we feel threatened, but we must learn to either find appropriate ways to release them or to contain them. For example, when someone cuts in front of you on the freeway, your heart will no doubt pump with adrenaline. You are initially frightened because you almost had an accident, then your fear turns to anger. What do you do? You could rev up your engine and drive so close to the other car that the driver feels the same fear you just felt. But you could cause an accident or anger the other driver even more, causing him to retaliate. And we've learned from the rise in cases of road rage that it isn't smart to respond to another driver in an aggressive way, no matter how threatened we may feel by his behavior.

In this case and in most others, it is best to control our impulse to become aggressive. Unfortunately, you may be unable to do so. As soon as you feel threatened and your adrenaline starts to pump, it is like you are on a one-way street with no way out. All reason is put aside. All you can focus on is getting back at the person who threatened you, no matter what the personal cost is to yourself, your loved ones, the person with whom you are angry, and innocent bystanders.

Although all humans have aggressive impulses, what makes some people aggressive is how frequently and pervasively they act on these impulses. If your primary anger style is aggressive, you will find yourself engaged in continual conflict with others because you are constantly feeling threatened and because you are unable to control your aggressive impulse to retaliate.

Sigmund Freud and other early psychiatrists believed that if people didn't release their aggressive impulses, they would build up inside until they suddenly exploded in anger, wrecking havoc and possibly endangering others. Some therapists still believe this. But Freud was only partly right. Sometimes when aggression is ventilated, the desire to keep it going actually increases. This is particularly true for those with an aggressive anger style or an aggressive personality. In actuality, although the impulse is to get a release from the built-up tension by forcing the angry energy out, in a sense you may just be priming the pump. The more you ventilate your anger, the more anger you feel you need to ventilate. This is partly due to the fact that aggressive anger increases rather than decreases frustration.

Many people report feeling better immediately after releasing their anger in an aggressive way. The instant release of pent-up energy feels like a relief. Unfortunately, the good feeling doesn't last very long. This is because aggression creates its own problems. It usually hurts other people, either emotionally or physically. Responding aggressively (e.g., yelling, throwing things, hitting walls, controlling, blaming) can hurt others' feelings (e.g., when you snap at them or criticize the way they do something), damage self-esteem (e.g., when you put them down, call them names, blame them for making your life miserable), frighten them (e.g., when you throw things or put your fist through a wall), or harm them physically (e.g., when you slap, hit, or punch others). As a result of being hurt by your aggressive action, other people may distance from you, reject you completely, or respond by physically assaulting you.

In addition to hurting other people and risking being rejected or harmed yourself, by responding in an aggressive way you set yourself up to feel guilt and shame. If you hurt someone emotionally, you may feel guilty when you recognize the effects of your words or actions (your child looks at you with fear in his eyes, your wife cries herself to sleep and is unable to be physically close to you for days afterward). If you hurt someone physically, you will no doubt feel terrible each time you have to witness the results of your anger (the blackened eye of your best friend, the bruised arm of your mate).

Last but not least, those who have an aggressive anger style are more likely to suffer from health problems such as cardiovascular disease, high cholesterol, and high blood pressure. For example, Dr. Ichiro Kawachi at the Harvard School of Public Health conducted research concerning the causes of heart disease. He found that high-anger men were almost three times more likely to have a heart attack or develop angina than low-anger men, even after other possible influences were taken into account, such as smoking, blood pressure, cholesterol, weight, alcohol, and family history of cardiac disease. This echoes the experiences of many doctors and psychologists who see a direct connection between how much anger people report and their overall health risk.

According to Redford and Virginia Williams in *Anger Kills,* hostile people are at higher risk not only for cardiovascular disease but other illnesses as well. This is true for a variety of reasons, including reduced social support, increased biologic activity when angered, and increased indulgence in risky health behaviors.

Assignment. Log your hostility and aggression. In order to determine just how much hostility and aggression you have, begin keeping a log of each aggressive action or urge (e.g., to blow your car horn, to slam a door), angry feeling (e.g., your face getting hot and red), or angry thought (e.g., thinking someone is incompetent or stupid) that you experience each day. For example, aggressive acts or urges can range from very mild expressions with your body (frowning at someone who appears to be taking too long to do something) to more extreme actions (shouting at someone or physically assaulting him). At the end of each day, review your entries. You'll probably be surprised to discover just how hostile and aggressive you are.

Find Alternative Ways to Release Your Anger Energy

Even though there are serious consequences to releasing your anger in aggressive ways, because there is such a feeling of temporary relief aggression can be difficult to give up. So what do you do when you

are angry and your adrenaline starts to pump? You'll need other outlets that will feel just as good and offer the same kind of release.

The most effective activities for releasing anger energy are taking a
brisk walk or run or playing a sport such as basketball, racquetball, or
swimming. If you are extremely angry and competitive, it is best to play
an individual sport in order to avoid physical skirmishes with others. I
suggest you shoot hoops, play one-person racquetball, go to a batting
cage and hit some balls, or practice your tennis game. Activities such as
boxing, wrestling, and hockey are usually not recommended for those
with an aggressive anger style because they are aggressive sports that
may actually reinforce aggressive behavior instead of releasing energy.
Instead find physical activities that make you feel calm and relaxed.

Writing your angry feelings down is also a good way of finding
some relief. Instead of telling someone off, write down all the negative, hateful things that are going through your head. Don't censor
yourself—just let it all come out. As a further way of releasing tension, you can then tear up what you have written.

Take a Time-Out

What if you are about to blow up in front of someone? This person
has said or done something that has really ticked you off and you're
just about to erupt. It takes about thirty seconds from the time you
begin to notice your anger signals before you finally explode. This
gives you just enough time to get away so that you can cool off.
There's no time for a discussion and no time to work off your anger in
a physically appropriate way. You just need a time-out.

A time-out will give you a chance to let your anger subside and
ultimately to regain control of yourself. Go to a place where you can
relax such as your car, your room, or a park. If you're inside, distract
yourself by watching TV, listening to music, or reading. If you're out-
doors, take a walk, ride a bicycle, or go for a run. Even though you
may feel like hitting a punching bag, throwing something, or chop-
ping wood, these activities may actually fuel your anger or even be
dangerous. And don't call up a friend or go to your local hangout
where you can talk and get more angry. The point is to calm down.

Once you've accomplished your goal, it is time to go back to the scene of your upset. Don't go back too soon or you will get angry all over again. Take all the time you need. It is far more important for you to avoid a blowup than to avoid keeping someone waiting.

If you were having a discussion with someone close to you when you started to get angry, go back and continue the conversation. Hopefully you will be able to stay calm this time. If not, table the conversation until you can remain calm. The goal is to be able to discuss things more reasonably—even issues that are controversial.

The following guidelines will help you to take time-outs when you need them:

1. *Tell people you are close to that you are going to try something new to help you manage your anger.* Explain what you are going to do from now on when you start to get heated. Do this in advance because you don't want people to come after you when you leave suddenly (a natural thing to do) or to think you're just running away from an argument or trying to punish them by not talking. Most people will want to support you with this endeavor, since your anger has likely been a problem for them as well as for you.

2. *Don't just leave.* Tell the person you are taking a time-out. Say something like, "I'm sorry, but I need time to cool off," or "I'm getting really angry, so I need a time-out."

3. *Assure the person you will be back, then keep your word.* Time-outs are not an excuse to avoid dealing with conflicts. You need to return to the scene of the upset so that you can learn to discuss things calmly.

4. *If you find yourself becoming angry with someone you don't know well or someone you haven't told about your need for time-outs, simply excuse yourself and tell the person you will be back in a few minutes.* He will probably assume you need to use the rest room or that you aren't feeling well. If after a few minutes you haven't calmed down sufficiently to avoid a confrontation when you return, call the person on the phone

or send a messenger to say that you have taken ill or you have an emergency. This strategy may seem extreme, but in some cases, such as certain business situations, it is a far better alternative than blowing up at your boss, the head of the company, or a potential client.

Grow Up

It is natural for us to want what we want when we want it. As children, we kicked and screamed and threw tantrums when we didn't get what we wanted. We may have even tried to hit those who wouldn't give us our way. For some, these tantrum-throwing behaviors continue into adulthood. Immature patterns of expressing anger include

- Impatience
- An inability to delay gratification
- A tendency to act out anger
- An inability to control impulses
- A low tolerance for frustration

Part of growing up is learning to take things in stride. Aggressive, immature people tend to demand fairness, agreement, appreciation, and that things go their way. We all want these things and we all get hurt and disappointed when we don't get them but those with the aggressive anger style demand them, and when their demands aren't met, their disappointment becomes anger or even rage.

Another part of growing up has to do with learning patience, being able to delay gratification, and not acting out all our feelings. Even though we might feel like hitting someone who gets in the way of something we want, we learn to control our impulses.

Laura: The High Price of Impatience

Laura, who was referred to me by the court for counseling, was arrested because of her impatience and inability to control her impulses. She was taking a flight from Los Angeles to New York for an important business meeting. After working several hours on her report, she managed to fall asleep for several hours only to be awakened by the announcement that the plane would soon be landing. She hadn't gone to the bathroom for several hours and now she had to go. There was a line for the rest rooms, so she waited impatiently for her turn. Finally, she was next in line, but before she got the chance to open the lavatory door, someone stepped around the corner and slipped in front of her. Laura was furious and pushed the woman aside. "It's my turn!" she scowled at the woman. "No, it's my turn," the woman countered as she pushed her way into the rest room. Undaunted, Laura grabbed the woman's hair and pulled her back. At this point, two flight attendants appeared to pull Laura off the frantic woman. Laura was livid and started yelling and trying to escape from the attendants. It took two more attendants to tackle her to the floor. When the plane landed, Laura was taken off in handcuffs and charged with endangering the flight and the passengers. After several witnesses were interviewed, Laura learned that there was another line coming around the back of the plane and that in fact it was the other woman's turn to go into the lavatory. Clearly, Laura needed to learn patience and to control her aggressive impulses.

Some people find it easier to tolerate frustration and control impulses than others. This is partly due to individual, constitutional, and temperamental differences, as well as how we are raised. The capacity to experience anger is at least partially programmed into us genetically. But it is also learned. For example, we become angry in situations today that remind our unconscious brain of similar situations from our past. Whereas anger may have served a positive purpose in one or more situations, it may not serve a useful purpose today, yet we are programmed to get angry nevertheless. What worked in the past may now actually work against us. In Laura's case, she was programmed to be impatient by well-meaning yet poorly informed parents who bent over backward to satisfy her every whim. Instead of delaying gratification once in a while to teach her patience, they gave into her demands just to keep the peace.

Own Your Anger

One of the best ways to learn to control your aggressive impulses is to begin to own your anger. Those with an aggressive anger style tend to get angry a lot and to hang onto their angry feelings too long (creating hostility) because they believe that the solution to their anger lies outside of themselves and is caused by the actions of others. They tend to believe that if other people would only act differently, they wouldn't get angry.

But the cause of your anger is not outside yourself. Instead of blaming other people for making you angry, you need to begin to focus on your own emotional response. You must stop getting stuck in the "if onlys": if only your wife had picked up the cleaning like you asked or if only your employee had done the job right, you wouldn't have gotten so angry. The cause of your anger doesn't lie in the actions of others. It lies within you—within your own biological and psychological makeup and reactions. Instead of focusing on what others are doing that makes you angry, you should be focusing on why you get angry at what others are doing.

Directing all your anger into coercing or forcing others to change their behavior is not only frustrating but futile. Instead of externalizing your anger, focus on what is happening inside of you. After all, it's your anger, not theirs.

You will never eliminate unhealthy anger from your life until you stop trying to change how other people treat you instead of focusing on changing your own behavior. As long as you externalize your anger—that is, viewing the cause of your anger as outside yourself— you will remain irritated, upset, and stressed. As long as you continue to believe that the reason you are angry so often is because other people are inappropriate, disrespectful, or incompetent, you will continue to have problems with your anger. Forget how others are treating you. Focus on what is happening inside of you.

Step Two: Identify Your Anger Triggers

The next step is to identify your triggers or hot buttons. Whenever you have an intense reaction to something, chances are high that one of your triggers or hot buttons has been pushed. Triggers are suppressed or repressed fears, insecurities, anger, resentments, or regrets that cause automatic and often intense emotional reactions when activated. These intense reactions are frequently experienced as abusive by other people. By identifying the specific situations, actions, words, or events that trigger these emotional reactions, you can begin to anticipate and manage them better, thus avoiding some of your aggressive or abusive behavior.

Assignment. What are your triggers?

1. Start keeping a log of the situations that consistently make you angry. Think about the last time you got angry. What was it about? Pay attention to the factors involved such as your general mood or the presence or absence of alcohol. Did something in your environment or something that was said remind you of a past experience?

2. Ask those closest to you to help by telling you what they notice tends to trigger your anger. This will require trust on your part, but if you really want to transform your aggressive anger style and gain control of your anger, it may be a necessary risk. Those closest to you may be able to help you discover patterns to your behavior, thus making it more predictable. Behavior that is predictable is easier to manage.

Common Triggers for Those with an Aggressive Style of Anger

- *Feeling out of control.* Often those with an aggressive anger style gain a false sense of control by dominating and controlling others. When someone refuses to do as they say, they become enraged because they no longer feel this sense of false control.

- *Having to wait or not getting their way.* Those with an aggressive anger style tend to be impatient and have a low tolerance for frustration. Therefore, when they are forced to wait or to adjust to not getting what they want when they want it, they often blow up in anger.

- *Being shamed.* Those who were heavily shamed as children or adolescents are often triggered by any treatment or attitude from others that appears to be disapproving, disrespectful, critical, or judging.

- *Being ignored or rejected.* Often those who become aggressive or abusive are triggered when they feel ignored or rejected. This is most likely due to the fact that they were neglected or abandoned when they were children.

- *Envy.* Some people are triggered by feelings of envy. If someone close to them has a good experience, it makes them feel bad about themselves. This may trigger memories of being a less favored child or of having a parent who ignored their needs.

Step Three: Identify the Beliefs That Trigger Your Anger

Unhealthy anger is often triggered by irrational, narcissistic, and unrealistic expectations or beliefs that we have about other people, the world, and ourselves in general. Examples of such beliefs include

- It's me against the world. I must remain on the defensive; otherwise, I'm going to get hurt or taken advantage of.

- I must do well and be approved of; otherwise, I'm no good.

- Those with whom I associate must treat me with consideration, kindness, and respect; otherwise, they are no damn good.

- The conditions under which I live (family, employer, etc.) must be exactly the way I want them to be; otherwise, it's catastrophic.

Assignment. Discover your problematic beliefs:

1. Spend some time thinking about what beliefs you have that trigger your anger.

2. Make a list of these beliefs.

3. Take a close look at your list to discover which of these beliefs have given you the most difficulties in life and which you are now willing to reevaluate.

Once you are aware of the beliefs that trigger your anger, you can decide whether you want to continue believing in ideas that cause you to become angry and that are probably not even true. Countering these beliefs can be difficult, but it is possible.

Letting Go of the Belief That It Is You against the World

Aggressive people tend to be more defensive than other people. In fact, their defensiveness can be described as a type of character armor. Most people with an aggressive anger style live with the motto, "It's me against the world" and "Everyone is guilty until proven innocent." They assume that other people are constantly using them, undermining them, manipulating them, or taking advantage of them.

It only stands to reason that if this is how you think and how you perceive others, you will constantly be involved in conflicts and altercations. But what if you are wrong? What if it is not you against the world? What if other people aren't using you or undermining you? And what if the people who constantly offend you don't even realize it and certainly don't intentionally set out to hurt you? The truth is, most of the time other people are not out to get you. In fact, they aren't even thinking about you. They are just innocently going about their own business, trying to get through each day the best they can. If they do something to offend you, it is probably not intentional. Therefore, begin to treat others as if they are innocent instead of guilty.

You can't change other people, but by treating them as if they are innocent, you can profoundly change the dynamics of your relationships.

Here are some suggestions that will help you begin to change your way of viewing other people:

- Assume that others are doing their best.

- Stop taking things so personally.

- Give others the benefit of the doubt. View them as innocent until proven guilty instead of the other way around.

- Take people's comments at face value instead of always looking for an ulterior motive.

- Practice patience. Don't constantly expect others to meet your unrealistic expectations. Give people a break.

- Instead of always focusing on trying to change how other people treat you, focus on how you can change your own behavior in reaction to theirs.

Of course, there will be people who come into your life who are not innocent—people who will try to take advantage of you or mistreat you. Ironically, the more you treat people as if they are innocent, the more likely you will be able to spot those who are not.

Think about how your life would be different if others saw *you* as innocent. You wouldn't have to be defensive and protective of yourself. You wouldn't have to work so hard to prove that you are right. You wouldn't feel so full of shame. You might even start liking yourself more.

Step Four: Discover the Emotions underneath Your Anger

It is especially important for those of you with an aggressive anger style to pay attention to what lies underneath your anger. If you are like most people with an aggressive anger style you tend to make a habit of ignoring the real cause of your anger. For you, anger is more than likely an all-consuming feeling that prevents you from experiencing other feelings. Anger has probably become a way of life and a way you are used to feeling, rather than a message that something is wrong. But without the message, there is no chance for positive change. Instead of anger being a force of empowerment, it has become a heavy burden.

There is almost always another emotion under your anger that will lead you to the real cause of your feelings of upset. Some people even believe that anger is not a primary emotion at all but a reaction to other emotions. Anger wells up when we feel afraid, humiliated, hurt, guilty, rejected, frustrated, threatened, or jealous. Reread the section on discovering the feelings underneath your anger from Chapter 5.

Anger and Fear

Often the angriest person is actually the most frightened. Those with an aggressive anger style are often covering up deep inadequacy and failure. We often intuitively sense this whenever we experience bullies. We sense that those who have to prove they are tough are actually compensating for deep feelings of inadequacy.

Cyrus: The Scared Little Boy Hidden under the Bravado

When Cyrus was a little boy, he used to run and hide when his father would come home. This was because his father was a very scary guy. He started yelling at Cyrus's mother the moment he came into the house, and he slammed doors and put his fist through walls when he got angry, which was often. If Cyrus made a mistake, like accidentally dropping a glass, his father would chastise him mercilessly and he was often hit for not doing his chores to his father's satisfaction.

Those who knew Cyrus outside his house would never recognize the frightened, intimidated boy described here. Cyrus was a loud, aggressive boy at school who liked to play rough with his friends. He was often in fights on the playground and hung out with a group of rough boys who liked to stand on street corners and intimidate younger, weaker boys who passed by. Eventually, Cyrus started bullying other kids on his own. He'd pick a kid at school who was clearly intimidated by him and harass the kid mercilessly until the boy started to cry. If the kid dared stand up to Cyrus, he'd pummel him with his fists until teachers would pull him off the boy.

Like Cyrus, if you have an aggressive anger style, the reason those who are weak, afraid, vulnerable, or incompetent bother you so much is that they remind you of a denied and rejected part of yourself. When you were a child, you too may have felt weak, afraid, and vulnerable, but there may have been no one there to comfort you. Your parents may have been too busy to notice you needed comforting, or you may have reached out for comfort only to be rebuffed with comments like, "You're too big to get on Mommy's lap" or "Big boys (or girls) don't cry. Be a man." Facing your vulnerable feelings alone may have felt too frightening, so you built up a defensive wall to hide behind. To the outside world you may have appeared strong and confident, but this was only a facade to cover up your real feelings of vulnerability. You may have become so good at pretending to be strong and invulnerable that you even fooled yourself. Soon you forgot what your real self was like.

The only time you are reminded of these softer feelings is when you experience them in someone else. But this reminder is not a welcome one. It doesn't feel good—in fact, it may be quite painful emotionally (although often only on an unconscious level). You become angry with the person who reminded you of these feelings. You hate yourself for feeling them and hate the other person for having them. You see your real self reflected back at you and you don't like the view. In order to break down the protective wall that you built around yourself, you may need to seek the assistance of a caring professional who will provide a safe environment in which you can revisit your childhood.

The Pain underneath Your Anger

Underneath your anger, your need to control, your need to blame, your impatience, and your intolerance of others' weaknesses is a great deal of pain. In fact, pain often causes you to become angry in the first place.

Unless someone has hurt us, we usually do not become angry with her or him, especially in an intimate relationship. Sometimes we hang on to our anger in order to avoid facing the underlying pain. This is what I did. As an adolescent and into my twenties, I built up a defensive wall to hide the overwhelming pain I felt about my childhood. I used my anger to motivate me to move away from my mother and my hometown and to start a new life in Los Angeles. All alone in the city with only $100 to my name, I hid my loneliness and my pain under a facade of strength and bravado.

It wasn't until my mid-twenties that the sadness I had been hiding became so overwhelming that I could no longer contain it. I decided to start therapy. During my first session with my therapist, I explained to her what I thought was wrong with me and what I felt I needed. I'll never forget her words. She looked into my eyes and said, "You certainly are controlling, aren't you? I wonder what you're hiding underneath all that control." She had seen through my facade and I instantly felt safe with her. For the next two years, I spent a large part of each session sobbing, letting out all the pain I'd held in for so long. My therapist acted as a compassionate witness to my pain, empathizing with me and soothing me. Slowly but surely, my wall of defensiveness came down, brick by brick.

If you find that you are angry most of the time and that your anger seems to linger on too long, take a peek underneath to see if there is pain that you have been avoiding. If you don't expose your pain, you will never have a chance to heal. Instead it will fester and worsen, causing you to become more bitter, defensive, and angry every day.

Anger and Shame

Shame can be one of the most devastating emotions, causing a shrinking sense of worthlessness and powerless. In reaction to this debilitating feeling and in an attempt to provide temporary relief from it, many people experience what is referred to as a humiliated fury.

While most people react with anger whenever they are made to feel humiliated, devalued, or demeaned, shame-based people tend to be extremely sensitive and defensive, and they go into rages when they feel criticized or attacked, which is often. Because they are so critical of themselves, they believe everyone else is critical of them. And because they despise themselves, they assume everyone else dislikes them. If you are shame-bound, one teasing comment or one well-intentioned criticism can send you into a rage that lasts for hours. Because you feel shamed by the other person's comment, you may spend hours making the person feel horrible about himself—in essence, dumping shame back on the other person.

Shame-based people feel very vulnerable underneath all their defensiveness. Another way that shame-based people use anger as a defense is by attacking others before they have a chance to attack. It's as if they are saying, "I'll show you. I'll make you feel like crap because that's what you think of me."

If you are shame-bound, you may also use anger to keep people away by raging at them. In essence you are saying, "Don't get any closer to me. I don't want you to know who I really am." This raging works—it drives people away or keeps them at a safe distance. Of course, this also makes you feel worse when you realize that others are avoiding you.

"YOU SHOULD BE ASHAMED OF YOURSELF"

Noah was raised by very strict parents who never seemed pleased with anything he did. They used shame and guilt as their primary disciplinary tools. Whenever Noah didn't meet their expectations, whether it was not getting all A's at school or not cleaning his room to their satisfaction, they would humiliate him mercilessly: "You should be ashamed of yourself. Most kids don't have your advantages. Some have to work after school to help their families. All you have to do is bring your lazy behind home and put your nose in a book. Is that too difficult for you?" As an adult, Noah is keenly sensitive to criticism of any kind. He immediately goes into a rage, trying to make the other person feel as bad as he was made to feel. He is extremely critical of himself, expecting perfection from himself and chastising himself whenever he falls short of his own expectations.

Step Five: Find Ways to Manage Your Anger

Now let's put it all together—your triggers, your beliefs, and the feelings underneath your anger. With this complete picture of your anger under your belt, you are in a much better position to control and manage it.

Assignment. Dissect your anger. The next time you become angry with someone, ask yourself the following questions:

1.   Why does this make me angry?

2.   What am I feeling underneath my anger? Am I feeling hurt? Afraid? Ashamed? Guilty?

3.   Does it remind me of anything from the past? Which one of my hot buttons was pushed?

4.   What is the belief that caused the anger? What beliefs do I have about the way people should or should not treat me?

Let's say that you are having a conversation with a friend when she answers the phone and starts talking to someone else. You become enraged. Why do you think you are so angry? Let's go through the questions:

- *Why am I angry?* Perhaps you are angry because you feel ignored. Perhaps you want your friend's undivided attention.

- *What am I feeling underneath my anger?* Perhaps you feel hurt because you don't think you are very important to your friend.

- *Does it remind me of something from the past?* Maybe you're angry because it reminds you of how your mother used to spend hours talking with her friends on the phone or around the kitchen table instead of paying attention to you. Or maybe it reminds you of all the times your mother was busy doing something else instead of being with you (e.g., going to bars, spending time with your stepfather).

- *What is the belief that caused my anger?* You may have a belief that others should give you their undivided attention. When someone becomes distracted while talking to you, it may trigger your anger. Or perhaps you believe that if your friend really cared about you, she would prefer to spend time with you rather than talking to someone on the phone. Or maybe you believe it is rude for your friend to interrupt her time with you to talk on the phone with someone else.

In order to learn how to control and manage your anger, you'll need to learn to communicate your feelings to others in nonthreatening ways (such as reporting your anger instead of attacking) by using "I" messages instead of "you" messages. And you'll need to learn to channel the energy and impulses that govern aggression into creative outlets, productive acts, and improved relationships.

You can't get rid of, change, or avoid the things or people who enrage you, but you can learn to control your reactions. The following models have been used successfully to constructively manage anger. See which model works for you.

The Assertive Model

Becoming more assertive means learning how to get your needs met more satisfactorily without aggression. It means being able to say what you want (or don't want) without having to get angry first. And it means taking care of yourself without abusing other people.

Those who have an aggressive style of anger often do not know how to communicate their feelings and needs in an effective way. By practicing the assertiveness techniques I provide here and in chapter 5, you will find a more constructive way of expressing your anger and learn how to more effectively communicate with others.

1. Identify the specific behavior in the other person that upsets you.

2. Decide if the issue or behavior is worth fighting over.

3. Pick a time that is convenient for both you and the other person and express your desire for a discussion.

4. Express your point of view using the assertive model of giving feedback; for example: *When*—"When you take time away from me by talking on the phone with your friends, . . . " *The effects are*—"I feel hurt and angry." *I would prefer*—"I would prefer it if you'd tell her that you'll call her back later or if you would limit the call to only a few minutes."

5. Negotiate a resolution to the problem once you feel the other person understands the issue and your feelings. For example, perhaps you and your friend can agree that she will limit her phone calls when you are talking together.

6. Make up. Let go of your anger and allow yourself to forgive the other person. Forgiveness involves acknowledging that the other person cannot be perfect. For example, while you may never completely approve of your friend or the way she behaves at times, you can accept the reality that she is who she is and that more than likely her actions are not deliberate attempts to hurt you. Ideally, both you and your friend will at least try to change some behaviors to avoid future conflict over the same issue, but you can't expect your friend to change who she is for you.

7. Ask yourself what you learned about yourself and the other person from this process.

You may have erroneous beliefs about assertiveness, which may get in your way of being willing to try these techniques. These beliefs are (1) that assertiveness is too rational to convey real anger, and (2) that anger has to be forceful, emotional, loud, or explosive to be effective. But the truth is that when you learn how to be effectively assertive, you will find that you are far better able to express the intensity of your true emotions to others and that others will be better able to listen to you and take in what you are saying. This is especially true if you tend to be a "blameaholic" who consistently finds fault in others and blames them for your problems. By using self-acknowledging "I" statements, instead of blaming "you" statements, others will be far more receptive to hearing your concerns and will give you the respect you are so hungry for.

Cognitive Restructuring

Simply put, this means changing the way you think. Unhealthy anger is often caused by the type of unrealistic, irrational, and narcissistic beliefs discussed earlier in this chapter. The cognitive-behavioral model helps people see alternative ways of thinking and reacting to anger. The following techniques have been proven highly effective in managing and preventing anger:

1. Anger, even when it is justified, can quickly become irrational. But logic defeats anger. So when you begin to get angry, use cold, hard logic on yourself. Remind yourself that the world is "not out to get you," just because things aren't going your way. You're just experiencing the normal ups and downs of daily life. Do this each time you feel anger getting the best of you and it will help you achieve a more balanced perspective.

2. Become aware of your demanding nature and begin to translate your expectations into desires. Instead of saying, "I insist" or "I must have" say, "Please" or "I would like." When you are unable to get what you want you will experience the normal reactions of frustration, disappointment, and hurt, but your tendency to become angry will lessen.

3. Aggressive people tend to swear or curse a lot. This reflects their inner thoughts, which can become very exaggerated, overly dramatic, and negative when they are angry. Try replacing these negative thoughts with more rational ones. For example, instead of telling yourself, "It's so terrible, everything is ruined," tell yourself, "It's frustrating and it's understandable that I'm upset about it but it's not the end of the world."

4. Be careful about using words like "never" and "always" when talking about yourself or someone else. Statements like, "You're always forgetting things," or "You never think of my needs" are not just inaccurate but they also serve to make you feel that your anger is justified and that there is no solution to the problem. They also alienate and humiliate people who might otherwise be willing to work with you on a solution.

5. Remind yourself that in your case, getting angry is not going to fix anything and that it won't make you feel better (and may actually make you feel worse).

6. Challenge/change the irrational beliefs/assumptions that cause your anger.

7. Give up shoulds and wants that are narcissistic or otherwise dysfunctional.

8. Acknowledge anger and learn constructive ways of releasing it.

9. Practice distracting techniques such as leaving the situation, taking constructive action, counting to ten, or saying the word *calm* to yourself.

10. Work on becoming more tolerant of others.

11. Don't take yourself so seriously. Use humor and see the absurdity of the situation.

12. Be your own critical parent: "I'm acting like a narcissistic two-year-old. I need to grow up."

13. Practice reframing (thinking of the situation in an entirely different way): "He must be pretty insecure to have done this to me. He's really pathetic."

14. Use imagery. Imagine the worst possible scenario, let yourself feel the anger, then imagine that all you will do is

express your point of view without becoming aggressive or otherwise inappropriate.

Nine-Step Process for Handling Your Anger

1. *Identify what you are feeling underneath your anger or what feeling is causing your anger.* Ask yourself, "What am I really feeling in this situation? Am I feeling frustrated, threatened, afraid, humiliated, rejected, hurt, or jealous?"

2. *Once you have identified the feeling underneath your anger, communicate your feelings to the person with whom you are upset.* Using the assertive model you've now learned, communicate what you are feeling using "I" messages and avoiding sarcasm, name-calling, or vindictiveness. For example, if you feel humiliated, say something like, "I feel so humiliated when you tell your friends about our problems. I don't think it is any of their business and it makes me really angry. I wish you wouldn't do it again."

3. *Avoid making statements that can devastate the other person or destroy your relationship.* Making derogatory statements like, "You're a whore" or "You're a loser," can devastate a person's self-esteem. Threatening to end a relationship, quit a job, or get a divorce can cause irreparable harm. Make sure you don't say anything in the heat of an argument that you can't take back.

4. *Avoid making sarcastic remarks, insults, or put-downs in order to get back at someone.* If someone has done or said something to anger you, instead of coming back at her with sarcasm or insults, tell her what you are feeling and that you do not like what she said. You may discover that she did not mean to upset you or was not aware that what she said or did would upset you. It also makes it clear to the other person that you do not want to be spoken to or treated like that again.

5. *Think through your responses.* Aggressive people tend to jump to conclusions and act on impulse. The next time you find yourself in a heated discussion, slow down and think through your responses. Think carefully about what you want to say instead of saying the first thing that comes into your head. At the same time, listen carefully to what the other person is saying.

When you feel critized it is natural to get defensive. But instead of immediately fighting back, listen to what the underlying message is that the other person is trying to convey. For example, if your significant other complains that you don't spend enough time with her, instead of getting defensive and retaliating by accusing her of trying to smother or possess you, try to understand that she probably feels unloved.

6. *Avoid hitting, pushing, shoving, shaking, grabbing, or physically abusing another person in any way.* If you feel you can't control yourself; leave the scene. You don't have to explain yourself; just get away as fast as you can for your protection as well as for the protection of the other person.

7. *If necessary, take a cooling-off period.* If you find that you are losing control, take a time-out. Take a short walk or go someplace where you can sit and think things out. When you have calmed down, discuss the situation that upset you.

8. *Find constructive ways to vent your anger.* Sometimes a conversation with the person who upset you is not possible or you continue to be so upset that a discussion is not a good idea. In these situations, physical exertion and sports are good outlets for your anger.

9. *Examine what part you had in creating the incident.* Taking responsibility for your part in the situation will prevent you from blaming others and will actually help you to feel more in control of your life.

Step Six: Find Ways to Prevent Anger from Building Up (Stress Reduction and Relaxation)

While the fight-or-flight response is still useful when we need to take emergency action in order to respond to a real threat to life and limb, such threats are quite rare in modern society. Unfortunately our low threshold for triggering the fight-or-flight response is more likely to damage our health than to help us function in today's world. Those with an aggressive anger style tend to experience an even quicker activation of their fight-or-flight response than the average person. This, in combination with a relatively weak parasympathetic calming response, puts them at higher risk of stress-related diseases as the result of too many unnecessary fight-or-flight responses. On the other hand, many people develop an aggressive anger style because their arousal level is high.

In order to reduce your reactivity and arousal levels, you must learn some general relaxation techniques. I've recommended some books on stress reduction in the Recommended Reading section at the end of the book, but here are a few more suggestions to get you started. Refer to chapter 5 for a more detailed description of some stress-reduction techniques.

- Focus on a word or image that will relax you. For example, say the word *calm* to yourself over and over. Visualize a scene that is relaxing to you (the ocean, the mountains).

- Get involved with a creative activity, especially one that involves using your hands.

- Learn and practice meditation or yoga.

- Practice deep breathing. Once every hour, stop and take ten to twenty slow, deep breaths. Breathe in through your nose, hold it a second, then breathe out through your mouth.

- Get a massage or give yourself a head and neck massage. (Gently massage your head by moving the flats of your fingers in small circles against the skin. Start with your scalp, then move to your ears, your face, your forehead, and temples. Continue the circular movements on the sides and back of your neck, then on both shoulders. An alternative way to massage is to simply press your fingertips deeply into the skin).

- Try turning the radio in your car off when you drive. Instead enjoy the calming silence.

- If you have a pet, spend quality time with it, stroking it, brushing it, and walking it. Watch how your pet relaxes and follow its lead. If you don't have a pet, consider getting one. Research shows that people who have pets generally have less stress.

- Use humor to get yourself out of a bad mood. Numerous laboratory experiments lead to the conclusion that amusing someone sharply reduces the likelihood that he or she will subsequently engage in overt acts of aggression. When you begin to get annoyed at someone, try seeing the humor in the situation. For example, I used to become very annoyed that no matter what line I got in at the grocery store it seemed to be the slowest one. The teller had to stop to get more change, the person ahead of me needed a price check, and so on. Now, instead of becoming annoyed, I have decided that I just don't have good grocery line karma and I laugh at all the circumstances that occur to make me have to wait longer. It is especially important that those with an aggressive anger style learn how to laugh at themselves. If you find yourself in a compromising situation, instead of becoming defensive and blaming or attacking someone else, try making fun of your own self-importance, impatience, need to be right, or tendency to control.

- Have a good cry once in a while. Stress chemicals are released through emotional tears.

- Find a spiritual outlet. Medical research has repeatedly shown that individuals who regularly attend a religious service have less stress-related illness such as heart attacks and high blood pressure.

Reducing Stress by Changing Your Attitudes and Behavior

If you have an aggressive anger style, certain attitudes and behaviors that you exhibit make life more stressful. This is because the very nature of these attitudes and behaviors creates tension in you and in others. By becoming conscious of these attitudes and behaviors and the damage they cause, you will be in a better position to change them. Here are some stress-producing attitudes:

1. *Having to be right.* We all like to be right and we all like to have others agree with our point of view. But if you have an aggressive anger style, you may carry this tendency to the extreme. In your need to be right, you often make others wrong. You may carry on a discussion until it becomes an argument or worse in your attempts at forcing the other person to agree with your point of view. If you are unwilling to consider any other point of view and are not even willing to listen to the other person's perspective, this is bound to create tension in all your relationships as well as continual power struggles. While it is perfectly fine to have strong beliefs and moral principles, when you try to impose your beliefs and opinions on others without respecting their right to have their own opinions, problems will continue to arise.

2. *Having to be the best.* Having an overly competitive attitude and comparing ourselves to others creates a great deal of tension. No matter how good we are at something, there is always someone better. No matter how smart or attractive we are, there is always someone smarter or more attractive. You can still continue to strive for improvement, but until you accept yourself as you are, you will never feel good about yourself no matter how much success you achieve. Once you feel good about yourself, you will also be less concerned about having to be the best.

3. *Having to be perfect and expecting others to be perfect.* You've heard it before—no one is perfect. But that probably hasn't stopped you from trying to be perfect or from pressuring others to be perfect. What may stop you is realizing that your need for perfection creates a great deal of tension and stress in you and in those around you, greatly contributing to your tendency toward aggressive anger. If you want to feel good about yourself, and be at peace with yourself, you will need to stop chastising yourself and others for not being perfect. Being imperfect does not mean you or others are a failure. We all have strengths and weaknesses. A more realistic goal is to strive for being the very best you can be in any situation and expecting the same from others.

4. *Continually striving for more.* If you cannot enjoy what you have, it isn't likely you will be content with more, no matter how much you acquire. True satisfaction comes from being able to appreciate and enjoy what you have.

Stress-producing behavior can manifest itself in the following ways:

1. *Trying to control others.* By trying to control or dominate others, you create tension. In order to maintain their sense of self and their integrity, others must resist being dominated, and this sets up a situation where there will be constant arguments or power struggles, creating stress for both you and the other person. Only by easing your controlling behavior can you reduce this stress and make the relationship more satisfying for both of you.

2. *Trying to change the other person.* Most people are very resistant to being changed unless they themselves are motivated to change a certain behavior. When you try to change someone, you will undoubtedly be met with resistance and even hostility, which in turn will lead to frustration and tension for both of you.

3. *Trying to possess or hold onto someone.* If you are insecure in a relationship and fear losing the other person, you will likely try to hang on to him by being possessive or holding on too tight. Unfortunately, this will likely cause the person to feel very uncomfortable and he will either rebel or pull away from you, creating tension for both of you.

4. *Seeing yourself as a victim.* It is much easier to blame another person for your own difficulties. But by blaming others we create tension in that relationship. The other person will either take on the blame and feel guilty and responsible for things she didn't do or she will become angry with you for trying to avoid taking responsibility for your own actions.

5. *Carrying grudges.* Carrying grudges against those who have hurt, disappointed, rejected, or betrayed you creates tension in your life and in the lives of those who are close to you. Carrying grudges depletes your energy and keeps you stuck in the past.

Although all the previous ideas and strategies for releasing anger and stress can be quite beneficial, some people with an aggressive anger style need outside help when learning to deal more constructively with their anger. If your anger continues to negatively affect your relationships, your job, or your health, I strongly recommend either anger management courses or individual psychotherapy. In some instances, aggressive anger may be a symptom of another emotional disorder or even of a physical problem.

Step Seven:
Complete Your Unfinished Business

We often take on a particular anger style based on our childhood experiences. For example, if one or both of your parents were controlling and dictatorial, you may have followed their example and become domineering yourself—with your partner, your children, and/or your coworkers. Whatever your pattern, it is important that you recognize it for what it is and that you begin to come to terms with it. You must be able to clearly see just how and why your anger style was formed and the role it plays in your aggressiveness.

You may resist the idea that it was the neglect or abuse by one or both of your parents or caretakers that set you up to become aggressive. Ironically, those who become aggressive often have a more difficult time admitting they were neglected or abused than do those who develop a victim-like stance. This is because many who take on the aggressive anger style do so because they cope by doing what is called identifying with their aggressor. This is particularly true for boys who feel especially humiliated when they are victimized. Instead of risking being seen as a victim, which is typically not acceptable for males in most cultures, they prefer to deny their victimization and take on the role of the aggressor against those who are weaker than themselves.

Understanding your pattern is one thing; changing it is something else. In order for this to occur you will need to work on your unfinished business. The following is a brief overview of what "completing your unfinished business" will entail:

1. Acknowledge the anger, pain, fear, and shame that you feel as a result of the neglect or abuse you experienced as a child. Those who were abused or neglected as children often become disconnected from their emotions as a way of surviving intolerable situations. Those who become aggressive or abusive as a way of coping are particularly prone to becoming desensitized to their feelings. For this reason it may be difficult for you to recapture these lost feelings and make them your own. But if you are to recover from your childhood and put an end to your aggressive behavior, this is exactly what you must do.

   The first emotion you need to access is your anger. Although you may have no difficulty becoming enraged with those who are in your life today, your anger toward your original abuser or abusers may be buried deep inside you. Fortunately, you can use your current anger to help you access your repressed and suppressed anger. Although you may not associate your tendency to be angry with what happened to you as a child, you will need to work on making these all-important connections.

EXERCISE: *Making the Connection*

- The next time you become overly aggressive with your partner, child, or friend, think of a time when one or both of your parents (or other caretakers) treated you in a similar way.

- How do you feel when you remember this incident? Angry? Ashamed? Afraid? Write in your journal about the emotions that you are feeling now and the feelings that you had as a child. Don't hold back—let it all out—all the rage, all the shame, all the fear.

- After you have acknowledged your anger about what was done or not done to you as a child, you will need to move beyond your blame and resentment. One way to do this is to realize that underneath your anger lies sadness, and that to get past your anger you must allow yourself to feel and express this sadness and pain. This may be even more difficult than getting in touch with your anger. You have probably built up a wall to protect yourself from these more vulnerable feelings and it will take safety and patience to bring this wall down.

  If you are having difficulty allowing yourself to feel sadness for the abused or neglected child who you were, I encourage you to reach out for help. A professional psychotherapist will work with you to bring down the wall in a safe, supportive environment.

2. Find safe, constructive ways to release your anger and pain concerning your childhood neglect or abuse. Writing in your journal is a very effective tool, as is expressing your emotions through poetry, painting, collage, or sculpting. These

types of creative endeavors are wonderful cathartic outlets, especially if you give yourself permission to express yourself freely without censor. Write about the pain you experienced, paint the rage you feel when you think of the treatment you received, or use clay to express how the abuse made you feel about yourself. If you need something more physical, express your anger through dance or physical exercise, scream into a pillow, or scream in the shower (if you can do so without anyone hearing you).

Write an "anger letter" in which you confront your parent or caretaker with your anger.

EXERCISE: *Verbalizing Your Anger*

- Have an imaginary conversation with the person you are angry with. Tell that person exactly what you feel; don't hold anything back.

- It may help to look at a picture of the person or to imagine that the person is sitting in a chair across from you. If you are still afraid of this person, imagine he or she is tied up and gagged and cannot get to you or say anything to you.

3. It is often important for those who were abused or neglected to confront their parents or other caretakers about the damage they inflicted. A confrontation is a way of formally challenging someone with the truth about what happened as well as with your feelings about it. It is not an attack and it is not meant to alienate the person. It is also not an argument. Its purpose is not to change the other person or to force someone to admit that they were wrong in the way they treated you.

    Confronting is different from releasing your anger. While your confrontation may include expressing your anger along with your other feelings, it is generally important that you have released a great deal of your anger in constructive ways before you confront because you will be less likely to lose control.

Confronting those who hurt you enables you to take back your power. It provides an opportunity to set the record straight, and to conmmunicate to your others what you need from now on.

Practice your confrontation by writing it down, speaking into a tape recorder, or just talking out loud. Use the following format as a guide. You may then pick and choose which points you wish to include in your actual confrontation.

- List the neglectful or abusive behaviors this person inflicted upon you.

- Explain how you felt as a result of those behaviors.

- List the effects those behaviors had on you, both as a child and as an adult, and how your life has been affected.

- List everthing you would have wanted from this person at the time.

- List everything you want from this person now.

  There are several ways you can conduct your confrontation: face-to-face, via telephone, or by letter or e-mail. Face-to-face confrontations are the most advantageous but sometimes this is not possible due to distance constraints or because you are not prepared to see someone in person. Choose the method that suits your needs and trust that whichever one you choose will work out.

4. Resolve your relationships with your abusers in some way. Unresolved relationships will continue to negatively affect your life until you get things out in the open.

Whereas healthy, constructive anger can be your way out of your past, blame keeps you stuck in it. Many people have difficulty moving away from blame and toward forgiveness. They insist they need an apology or at the very least an acknowledgment of the fact that they were hurt or damaged before they can forgive. Although apologies can be tremendously healing, an apology or acknowledgment is not always forthcoming, especially in cases of parental abuse or neglect. Holding onto your anger and blame will not only keep you stuck in the past but will imbue all your present and future relationships with hostility and distrust.

Not everyone can forgive their parents for their mistreatment as children, but many in recovery feel this is the only way to truly move on. Allowing yourself to acknowledge and release your anger in constructive ways and confronting those who damaged you were the first steps. The next step is to develop empathy for those who hurt you. For example, by learning more about your parents' background, you may come to understand why they treated you as they did. Many of us know very little about the forces that shaped our parents' lives. If this is your situation, I urge you to spend some time discovering more about your parents' histories. Others, including myself, have gained empathy for those who harmed them by recognizing that they, too, have hurt people in similar ways.

General Prescription for Those with Aggressive Styles

1. Instead of trying to rid yourself of your anxiety or discomfort by making someone else bad or by ending a relationship, work on containing your anger. When you stay with your discomfort, you create a rich environment from which to better learn about your true self and the feelings underneath your anger.

2. Get to the cause of your anger. It may just be a buildup of stress and frustration or it may be that a particular hot button of yours has been touched.

3. Focus your anger on the real source, such as unfinished business with your family of origin.

4. Learn and practice calming techniques.

5. Learn more effective ways of communicating needs (i.e., assertiveness).

6. Realize that anger is not a solution to a problem. In fact, in your case, it is part of the problem. Find other ways to

communicate your feelings instead of flying off the handle or trying to intimidate and control others.

7. Instead of attacking, give a feelings report. Verbal aggression is ineffective because it tends to cause the other person to become defensive and to be more inclined to strike back. Instead of attacking the other person or complaining about his or her behavior, try describing your feelings or your state of mind. The other person will be more likely to really hear you, empathize with your feelings, and it may inspire him or her to apologize or promise to change.

8. Learn how to empathize with others. Those who have an aggressive anger style often have difficulty putting themselves in the other person's place and imagining how that person feels. They are often so caught up in their own feelings that they can't connect with the feelings other people may have.

9. Work on giving up your victim mentality so that you can begin to recognize your abusive behavior. It is amazing how many aggressive, even abusive, people constantly feel victimized by others and remain blind to how their own behavior negatively affects others. In order to work past this tendency, begin to listen to others when they try to tell you how your behavior affects them instead of focusing only on your own hurt feelings. Instead of constantly complaining about how others hurt or disappoint you, ask them how your behavior affects them. And instead of telling yourself that they are exaggerating or that they are simply too sensitive, believe them when they tell you how your aggressive behavior frightens them, hurts them, or causes them to distance from you.

Specific Advice for Eruptors

If you have an eruptive style, you no doubt feel out of control of your anger. Even though your anger seems to come from out of nowhere, you need to recognize that anger doesn't just happen. There is always a reason for your anger and there are always warning signs that your anger is building up. Your problem has been that you haven't paid attention to the warning signs. This is one of the main reasons why you have more trouble controlling your anger than the average person.

The first thing you will need to do is begin to pay more attention to what you are feeling at any given time and notice any changes in your body that may indicate anger. For example, if you suddenly become agitated and nervous, it may be a sign that you are becoming angry. The same holds true if you begin to feel the buildup of tension anywhere in your body, especially in your head, jaw, eyes, neck, back, shoulders, chest, stomach, hands, or feet.

It may help to remember the last time you became angry. Do you remember what you were feeling in your body just before you exploded? Did you feel pressure building up inside? Did you feel your muscles tensing up? Did you stop breathing?

Notice your actions as well. Do you tend to do certain things whenever you are becoming angry? For example, do you tend to clench your jaw, make fists, or pace up and down the floor?

In addition to body signals, another indicator can be the type of thoughts you are having or the dialogue that is going on inside your head. Again, think back to the last time you blew up. What were some of the thoughts you were having just before you exploded? Eruptors tend to think in very characteristic ways as they build up anger, including feeling like a victim, being critical of other people, feeling hopeless, or feeling like others deserve to be punished. Try to remember what you were saying to yourself. Maybe you were thinking something like, "I can't stand this guy," or "If she says one more thing about the way I'm dressed, . . . " or "You can't talk to me like that."

Another way to begin to discover your anger signals is to ask those close to you what signs they see just before you blow up. They no doubt have come to notice physical signs of anger in you and they may have learned to modify their behavior or to avoid you when they see these signs. If you wish to gain control of your anger, you should at least know yourself as well as others do.

EXERCISE: *Your Anger Signals*

1. Make a list of the physical signals your body gives when you are becoming angry (e.g., splitting headache, stomach churning, tightness in your chest).

2. Now make a list of the things you tend to tell yourself when you are becoming angry (e.g., "I never do anything right as far as she is concerned," "No one can talk to me that way and get away with it").

3. Finally, make another list of the things you begin to do with your body—the ways you begin to show your anger—as you are building up steam (e.g., tapping your foot, grinding your teeth, glaring at the person with whom you are angry).

Once you've become more aware of your anger signals, your anger will no longer be such a mystery to you. You now have the power to gain control of your anger. The next step will be to slow your anger down.

When You Are Unable to Determine Your Warning Signs

For some Eruptors it is difficult or even impossible to spot your anger signals or to determine the exact cause of your anger at any given time. Some people are in a constant state of anger, even though they are able to suppress it a great deal of the time. But when their defenses are down, when they are feeling particularly vulnerable, when they are adversely affected by circumstances (inner or external), or when they are triggered by painful memories, this suppressed anger suddenly bursts out of them. In his or her early, formative years this type of Eruptor was usually unable to express anger and direct it at "forbidden" targets, usually his or her parents. Because the anger was a justified reaction to abuse or mistreatment, this person was left to harbor a sense of profound injustice and frustrated rage that gets projected onto the world in general.

While healthy anger usually has an external cause, this type of unhealthy, eruptive anger is not externally induced. It emanates from inside and is diffuse and excessive. While you may be able to identify the *immediate* cause of the anger, upon closer scrutiny, the cause will be found lacking. This is because you may be expressing and experiencing two layers of anger at the same time. The first, more superficial layer, is directed at the alleged cause of the eruption. The second layer is anger directed at yourself for being unable to vent normal anger in a constructive way. You may be afraid to show that you are angry to meaningful others because you are afraid to lose them. Instead you prefer to direct your anger at people who are meaningless to you, like waitresses and taxi drivers. From time to time, unable to pretend and to suppress, you may have it out with the real source of your anger and erupt in a rage, shouting incoherently, making absurd accusations, or swearing obscenities. This will only last for a short time before you are overwhelmed with remorse and a fear of being abandoned. In order to achieve forgiveness you will do anything, including groveling and demeaning yourself.

If you identify with the description of this type of eruptor you will benefit in particular from the information on triggers, from working on your unfinished business, and from the advice I offer Ragers and Abusers. But you may also need professional help in order to change your anger style. You erupt in anger due to self-loathing and an accumulation of prior negative experiences, and you will need the guidance of a therapist to help you navigate through this difficult terrain.

Learn to Relax

In addition to ignoring the warning signs that you are becoming angry, if you are an Eruptor you have also been ignoring how much built-up stress you have. While you do tend to be impatient and have a problem handling frustration when you finally do blow up, it is often not only due to the current conversation or situation but an accumulation of all the frustration and stress you've been feeling all day or maybe all week.

Much of your battle against uncontrollable anger can be won if you learn how to relax the physical tension in your body that accompanies anger. If you can relax your body and keep it relaxed, it is almost impossible to become angry. Learning stress-reduction techniques can help you calm down, think more clearly, and handle almost any provocative situation in a more effective manner. Refer to chapter 5 for stress-reduction techniques.

Learn to Contain Your Anger

Even though you feel temporarily relieved after ventilating your anger, you aren't really solving the problem. In fact, ventilating your anger actually creates more problems. First, although you may initially feel better once you've blown off steam, you probably end up feeling stupid, childish, or guilty after an episode. You realize that screaming or yelling isn't exactly adult behavior and that your actions hurt those close to you. You also realize that blowing up causes others to lose respect for you and may even jeopardize your success at work, your marriage, or your relationship with your children.

Second, anger doesn't really solve the problem. Erupting in anger prevents you from engaging in a constructive conversation about what is really bothering you. Others will be far more receptive to you if you learn to express your concerns in a rational and direct way.

As with all aggressive anger, your anger is actually a defense against feeling another emotion or against feeling your vulnerability. By immediately erupting in anger when you are upset, you avoid feeling the hurt that caused the anger. Instead of directing your anger outward, toward other people or objects, try containing your anger.

By containing your anger and allowing yourself to feel the emotion underneath your anger, you not only end up being more true to yourself but prevent yourself from saying or doing things you will regret in the future. Once you become aware of your hurt or shameful feelings, you can then communicate them to the other person and facilitate communication between the two of you instead of creating distance. When you automatically react with anger, there is little chance of real communication and little chance of healing either your wounds or the relationship.

Third, realize that every time you blow up, you're teaching yourself to be more angry. Carol Tavris, author of *Anger: The Misunderstood Emotion,* believes that ventilating anger "rehearses" it—that is, the more you practice erupting, the more times you will explode. Ventilating anger in your usual ways simply doesn't work to make you less angry. Every time you erupt, you are actually training yourself to be more explosive. The madder you are, the madder you get.

Specific Advice for Ragers

Your sudden bursts of anger and rage often signal hidden shame. When you start to feel ashamed, you get angry. Since shame is the key to your rage, you will need to first focus on how to manage your shame before you can get a handle on your anger. In order to do this, you will need to begin to recognize your shame, to become intimately familiar with it.

Shame is the feeling that you are the worst person in the world—the lowest of the low. Everyone experiences it differently, but most people describe it as feeling exposed, unworthy, having a sinking feeling, or feeling wounded. Some people actually become dizzy or disoriented and others become nauseated.

Your Shame Inventory

1. Notice what triggers shame in you. Is it criticism from others, being called on your "stuff" (or as one client described it, "having my covers pulled"), or being rejected?

2. When are you most likely to feel shamed? Is it when you are feeling the most insecure? Is it when you are trying to impress someone?

3. Who is most likely to trigger shame in you? Is it the people you care about the most? Or is it those you are trying to impress? How about the people you feel inadequate around or those who have rejected you in the past?

4. Pay attention to the ways in which you convert shame into anger. Do you put other people down because you feel rejected by them? Do you go on a verbal rampage in an attempt to shame anyone who dares to criticize you? Do you

yell at anyone who makes you feel inadequate? Do you become difficult or insulting when you feel like a failure?

In order to break the shame/rage cycle, you will need to ask yourself, "What am I ashamed of?" each and every time you get angry. Think of your anger as a red flag signaling the fact that you are feeling shame. This is especially true whenever you experience sudden bursts of anger or when you become enraged. It may be difficult to find your shame at first and you may not be feeling shame each and every time you feel angry, but with some practice you will be able to recognize those times when you are feeling ashamed and discover what has triggered it.

Once you've identified the shame/rage connection, you will need to break it. This means you will have to stop yourself from becoming angry as a way of defending against your shame. The following suggestions will help:

1.   The next time you become angry at another person, try to get away from him or her as soon as possible. Excuse yourself and go for a walk. If you can't do that, say you need to go to the rest room. Do anything you can to put some distance between you and the object of your anger and some distance between yourself and your anger.

2.   Ask yourself, "Why am I feeling ashamed? What happened? What did this person say or do to trigger shame in me?"

3.   If you are having a full-blown shame attack, you may need to talk to a trusted friend or someone else close to you (your therapist, your sponsor, a member of your support group, someone at a hotline). Explain that you are having a shame attack and that you are feeling horrible about yourself. Don't blame the person who triggered your shame for making you feel bad; take responsibility for your own shame. Try to make a connection between this current incident and what it is reminding you of (from your childhood, from a more recent traumatic shaming). Ask your friend to remind you that you are not a horrible person by telling you at least one good attribute you have.

4. If you can't find someone you trust to talk to, write your feelings down on paper or in a journal. Describe what you are feeling in detail, including your physical reactions. Trace these reactions back to other times and incidents when you felt similar feelings. If you find a connecting incident, write about it in detail. Then spend some time reminding yourself of your good qualities and accomplishments.

Shaming and attacking others may temporarily hide your shame, but it doesn't heal it. In order to heal your shame from the past (e.g., childhood neglect, abandonment, or abuse), you will need to share your experiences with someone you love and trust (your partner, a close friend, a therapist, members of a support group).

You will also need to consciously work on believing that it is okay to be who you are. The following suggestions will help:

1. *Stop relying on anyone who treats you as if you are not okay the way you are.*

2. *When someone treats you poorly, tell him or her to stop it!* Tell this person that you do not deserve to be treated poorly even if you don't believe it yet. The more often you say it, the more you will believe it. If the person continues to treat you poorly, don't continue telling him over and over. This is like begging, and it makes you look weak in his eyes and makes you feel weak, causing you to lose respect for yourself.

3. *When someone treats you poorly or insults you, make sure you don't absorb it.* Those who really care about you will not insult you if they don't like something about you; they will kindly take you aside and have a talk with you. Even then, you are not obligated to take in everything that is said because often people have a hidden agenda in pointing out your faults. The important thing is that you do not allow someone else to make you feel bad about yourself or make you feel like you are not a valuable human being. Most especially, don't allow yourself to replay negative messages over and over in your mind.

4. *Spend more time with people who know you and accept you for who you are.* Choose your relationships based on how you are treated as opposed to whether the person makes you feel comfortable. We are often most comfortable with the kind of people we are used to being around, including those who treat us poorly and remind us of people from our childhood who treated us poorly.

5. *Open up more with those who already accept you as you are.* The fewer secrets you have, the less shame you will experience.

6. *Treat others the way you want to be treated.* If you treat others with respect and consideration, they are far more likely to treat you the same way. And the better you treat others, the less shame you will experience.

7. *When someone treats you well, make sure you absorb it.* When someone does something nice for you, take a few minutes to take it in and feel good. Don't doubt the person's sincerity or tell yourself that she is being nice because she wants something. Trust that she is being nice because she simply wants to be and because she likes you. If someone gives you a compliment, take a deep breath and really take it in. Don't negate the compliment or talk yourself out of believing it. Most people don't give compliments unless they really mean them.

8. *Let people know you appreciate their kindness.* This will encourage them to continue being kind.

Specific Advice for Controllers

If you are a Controller, you use your anger to manipulate, intimidate, and gain power over others. Most people avoid anger because the strong feelings associated with it are frightening. They fear they may lose control and do something they might regret. But your anger is often intentional and deliberate. If you get angry enough, people will feel intimidated and do what you want. If you threaten others with your anger and power, they won't hurt you or try to control you. Some

Controllers even enjoy frightening and hurting others because it makes them feel more powerful and in control.

I don't necessarily mean that you consciously decide to get angry in order to control others, although some Controllers are guilty of doing just that. But your anger works. You've learned through trial and error (or by watching the example of your parents or other caretakers) that by getting angry you can get what you want. You may actually feel a little angry but decide to pretend you are furious in order to scare others into submission. Or, if someone dares to resist or argue with you, you may actually become enraged. The point is that you don't try to avoid getting angry or to control your anger. Instead you use your anger to your advantage. The first thing you will need to do in order to begin to change your controlling anger style is to be honest about this fact.

The second thing you will need to do is examine the payoffs you receive from being controlling and getting angry. In other words, what do you gain? For example, those with a controlling anger style make a particular effort to control their families. They demand unquestioning obedience from their children and even expect their spouses to submit to them. This desire to control is often an attempt to demand the respect of others. Their exercise of power may temporarily boost their low self-esteem.

Assignment. Make a list of the benefits you get out of being controlling and angry. For example, "I get my way," "I keep people away," "I frighten people into submission," and "I need for others to see me as strong and powerful."

In order to give up these payoffs, you'll need to know you can replace them with something else. The truth is you wouldn't be reading this book if you didn't realize that there is a price to pay for controlling and dominating others. Perhaps you've lost several relationships because of your anger, or perhaps your career has suffered. You may be estranged from your children or other family members. Perhaps you've gotten in trouble with the law and have been sent to an anger management course. But aside from these reasons to work on giving up your controlling anger, there are some even more important ones:

1. Controlling others with your anger keeps you from facing your real feelings and seeing who you really are. More than likely there is a lot of sadness and fear underneath all that anger. There's also a vulnerable human being. It takes real courage to find out what you are really feeling and who you really are—a lot more courage than it takes to intimidate other people.

2. Controlling through anger gives you a false sense of being in control when you are really out of control. Those who have a strong need to be in control usually feel out of control in life. You can't actually control anyone else. The only person you can control is yourself, and right now you are out of control.

3. Controlling others through anger keeps you from experiencing true intimacy. No one can feel close to a bully or a tyrant. Instead of feeling love and closeness, others feel fear, anger, resentment, and even hatred. By letting go of control, you will gain the respect and love of your partner, children, friends, coworkers, and other family members.

Specific Advice for Blamers

Blamers may not seem to be as overtly aggressive as many of the other variations of the aggressive anger style, but the consequences of their actions are actually just as damaging. Make no mistake about it, blaming is a very aggressive, hostile act. It is also a form of emotional abuse. This is because when you blame others, you also shame them, and shaming them can be extremely destructive to their self-esteem.

When you simply tell someone that you are angry, there is none of the shame that goes along with blaming. You aren't telling the person that he is a horrible human being. You're not blaming him for your feelings or circumstances. You're just stating the fact that you're angry. This frees the other person up to listen to what you have to say instead of having to defend himself.

Many people get stuck in blame and never get over hurtful incidents. Instead they wallow in self-pity or continuously entertain harsh, negative feelings toward the person who harmed them. This keeps them stuck in blame and stuck in the past, unable to go forward, unable to forgive. Consider the following suggestions to break your cycle of blame:

1. *Learn how to express your angry feelings without blaming the other person.* If someone does something that hurts or offends you, by all means tell him about it. But instead of trying to make him feel guilty or bad about himself, tell him how his actions made you feel. Don't go on and on about it; simply state the facts. There is no need to humiliate this person, chastise him, or belittle him. That is blaming behavior, and no one deserves to be treated like that. It is not your job to make this person change his behavior or attitude, so don't preach or lecture.

2. *Stop exaggerating the other person's behavior by using words like* every, always, never, nobody, *and* nothing *to make accusations and threats.*

3. *Start taking responsibility for your actions instead of blaming others.* If you are a blamer, you probably have a difficult time accepting responsibility for your part in any problem or conflict. Instead you tend to automatically assume that whenever something goes wrong, it is someone else's fault. In order to change your anger style, you will need to stop blaming others, telling others that they provoked you into doing what you did, or rationalizing and justifying your actions. You need to take responsibility for yourself and for your actions.

4. *Start taking responsibility for your feelings.* Most critics and blamers focus on the faults or shortcomings of others as a way of avoiding their own feelings of inadequacy or shame. While you may feel empowered by your anger, it can be a false, temporary empowerment if it is shame induced. Instead of criticizing or fighting with others or expending all your energy

trying to change someone who does not want to change, begin to pay more attention to owning your own fear or shame.

5.   *Work on being less critical and judgmental of others.* The next time you feel critical of someone (e.g., your partner or your children), do the following: (a) Make sure you aren't feeling critical of yourself and projecting it on to others. (See Chapter 9 for more information on projection.) (b) Before you say anything to the other person, write in your journal, take a walk, or just let some time pass—and with it, your mood.

6.   *Realize that holding onto blame keeps you attached to the other person and caught up in the problem.* The more you blame someone, the more you give your power to this person. Express your anger directly to the person or release your anger in a constructive way, then let it go. Anger is empowering, freeing, and motivating. Blame, on the other hand, depletes your energy and keeps you caught up in the problem, not the solution.

7.   *Realize that it is not always necessary to determine fault.* Blamers tend to need to blame someone for every mistake or unpleasant situation. They usually look for someone or something else to blame for whatever went wrong so that they don't have to blame themselves. But you can't control everything and mistakes will happen, no matter how much you try to control others and yourself. Blaming doesn't fix problems and it doesn't prevent the same thing from happening in the future. Instead of blaming, analyze the situation to discover how the problem can be prevented in the future. If there is nothing you can do differently or if it was out of your control, accept it as bad luck.

Specific Advice for Abusers

No one wants to admit that his or her style of anger is abusive. The reason you tend to be so good at fooling yourself and making excuses for your abusive behavior is that deep down inside you know that once you admit you are abusive and recognize the damage you've caused others and yourself, you will be overwhelmed with shame until you change the situation. Denial often lulls us into a false security, while the hard truth is like a cold shower or a slap in the face.

Unfortunately, most people are unaware of the feelings that cause them to become abusive. Your anger journal can help you identify your triggers and your false beliefs and help you gain insight into your behavior. Keep a log of each incident of abuse. Ask yourself, "What is it about me that caused me to respond in that manner?" For example, you may find that one of the things that triggers your anger is when things seem unfair or when you feel you have been treated unfairly. Instead of constantly becoming upset over this, it might be far better to work on accepting the fact that there is inequity in the world and concentrate on developing coping skills when you are treated unfairly.

The most effective way of countering your abusive tendencies, of course, will be to continue working on the unfinished business that caused you to be abusive in the first place. Your problem is not that you *get* angry; it is that you *are* angry. In fact, your life is dictated by your anger. Unless you discover the root cause of your anger, you will not be able to let go of your abusive anger style.

Make the Connection between Your Abusive Behavior and Substance Abuse

Research also strongly supports the link between substance use and violence. When one or both partners have been addicted to alcohol or drugs it is also likely that incidents of domestic violence have occurred in the relationship. In the United States in particular, substance abuse has shown to increase the risk that men will batter their partners. Half of domestic violence incidents involve alcohol use by both partners.

Although substance abuse is not a risk factor per se it can strengthen the probability of occurrence by causing a loss of control, decreased inhibitions, and impaired judgment. Alcohol and drug use may facilitate miscommunication and resentment and reduce the ability to take into account the consequences of aggressive actions.

Alcohol abuse seems to be a particularly potent risk factor for men's violence. The Research Institute of Addictions found that heavy drinking by husbands is a key contributor to marital violence. Alcohol intoxication may serve to legitimize men's violence and men are more likely than women to associate alcohol use with a decreased ability to manage anger and increased feelings of superiority over others.

Recognize the Ineffectiveness of Aggression

Verbal aggression (yelling, name-calling, belittling) is not an effective way of communicating your feelings. It simply doesn't work—for you or for the other person. When you are verbally aggressive, the end result will be that you will antagonize the other person and cause him or her to strike back, or it will intimidate the other person and shut him or her down. In either case, genuine communication cannot occur. Your true feelings will not be heard and the issue will not be resolved. By describing your state of mind, on the other hand, and explaining why you are feeling a certain way, you are opening the door to communication and giving the other person a chance to really understand you. For example, notice the difference between the following two exchanges:

1. "You're such a tramp. You flirted with that guy all night long, right in front of me and everyone else. You might as well have had sex with him right there—it was so obvious you wanted to."

2. "I feel really hurt and angry with you for flirting with that guy. It seemed to me like you were really sexually attracted to him. And it felt like you didn't respect me because you were flirting right in front of me and everyone else at the party. That was really humiliating."

In the first exchange, the other person is obviously going to feel insulted and attacked. She will either attack back, tune out, or try to get away from the attacker as soon as possible. And the words are so accusatory that she will find it nearly impossible to hear the hurt under the anger.

In the second exchange, the other person will be more likely to be able to stay connected to the speaker. She knows how he is feeling, and although she may become defensive (especially if she really was guilty of blatantly flirting), she may also be touched by the fact that he is feeling hurt and humiliated. If she cares about him, she will feel badly about this and will want to express regret.

Those who yell and throw insults when they are angry don't usually get the results they hope for. What you really want is to be heard and for your feelings to be understood. You also may want an apology and assurance that the person will not repeat the act. But because you are going about it all wrong, you aren't likely to get any of your needs met. This sets up a vicious cycle where you tend to yell louder the next time, causing the other person to either counterattack or to ignore you.

Develop Empathy

If you are abusive, you tend to lack empathy for other people. Instead of being able to put yourself in the other person's place to get an understanding of how he or she might feel, you tend to focus only on how you feel. No matter how inconsiderate, impatient, selfish, caustic, or abusive you are toward others, you probably tend to feel like the victim when you have a conflict with someone. In order to stop your abusive tendencies, you will need to learn how to step outside of yourself and empathize with others. The following exercise will help.

EXERCISE: *Practice Being Empathetic*

Think of someone with whom you are having difficulties. Write about the situation from the perspective of the other person. You might be surprised at the insights you gain from doing such an exercise. There are really two sides to a story, and you need to be reminded of this, especially when you are locked into a conflict.

Counter Your Negativity

Abusive people tend to be critical and negative. They especially tend to find fault in those who are close to them. This serves several purposes: it protects them from being vulnerable, it keeps people around them off center, and it helps them avoid dealing with their own issues. The following exercise will help counter your negative/critical stance.

EXERCISE: *An Attitude of Gratitude*

1. Before you go to sleep at night, think about the good things that happened that day. If you start to focus only on the things that went wrong, bring your mind back to the things that went right. As one of my clients shared with me, "This really helped me to get some perspective. My tendency is to only remember the things that went wrong, the things that didn't go the way I wanted them to go. But when I stopped myself and said, 'Wait, there has to be some good,' it reminded me of how often things work out and go smoothly."

2. Think of at least three things that your partner did that were caring, considerate, or thoughtful toward you or someone you care about (such as your parents, your children, etc.).

3. Now think of at least three reasons to be grateful for your partner. For example, "I'm grateful because she is still with me," "I'm grateful he's stopped drinking," or "I'm grateful that she's so patient."

Prevent Abuse

In order to prevent yourself from becoming verbally or physically abusive toward your loved ones (your children, your partner) and others, practice my ALERT program.

Admit that you have a tendency to be abusive with your anger.

Leave the situation as soon as you become aware that your anger is getting out of control.

Express your emotions in a constructive way (go for a walk and tell the other person off in your mind, write everything down on paper that you would like to say to the person with whom you are angry).

Relax. Find a way to reduce the stress that has built up (practice relaxation exercises, take a few deep breaths, meditate, pray, play calming music, read scriptures, light a candle and put on some relaxing music).

Trace your triggers. After you have calmed down, spend some time going back over your day in order to track down exactly what happened to get you to such an explosive state. Remember, don't blame others. Take responsibility, but at the same time look for triggers.

CHAPTER 7

From Passive to Assertive

I'm afraid of my anger. I'm afraid that if I finally start letting it
out, I will lose control and go crazy.

—LARRY, AGE 24

Even though there have been some famous pacifists such as Mahatma Gandhi, passivity has probably not gotten you very far. Otherwise, you wouldn't be reading this book. It is one thing to passively and quietly protest when you disagree with someone or something and another matter entirely to simply allow others to walk all over you. Because anger is a natural defense mechanism designed to protect us from pain and abuse, it is not a good idea to deny feeling angry. It is extremely beneficial to feel and acknowledge angry feelings when they occur. Otherwise, we lose out on the benefits of anger—empowerment, protection, energy, and motivation. Anger energizes us and can serve as a catalyst for resolving interpersonal conflict. It can promote self-esteem and can foster a sense of personal control during times of peak stress.

Those with a passive anger style don't stand up for themselves. They don't take the necessary and appropriate actions to make certain that they will be treated fairly and with respect. If you have this anger style, you don't need to turn yourself into a screaming maniac in order to work past your passivity, but you do need to learn to give yourself permission to voice your feelings and needs and to communicate assertively. In this chapter we will focus on the following aspects of these goals:

1. Discovering the origins of your passive anger style

2. Working past your fear of expressing your anger

3. Working past societal expectations concerning female passivity (for women only)

4. Recognizing the damage you cause yourself and others by not expressing your anger

5. Learning to express your anger assertively

Step One: Discover the Origins of Your Passive Anger Style

The first thing you will need to do is discover why you have chosen the passive style in the first place and what core beliefs about anger have motivated you to remain passive. As you learned in chapter 5, early childhood usually holds the key to choosing one anger style over another. Go back over your anger beliefs list to remind yourself of your core anger beliefs and where they came from. Later on in this chapter, I also offer you help in determining the origin of your secondary anger style, whether you are a Denier, an Avoider, a Stuffer, or a Self-blamer.

Some people are born with a passive interactive style—it is part of their temperament. These people, who have a shy temperament, are incapable of spontaneous and uninhibited expression of emotion, including anger. If you are shy, it does not mean you are unable to feel emotion, only of freely expressing it. Shy people tend to withdraw when frustrated and are reluctant to react when provoked by others. In other words, they lack assertiveness.

Many people adopt the passive interactive style as a result of negative social experiences. They learn to be passive and submissive and to keep their anger hidden. This is especially true of those who experienced emotional, physical, or sexual abuse as children. Those who were victimized in any of these ways tend to suffer from learned helplessness, which is the belief that you cannot control the outcome of any situation through your own actions. Those with this mindset believe that nothing can be gained by standing up for one's rights or protecting oneself from harm. Therefore, even though you may feel angry about the way someone is treating you, you might think to yourself, "What good will it do to tell him how I feel? It won't change anything."

EXERCISE: *Words of Anger*

1.   Make a list of all the words that come to mind when you think of the word *anger.* Don't think about it—just write.

2.   Notice how many of the words that you wrote down have negative connotations.

3.   Now think of as many words as you can that have a positive or affirming connotation when you think of the word *anger.* See if you can come close to balancing the number of negative words you wrote in item 1.

Step Two: Work Past Your Fear of Expressing Your Anger

There is a strong likelihood that the main reason for your passive anger style is that you are afraid of getting angry. We often become frightened when we feel anything intensely, whether it is anger, sadness, fear, or even love and joy. We are afraid that our feelings will overpower us or that we will get out of control. We imagine our emotions spilling out all over the place, creating havoc. The irony is that it is what you don't express that can get you into trouble. The more you suppress and repress your anger, the more likely it will burst out of you when you least expect it.

In order for you to begin to overcome your fear of anger, it is important to understand these specific reasons for it:

- *The fear of retaliation.* This is a very real fear if you were punished when you were a child every time you got angry or if you have been abused as an adult for standing up to your partner. As one client told me, "When I was a kid, I got beaten very badly the one time I talked back to my dad. I learned never to do that again."

- *The fear of rejection.* This is also a very real fear if you experienced rejection when you stood up for yourself. My client, Joseph, shared his experience with me: "When we first got married, my wife would stop speaking to me when I got angry with her. I wouldn't yell at her or anything, just let her know I didn't like what she was doing. But she said it hurt her feelings and that I shouldn't get angry with her if I loved her. She even threatened to leave me if I got angry with her again. So I stopped getting angry."

- *The fear of hurting another person.* This fear is especially strong if you hurt someone when you were angry. This is a story a friend told me: "When I was growing up, I had a bad temper. I used to yell and scream and throw things when I got mad. One day I got so mad at my younger brother that I threw a plate of food at him. The plate hit him in the head and cut it open. He had to be taken to the hospital to get stitches. Since that time, I've never gotten angry again."

- *The fear of becoming like those who abused you.* If you were emotionally, physically, or sexually abused as a child or adolescent, your primary reason for not expressing your anger is probably your fear that you will become an abuser yourself. This is a genuine concern. But if you fear continuing the cycle of abuse, there is even more reason to begin to communicate openly about your angry feelings. If you continue to hold in your anger, it is likely that you may one day explode in a rage.

And it is very likely that you are already taking your anger out on your loved ones in a negative way (belittling or berating, punishing with silence, unreasonable expectations). Your old anger toward your abusers needs to be released in constructive ways and your current anger needs to be spoken. Then you can be assured that you will not become like those who abused you.

- *The fear of losing control.* To you, expressing or communicating your anger may seem as if you are losing control. You may be afraid that once you begin to express your anger, you will go crazy and hurt others or yourself. Ironically, it is often the person who represses her anger who is most likely to become destructive or to have rage erupt in inappropriate ways at inappropriate times. You will not go crazy if you allow yourself to feel and express your anger. If you learn to consistently allow yourself to express your anger instead of holding it in, you will find that you will actually feel more in control of your emotions and yourself.

- *The fear of becoming irrational or making a fool out of yourself.* Far from making you irrational, anger can often cause you to think and see things more clearly. It can also empower you to make needed changes in your life. This is especially true if you don't allow your anger to build up to the point where you lose it and begin to yell, act irrationally, or lash out at someone.

EXERCISE: *Getting Past Your Resistance*

If you are reluctant to express your anger openly, the following exercise may help uncover additional reasons why you are afraid of your anger:

1. Write and complete this sentence: "I don't want to express my anger because. . . ." Don't think about your answers beforehand, just write.

2. Continue completing this sentence for as long as you have responses.

Step Three: Work Past Societal Expectations Concerning Female Passivity

The following information pertains to women only and to those who are partners to women with a passive anger style. Although there are certainly men who operate primarily out of a passive anger style, women most often have difficulty acknowledging and expressing their anger. Various reasons are presented for the repression of anger in women, including

1. The fear that the expression of anger will cause retaliation

2. The fear that expressing anger will deny the nurturing aspect of women's socialization or drive away the love and closeness women seek

3. The need for change that is signaled when something is wrong

4. The need to be seen as the good woman or the nice lady as opposed to being perceived as unfeminine or the bitch.

While there is considerable disagreement as to whether women's difficulty in acknowledging and expressing anger is caused by gender differences or status and power discrepancies, it is likely a combination of the two. For example, some contend that our society permits women the expression of anger in defense of those more vulnerable than themselves (such as their children) but discourages them from expressing anger on their own behalf (probably rooted in the belief that women's power unleashed is considered devastating). It is clear that females have been trained to contain their anger at violation, fearing retaliation of those more powerful.

Researchers such as Belenky and Gilligan have found that relatedness is primary for women. With this in mind, it becomes clear why a woman will go to any lengths, including the altering of herself, in order to establish and maintain intimate ties.

The Ten Most Common Mistakes Women Make Concerning Their Anger

In my experience working with female clients, I have found that women tend to make the following predictable mistakes when it comes to anger:

1. Crying when they are really angry

2. Telling themselves that they don't have a right to be angry

3. Telling themselves that they aren't really angry even though they know they are

4. Becoming an Anger Magnet—that is, attracting those who will act out their anger for them

5. Pretending to forgive someone when all the while they're plotting ways to get back at him or her

6. Becoming withdrawn or distant from the person with whom they are angry

7. Taking the anger they feel at someone else out on themselves (by becoming self-critical or blaming themselves)

8. Stuffing their anger (by overeating, drinking too much, smoking cigarettes, taking drugs, shoplifting, becoming addicted to sex)

9. Taking the anger they have at one person out on someone else (becoming impatient with their children even though they are really angry with their husband)

10. Holding anger in, then suddenly exploding in a rage and saying hurtful things to those around them

Anger by Any Other Name

As you will notice, most of the mistakes women make concerning their anger involve expressing their anger in passive rather than assertive or even aggressive ways (with the exception of item 10).

Because the expression of anger has been socially unacceptable for women, they have learned to disguise or transform their anger into hurt, sadness and worry, attempts to control, or headaches, insomnia, ulcers, back pain, and obesity. When women are under stress, anger is often turned into tears, hurt, self-doubt, silent submission, or nonproductive blaming. Women often become distant or under- or over-achieving. Anger is frequently accompanied by crying, an expression of the impotence and powerlessness many women feel when victimized by injustice. Tears also accompany anger when there is a power differential between a woman and the object of her anger—when action is denied because the forces that frustrate her are too powerful. Commonly misinterpreted as a sign of sorrow, crying is a signal of the righteousness of women's anger along with the strength of the hurt.

What's So Good about Feeling Mad?

In order to counter negative cultural conditioning concerning anger, women need to learn about the positive benefits of expressing their anger directly. Anger can perform many valuable functions, including the following:

- Anger serves primarily as a messenger, providing a clue that something is not right.

- Anger can serve as a teacher, imparting the awareness that all emotion, even rage, carries knowledge, insight, and what some call enlightenment.

- Through their anger, women can learn to identify problems, mobilize their energy to respond to a perceived threat, and discern how to change, develop, and protect themselves.

- Anger directed against societal and personal injustice is a source of power.

- Expression of anger can actually promote health. Women with cancer who express their anger are found to live longer than those who express no anger.

- Anger and even rage can be a survival tool and a grounding technique by which women become centered and reconnected to themselves.

- As uncomfortable as anger may be, it can be preferable to anxiety, as it lays the blame outside ourselves.

Step Four: Recognize the Damage You Cause Yourself and Others by Not Expressing Your Anger

If you have a tendency to repress or suppress your anger, you have lost touch with an important part of yourself. Getting angry is a way to assert your rights, express your displeasure with a situation, and let others know how you wish to be treated. It can motivate you to make needed changes in a relationship or other areas of your life. And it can let others know that you expect to be respected and treated fairly.

Don't fool yourself into thinking that just because you don't express your anger it will miraculously go away. Each emotion has a purpose, and that emotion will remain with you, buried inside your body, locked up in your psyche, until that purpose is recognized and understood. Anger arises within you to tell you that what is occurring is undesirable or unhealthy. Suppressing your emotions—that is, consciously trying to bury them—does not eliminate them. In addition to causing you to become numb to your feelings, including your positive feelings, your suppressed emotions will often cause physical symptoms such as muscle tension, back problems, stomach distress, constipation, diarrhea, headaches, obesity, or maybe even hypertension.

Your suppressed anger may also cause you to overreact to people and situations or to act inappropriately. Unexpressed anger can cause you to become irritable, irrational, and prone to emotional outbursts and episodes of depression. If you carry around a lot of suppressed or repressed anger (anger you have unconsciously buried), you may lash out at people, blaming them or punishing them for something that someone else did long ago. Because you were unwilling or unable to express how you felt at the time, you may overreact in the present, damaging your relationships.

The passive anger style is not compatible with a healthy relationship. Denying you are angry or withdrawing from your partner does not give the two of you the chance to work out your problems. Instead you are likely to build up tension, then finally blow up. After your tirade, your partner is likely to feel wounded and angry and wonder why in the world you didn't say something before.

It is also important to realize that as long as you are angry, you will exude a certain kind of angry energy. Sometimes this energy is palpable and is consciously experienced by others. Other times it is felt only subliminally by others, but it is felt nevertheless. Other people are affected by your anger whether it is overt or not and whether they are aware of it or not. They will respond by getting angry along with you, by acting out your anger for you (read more about this in chapter 9), or by being on guard around you.

Not responding to a provocation, turning the other cheek or letting things go, won't stop the other person from continuing his unacceptable behavior. It won't make the other person back off and leave you alone. In fact, reacting passively to inappropriate, even abusive, behavior actually invites the other person to continue his behavior. The less you react to provocation, the more provocation you will invite.

Anger can be the most threatening and frightening of emotions. Your fear of anger may have kept you imprisoned in the past, afraid to stand up to those who have hurt you and afraid to go forward. But the more you express your anger, the less afraid of it you will be. Anger is energy—a motivating force that can empower you to feel less helpless. By discovering it, then releasing it, you will find you can rid yourself of the physical and emotional tension that has sapped you of energy that you could otherwise use to motivate yourself to change your life.

Assignment. Make a list of the ways you have hurt yourself and others by suppressing or repressing your anger.

Step Five: Learn to Express Your Anger Assertively

If you have a passive anger style, assertiveness is especially important. We began our discussion about assertiveness in chapter 5. Here we will focus on the specific benefits of assertiveness.

Assertiveness is an alternative to personal powerlessness and manipulation and a tool for making your relationships equal, for avoiding the one-down feeling that often comes when you fail to express what you really want. Being assertive may increase your self-esteem, reduce anxiety, help you gain a greater respect for yourself and others, and improve your ability to communicate more effectively.

There are many other benefits to assertiveness, such as:

- *Promoting equality in your relationships.* Assertiveness will help restore the balance of power in your relationships by providing you with personal power and by making it possible for everyone to gain.

- *Helping you to act in your own best interest.* Assertiveness encourages you to make your own decisions rather than to allow others to dictate how you should run your life. It encourages you to take initiative and to trust your own judgment.

- *Helping you to stand up for yourself.* This includes assertive behaviors such as saying no, setting limits on time and energy, responding to criticism or put-downs, and stating and defending your opinions.

- *Helping you to express your feelings honestly and comfortably.* This includes being able to disagree, show anger, admit to fear or anxiety, and being spontaneous without anxiety.

- *Helping you to stand up for your personal rights.* This includes the ability to respond to violations of your rights or those of others and the ability to work for change.

- *Helping you to respect the rights of others.* Ultimately, assertiveness is the ability to accomplish all of these items without hurting others, being unfairly critical of others, or having to revert to manipulation or controlling behavior.

Overcoming the Obstacles to Self-Assertion

In order to learn how to value yourself and express your feelings directly and honestly, it is necessary to overcome these beliefs about assertiveness:

- *Believing you don't have a right to be assertive.* Even though you may have learned otherwise, we all have a right to be assertive about getting our needs met. This doesn't mean you have a right to be aggressive, however. Assertiveness does not mean you have the right to take advantage of other people in order to take care of yourself or that you have the right to insist on having things your way. It does mean that you have the right to stand up for yourself and look after your own interests.

- *Being afraid to be assertive.* Many people are reluctant to be more assertive because they are afraid people will think of them as overbearing, pushy, or obnoxious. But if you try to please everyone else, you will continue to feel frustrated and powerless. This is because what others want may not be what is good for you. You are not being mean when you say no to unreasonable demands or when you express your ideas, feelings, and opinions, even if they differ from those of others. Asserting yourself will not upset people as much as you think it will, and even if it does, they will get over it. When you decide to make changes in the way you deal with people, you will be surprised at how quickly they will get used to your new approach. Some people will actually prefer the new you.

- *Overcoming familial and cultural negativity about being assertive.* This can be a difficult process. We discussed the problems that women have overcoming the cultural expectation that they remain passive. The messages you received from your family or your childhood experiences may have caused you to believe that assertiveness is unacceptable or even dangerous.

Practice telling yourself the following to counter these messages:

1. I have the right to be treated with respect by others.

2. I have the right to express my feelings (including anger) and opinions.

3. I have the right to say no without feeling guilty.

4. I have the right to ask for what I want.

5. I have the right to make my own mistakes.

6. I have the right to pursue happiness.

Assertiveness Skills

The following information will guide you step-by-step through the process of initiating an assertive exchange with someone with whom you are having difficulties, or with someone who has hurt your feelings or angered you.

1. *Start with an "I" statement that expresses your feelings and describes the problem very specifically.* Begin your exchange with an "I" message such as "I'm frustrated" or "I'm angry." Depending on the context and the relationship, you may need to be more or less tactful. Positive example: "I need to talk. I'm very frustrated with the fact that the yard is such a mess. You promised to clean up the yard two weeks ago when I told you about the barbecue for my father's birthday and it still is not done."

2. *Avoid blaming statements.* In addition to avoiding blaming "you" statements such as "You never do what you say you're going to do," also avoid provocative, judgmental ones such as "What's wrong with you?" or "Why are you so lazy?" Positive example: "I've asked you twice now to clean the yard and you promised to do it last weekend. What's going on here?"

3. *Explain why you are upset.* Include any effects the person's behavior has had on you. Positive example: "I planned to invite my family over for a barbeque to celebrate my dad's birthday, but I'm so embarrassed about the shape the yard is in that I canceled it." Resist the urge to blame or whine. Just state the reasons you are upset.

4. *State your expectations clearly and specifically.* Express firmly but in a nonblaming way what your needs, desires, or expectations are concerning the problem. Positive example: "I do not want to continue stressing out about the yard. Let me know if you are willing to do it or not. If you are unable or unwilling to clean up the yard by next weekend, I am going to hire a gardener."

5. *Notice your flow of speech.* A smooth flow of speech is a valuable asset in terms of getting your point across. Clear and slow comments are more easily understood and more powerful than rapid speech that is erratic and filled with long pauses.

6. *Notice your timing.* Hesitation often diminishes the effectiveness of your assertive statements. The more you practice being assertive, the more courage you will have to confront people at the time of the offense instead of waiting and obsessing about what you could have said. On the other hand, it is never too late to be assertive. Even though the ideal moment may have passed, you will usually find it worthwhile to go to the person later and express your feelings.

7. *Acknowledge the other person and ask for input.* At this point you can ask the other person where he is coming from and for any suggestions he might have for solving the problem. Why not begin your encounter with this more empathetic approach? The reason is that those with a passive anger style generally have too much empathy for others and not enough empathy for themselves. They also get easily sidetracked by

others' perspectives and excuses. Once you have let off some steam and made your needs and expectations clear, you can better afford to listen to the other person's point of view and give him or her a chance to be a problem-solving collaborator. Positive example: "Thank you for listening to me. Now I'd really like to hear what you have to say about the situation and what suggestions you might have to solve the problem."

How to Respond to Sabotaging Attempts

Just because you are beginning to be less passive and more assertive doesn't mean that others will welcome your changes. In fact, those around you will likely resist and resent your attempts at being more direct with your needs and your anger. After all, they are used to being able to get their way around you. It will take time before others will come to realize that you are no longer going to keep quiet or back down when there is a conflict.

Some will actually try to sabotage your efforts by using these blocking strategies to avoid dealing with conflict or acknowledging the behavior that has provoked you:

- *Laughing it off.* The other person responds to your confrontation by making a joke or making light of the situation.

- *Ignoring you.* The other person completely ignores what you are saying.

- *Denying.* The other person tells you, "That's not true. I didn't do that," or acts as if he doesn't know what you are talking about.

- *Minimizing.* The other person tries to minimize the importance of what you are saying: "I don't know why you are making such a big deal out of this."

- *Debating.* The other person wants to debate with you about the legitimacy of how you feel or the importance of the problem: "You shouldn't feel that way."

- *Guilt.* The other person responds with tears and acts as if you are being mean: "How could you say such horrible things to me?"

- *Putting you off.* Your confrontation is met with a statement like, "So what?" or "I'll talk about it later."

- *Questioning.* The other person responds with a series of questions, such as "Why do you feel that way?" or "Why didn't you tell me before?"

- *Reversing.* The other person blames you for the problem.

- *Retaliation.* The other person responds by attacking you.

- *Threatening.* You are threatened with statements like, "So, if you don't like it, I'll just find someone who does," or, "If you keep nagging me, this relationship is over."

The following techniques have proven helpful for overcoming blocking strategies. Although most of the techniques work for any of the blocking strategies, some work best for specific types as noted.

- *The broken record.* Repeat your point calmly and quietly. Do not get distracted by irrelevant issues, do not get defensive, and do not get caught up in a debate. For example, "Yes, I know, but my point is. . . ." This is especially effective with laughing it off, putting you off, and debating.

- *Refocusing.* Shift the focus and comment on what is going on between the two of you: "It feels like we are getting into old issues here. Can we get back to the issue I brought up?" This is especially effective with questioning, threatening and debating.

- *Hedging.* You appear to give up ground without actually doing so. Agree to the person's argument, but don't agree to change: "That's a good point. I probably could be more patient." This is especially effective with reversing and retaliation.

- *Defusing.* Put off further discussion until the other person has calmed down: "I see that you are very upset right now. Let's discuss this later on today." In order for this to be effective, you must return to the issue later. This is most effective with retaliation.

- *Cutoff.* Respond to the provocative statement with only a short word and quickly get back to the point. This helps prevent escalation. This is most effective with threatening.

Knowing how to deal with blocking strategies will give you confidence and help you stick to the issues at hand instead of being discouraged, distracted, or defensive. Unfortunately, if you are in an emotionally abusive relationship or dealing with someone who refuses to change, even these techniques will not necessarily work. If this is your experience, give yourself credit for being assertive in the first place instead of silently allowing yourself to be controlled, dominated, or victimized. The more you practice assertiveness, the stronger you will feel, which will hopefully give you the courage to end relationships that are not mutually satisfying.

Advice for Those with a Passive Anger Style

- Resist the temptation to take the easy way out by responding passively and avoiding conflicts at all costs.

- Understand that by being passive, you actually encourage others to be controlling or abusive.

- Understand that by being the silent partner—that is, allowing your mate to be emotionally, physically, or sexually abusive to your children—you have an equal part in the damage caused to your children.

- Practice saying no. Say it out loud when you are by yourself. Say it silently to yourself whenever you would like to say it to someone out loud but are afraid to do so. If you continue practicing and telling yourself you have the right to say no, eventually you'll gain the confidence to speak your mind out loud.

- Remind yourself that being assertive is different from being aggressive. You are not being mean, demanding, or abusive when you say no to unreasonable demands or when you express your own ideas, feelings, and opinions.

- Practice being assertive in low-risk situations in order to build up your courage. For example, would you be more comfortable being assertive toward someone you know or toward a stranger? Would it be easier to be assertive over the telephone or in writing instead of in a face-to-face encounter?

- Don't fool yourself into thinking that just because you don't express your anger directly, others are not aware of it or not affected by it.

- Don't confuse anger with blame. Many people with a passive anger style believe that it is wrong to get angry. They think it is a sign of weakness or evidence of an unevolved spirit. One of the reasons is that they confuse anger with blame. Whereas anger is a natural, healthy emotion when ventilated properly, blame is a wasted and negative experience. The difference between anger and blame is that blaming keeps you caught up in the problem while releasing your anger constructively allows you to work through the problem. Continually blaming others for what they have done to you keeps you stuck in the past. But when you release your anger in healthy ways (such as writing anger letters) toward those who have hurt or damaged you, you are able to step out of blame and let go of the past.

Specific Advice for Deniers

Why does someone take on this variation of the passive anger style? I believe that there are three factors in play: (1) parental examples and messages; (2) fear of separation; and (3) fear of facing the truth.

Parental Examples and Messages

Many people learn the denial anger style from their parents. This was the case with Sarina. When I first met her, I would best describe her facial expression as flat. There was very little expression on her face, and her eyes and skin seemed very dull—almost gray in appearance. Her body movements seemed almost robotic.

Sarina came to see me because she had never been married, was forty years old, and desperately wanted to have children. She said, "I keep choosing men who are unavailable in some way. They are either already married, gay, or they just can't commit. I'm afraid I'm going to miss out on having a family unless I can figure out what's going on with me."

After taking her family history, it became clear that part of Sarina's problem was that she had not received much affection from her parents. Unfortunately, as so often happens, in her attempts to gain the love she hadn't received from her parents, she continually picked partners who were very much like them—distant, unemotional, and unavailable. Once she became aware of her pattern she began the work of changing it. She started by saying no to her usual type and yes to men who initially didn't attract her but were available.

Sarina also needed to work on her unfinished business with her parents, namely her anger at them for not being loving toward her. But even though Sarina recognized that she should be angry at her parents, she couldn't bring herself to feel it. This was mostly because Sarina was never given permission to get angry as she was growing up and she never saw either one of her parents angry. She explained, "My parents never got really excited about anything. They were very uptight people. I guess that's why I have a difficult time getting angry. I just never had any role models."

Sarina's parents were actually role models for never showing their anger. The message she received from their example was "It isn't okay to get angry. If you feel angry, just keep quiet about it." And it wasn't just anger that Sarina's parents didn't express. It was all emotions. Sarina's parents didn't express sorrow either. When her grandfather died, no one in the family cried.

Once Sarina became aware that she was closed down emotionally and that it was largely due to parental modeling, she eventually began to give herself permission to feel her emotions, including her anger. It was extremely difficult at first, since she had been so conditioned to repress and suppress her emotions, but gradually, with my encouragement, she began to feel and then express her anger.

Fear of Separation

Sometimes people deny their anger, because if they were to acknowledge it, they would also feel the separation that comes with anger. Anger separates people. It creates a distance between them. Anger deniers are often enmeshed with the people in their lives—their parents, their spouse, their children. Enmeshment is an unhealthy connection with someone. It indicates overinvolvement, a loss of self, or an inability to emotionally separate from someone. Young children often deny their anger toward their parents because they don't want to feel separate from them. This is normal and healthy. But as we mature, we need to feel separate from our parents in order to develop an individualized sense of self. This is why it is typical and healthy for adolescents to frequently feel angry with their parents. It is part of what is referred to as the individuation process.

Unfortunately, some adolescents don't go through this normal stage of development. They remain enmeshed with their parents, refusing to acknowledge or express their angry for fear of feeling separate from them. Ironically, children who have been neglected or abused by their parents often have the most difficulty getting angry and separating. They tend to tenaciously hold onto the hope of getting what they didn't get as children. As long as they hold onto this hope, they can't afford to get angry.

This same phenomenon occurs when someone is too enmeshed with a partner. If a battered wife were to admit being angry with her abusive husband, she might have to face the fact that she needs to leave him. If she is totally dependent on him either emotionally or financially or both, she can't afford to risk feeling her anger. If an overly dependent man whose partner continually flirts with other men were to admit his anger, he might have to face the possibility that his partner does not love him. If he were to confront her with his anger, he would also risk finding out how she really feels about him. She might just be waiting for an excuse to leave him. So, instead he pretends he doesn't notice her flirting; he pretends he isn't angry at all.

In order to risk feeling your anger, you need to be willing to feel your separateness from the person with whom you are angry. Anger distances you from this person. If you don't want to feel that distance, you can't afford to acknowledge or feel your anger. This is why feeling and expressing anger is often the first step in releasing yourself from an unhealthy situation or relationship. You need to begin to release yourself from the feeling of enmeshment and learn that you have a separate identify. You need to learn that you can survive as a separate person.

Fear of Facing the Truth

Many Deniers have repressed or forgotten significant parts of their childhood because they don't want to have to face the truth about what it was really like. Unexpressed and buried emotions can interfere with your life. It may be necessary for you to find a way to uncover and express your repressed anger in order to free yourself from the past, find your voice, and live more assertively in the present. There are many ways of voicing your anger and pain from the past. Here are some suggestions:

- Write about your anger, fear, pain, and shame in your journal. Getting your feelings down in black and white can act as a catharsis, helping you to get the feelings out instead of continuing to allow them to fester and grow inside you.

- Write a letter to each of the people who hurt you in the past. Don't censor yourself. Say everything that comes to mind and don't hold anything back—even your most hateful feelings. The purpose of the letter is to help you come out of denial, to face the truth about what happened to you and how you feel about it, and eventually to help you gain some closure. You need not mail the letters; in fact, it is best if you do not. If you wish, you can keep the letters for future reference or tear them up or burn them as a symbolic act of closure.

- Pretend that those who hurt you in the past are standing in front of you. Individually tell them exactly what they did to hurt you, how their actions or inaction harmed you, and how you feel about them now.

Coming Out of Denial

If you are a Denier, you will have a difficult time admitting to yourself that you are really angry. Although I am telling you that you are angry under all that denial, and it makes sense to you that you would be angry considering what has happened to you, and even though you may have finally come to believe you have a right to your anger, it may still be difficult for you to access your anger.

My client, Lorraine, is a perfect example of a Denier who had difficulty finding her anger. When she was a child, she was severely neglected by both of her parents, yet she insisted that she was not angry with them. She made excuses for their neglectful treatment of her, saying that they were too busy earning money for the family, or, in the case of her mother, that she did the best she could given the fact that she had emotional problems.

Lorraine came to see me because she had a pattern of getting involved with men who were emotionally unavailable to her. During therapy I was able to help her see the connection between her pattern with men and the fact that her parents were not available to her. But in spite of the fact that she was able to recognize the origin of her current pattern, she remained unable to access any feeling of anger toward her parents.

Her father had died, but she remained very close to her mother, who, after her father's death, had looked to Lorraine to take his place. Eager to have the connection with her mother that she'd always craved, Lorraine ended up comforting her and in essence becoming her parent. Lorraine moved closer to her mother and became her mother's confidante, housecleaner, and errand runner. She loved being closer to her mother, even though she sometimes complained that it was difficult to maintain her own life.

Lorraine's mother became more and more demanding. She called at all hours of the day and night, expecting Lorraine to drop whatever she was doing to take care of her needs. Lorraine's job as a waitress was beginning to suffer because she often went to work exhausted. Her mother would even call in the middle of the night insisting that she needed some medication from the drugstore. Lorraine reported becoming more and more impatient with customers, and her boss had warned her about her increasingly negative attitude. When I suggested to Lorraine that perhaps she was taking the frustration she felt at her mother out on her customers, she denied any such possibility. I also suggested that she ask her mother to stop calling her in the middle of the night, but she refused, saying that she'd feel horrible if something happened to her mother because she didn't get her medicine.

Months later, Lorraine's anger finally erupted. Her mother had once again called late one night insisting that she needed aspirin because she had a headache. Lorraine dutifully went to the drugstore and brought the aspirin to her mother. But when she went into the kitchen to get her a glass of water, she was surprised to see a bottle of aspirin on the counter. When Lorraine told her mother that she already had some aspirin in the house, her mother simply said, "Well, it was a lot easier to call you than to get up and go in the kitchen." Lorraine tried to explain to her that she was tired, she had to get up in the morning, and she'd appreciate her mother getting up to look the next time. Her mother countered: "Don't get smart with me, young lady. I went to work every day when you were growing up—you owe me." This was the last straw. Lorraine screamed at her mother: "I can't believe how selfish you are. You don't think about my feelings at all, do you? You never have. It's always been about you—your needs, your feelings, never mine."

Lorraine was surprised at the intensity of her anger. "All the anger I ever felt toward her came out in that one moment," she explained to me. "I guess I'm a lot more angry with her than I realized." Lorraine needed to be confronted with her anger in order to believe it really existed.

Uncovering your anger is like digging for gold. It may take a lot of work and you will need a great deal of commitment because often you will have to dig very deep with few results. But once you find your repressed anger, it can be a treasure that provides you with a wonderful avenue for healing. Your anger can provide you with the strength, motivation, and resolve to heal unfinished childhood issues and to start your life anew. It can provide you with the courage to confront the people and situations in your life that are unhealthy or abusive. And it can give you the motivation and strength to pursue goals you might never have the energy or courage to pursue otherwise.

Prescription for Deniers

1. Be open to the possibility that you may express anger more than you realize. Ask your friends and loved ones if they ever experience your anger. If they say they do, ask them to give you some examples of the ways you express anger or some examples of situations in which they have seen you angry.

2. We often mislabel anger as feeling impatient, frustrated, disappointed, or upset. The next time you find yourself using any of these terms, ask yourself if you are really angry.

3. Even though you may not be able to express anger toward those with whom you are close, you may be misdirecting your anger and taking it out on innocent people. Notice with whom you become impatient and with whom you seem to be frustrated or have conflicts. Are they people with whom it is safe to be angry (even though you aren't labeling it anger)?

4. Pay attention to signs of repressed anger in your body. Your body doesn't lie. It stores up the emotions that you don't release, and these stored-up feelings are often manifested as physical symptoms. Common symptoms of repressed or suppressed anger are clenched jaws, grinding of teeth, tense shoulders and arms, clenched fists, headaches, stiff neck, and tightness in the chest. Notice where you store your anger. Pay attention to what your body is telling you and begin to release the tension with exercise and anger-release techniques such as screaming into a pillow, stomping on aluminum cans, and pounding pillows with your fists. The pent-up anger may surface the more you move your body.

Specific Advice for Avoiders

Unlike Deniers, Avoiders consciously choose to squelch their anger. They may do so because they are afraid that they will lose control and damage property or hurt someone if they allow themselves to become angry. Or, they may be critical of people who express their anger and feel morally superior to them. From their perspective, if they were to express their anger openly, it would be an indication that they are weak, out of control, or less evolved.

This is what my client, Holly, told me: "I begin to get angry at someone and then I switch it off—just like that. I start thinking about why they are the way they are, what their childhood was like, or what obstacles or problems they've had to face in life, and I am suddenly overwhelmed with empathy for them." Although this may sound like a very evolved way of dealing with anger, it wasn't working for Holly. She exuded a great deal of silent hostility. You could feel it. She kicked her leg almost continuously and she frequently made disapproving faces and gestures. When I would note her angry gestures and ask her what she was feeling, she would usually say she wasn't feeling anything. "People always think I'm angry when I'm really not," she explained. "I guess I just have that kind of face."

As it turned out, Holly had been raised to always think about the other person's feelings before her own. For example, when she would come home from school and tell her mother about being bullied by another child, instead of her mother comforting her, she would say, "What did you do to make that child angry? People don't just hit you for no reason." When Holly would tell her mother that she'd done nothing, her mother wouldn't believe her. "People always have a good reason for their behavior," her mother would tell her. "If you just put yourself in their place, you'll understand, and you won't ever have to get angry." While Holly's mother may have had good intentions concerning teaching Holly empathy, her attempts were convoluted and extremely negating of Holly's feelings—so much so that Holly was unaware of what she was feeling at any given time.

As much as anger avoiders don't want to own or express their own anger, they don't want to deal with other people's anger either. Some feel afraid of others' anger and some simply get turned off. Others are uncomfortable around those who get angry because on an unconscious level it reminds them of their own suppressed anger. "I'm uncomfortable around angry people," my client, June, told me. "You never know what they'll do or say. I try to avoid them as much as possible." Little did June know at the time that the reason she was uncomfortable around angry people was that it touched a very angry part of her—a part that she worked hard to keep under wraps.

Avoiders pay a heavy price for ignoring their anger. They are often seen as weak because they have lost their voice and their ability to stand up for themselves. In my book *Loving Him without Losing You: How to Stop Disappearing and Start Being Yourself,* I wrote about how many women complain about not being listened to, heard, or "seen" by their partners. These women often feel that their partners ignore their feelings and needs and that they are taken for granted. When they do muster up enough strength to voice an opinion or to disagree with their partner, they usually have the experience of being ignored or discounted. This is what Denise told me: "I learned early in my marriage that it just wasn't worth it for me to get angry with my husband or even to disagree with him. He'd end up getting even more angry with me than I was with him. He'd rant and rave for hours and I'd end up feeling really small. So now I just go along with whatever he says or does." Unfortunately, Denise was becoming more invisible every day. Although it may have seemed hopeless to communicate her feelings to her husband, by giving up trying she had sacrificed a part of herself. And by keeping quiet, she was sending the message that it was okay for her husband to treat her inappropriately.

Some women don't give up stating their grievances altogether, but they simply choose to do so in a passive way. The most common way women tend to make their complaints known is to whine. But whining makes others perceive them as victims, martyrs, or losers, and others lose respect for them.

By not voicing their anger when it is appropriate, many women damage their self-esteem. They become angry with and ashamed of themselves for putting up with inappropriate behavior. The more they put up with, the worse they feel. Soon they begin to believe they don't have the right to complain. They convince themselves that they are making a big thing out of nothing or they become so dependent that they are terrified of making their partner angry and being abandoned.

Anger is a great motivator and provides us with a great sense of power. Those who cannot access their anger deprive themselves of this motivation and power and often end up feeling listless, helpless, and powerless. They allow other people to walk all over them and to dictate how they should run their lives.

Many Avoiders put up with unacceptable, even abusive, behavior for months and even years until one day they finally blow up. This was the case with Janine:

"For years I avoided getting angry with my husband and kids, even though they walked all over me. I put up with their mistreatment because I didn't want to become like my mother, who was a raving maniac. But all of a sudden, one day I just lost it. I started screaming, 'I can't take this anymore. You all treat me like I'm a servant. I refuse to do one more thing for any of you!' I started throwing dishes all over the place and continued screaming about how they took me for granted and how I'd never cook another meal for them. My husband looked at me like I'd gone nuts. My kids just stood paralyzed with fear. They'd never seen me like that.

"After I calmed down, I felt terribly guilty. I couldn't believe I'd done what I had done. I'd become my mother after all. I knew then that I better start working on my anger before I had another incident like that one."

Avoiders often develop physical and emotional illnesses. Many become depressed because they feel so hopeless and helpless about being able to change their lives and because they tend to turn their anger inward. Many Avoiders are prone to certain types of headaches, muscle tension, nervous conditions, and insomnia.

Avoiding anger causes people to lose touch with their other emotions and to close down emotionally. We can't just pick and choose which emotions we are going to feel. If we decide to push down our feelings of anger or sorrow, we inhibit our capacity to feel joy as well.

Prescription for Avoiders

1. Recognize how often you are blind, deaf, or silent when it comes to anger.

2. Recognize that anger is not your enemy. It is a natural part of life and a part of being human. Becoming angry is not a negative thing. In fact, it can be a very positive one if we use our anger to change things in a positive way or to take care of ourselves or those we love. Think of some positive role models to replace the negative ones you grew up with—people who use their anger in positive ways.

3. Instead of ignoring your own anger or the anger of others, start paying attention to the messages that anger is sending. Earlier in the book, I wrote about how anger is a signal that there is something wrong. If you pay attention to the signal, you can often figure out what you can do to change things.

4. Begin to recognize the price you pay for avoiding your anger. Not only do you neglect to find solutions to problems by ignoring anger signals but your anger avoidance often prevents you from getting what you want. Whether it is telling your husband you are tired of sitting home every weekend or telling your boss that you need a raise, without your anger you have lost your voice, your motivation, and your courage to get the things you need and deserve.

5. Practice being assertive by making your needs and grievances known. Instead of withholding your anger or whining, state your grievances when they first come up in as honest a way as you can. Make your needs known in a very direct, assertive way. Don't name-call and avoid using "you," "always," and "never" statements like, "You never take me out anymore" or "You always make fun of me." Instead use "I" statements, such as, "I would appreciate it if we could go

out at least once a month" or "I don't like it when you make fun of me."

6. If you confront someone on inappropriate behavior, don't back down. If you end up giving in, the next time the person behaves in the same inappropriate way, your words of confrontation will mean nothing. The other person will just assume you are spouting off and that he doesn't need to take you seriously. State your position and stick to it. Don't back down and don't apologize for bringing up the issue. There is also no need to argue about what you have said. If the other person defends himself, listen carefully, then say something like, "I understand you don't agree with me and you have a right to your point of view. But I would appreciate it if you'd think about what I've said."

7. Be consistent and state consequences. For example, don't complain endlessly about your mate's excessive drinking, then get drunk with him one night. And don't threaten to end a relationship unless you are willing to stand by your words. Otherwise, you'll weaken your words and your position.

Specific Advice for Stuffers

Many women and men stuff their anger down by overeating, smoking, drinking alcohol, or taking drugs. In fact, there is a strong correlation between addictive behaviors of all kinds and the repression of anger. For example, many people smoke cigarettes as a way to tranquilize themselves whenever they have to deal with anger-provoking situations and as a way of stuffing down their anger. Angry smokers are much more resistive than others to traditional smoking cessation programs. In one study done at the University of Montana, 61 percent of angry smokers either dropped out of treatment early or continued smoking after treatment was completed. This result was in sharp contrast to the quit/failure rate of only 5 percent for nonangry smokers who completed treatment.

Smoking can also be a way of denying that you are an angry person. As my client, Emily, told me, "Whenever I try to stop smoking, I just end up snapping at everyone. But when I smoke, I seldom get angry." Research shows that many smokers self-medicate with nicotine in an attempt to suppress anger (as well as depression and anxiety). The more nicotine a person ingests, the less likely he or she is to react aggressively when provoked. The increase in irritability that many ex-smokers experience after they quit appears to extend well beyond what could realistically be called the withdrawal phase. In a study of 150 French ex-smokers, 94 percent of those who were smoke-free at the end of one year remained more irritable than when they were smoking.

Episodes of intense anger often cause ex-smokers to relapse. In one nationwide study, it was noted that anger was the second most often cited reason for relapse (26 percent), anxiety was the most frequently cited at 42 percent, and depression was a close third at 22 percent.

Anger and Unhealthy Eating Behavior

Research shows that women, in particular, identified eating as a way to deny feelings. Excessive eating is viewed among women as a means of gaining control and power, and is cited as a socially acceptable way to appease anger.

I have counseled many clients who use food as a way to protect themselves from their rage. Pamela, a client who recently lost a great deal of weight, reported suddenly feeling enraged a great deal of the time. "It totally surprised me. I didn't know all this rage was hiding underneath that fat," she reported. At first, Pamela's rage was frightening to her and so out of character that it was alarming to others. But I encouraged Pamela to accept her rage and feel positive that she was now able to express it freely. "I guess I don't have a choice," she told me. "It seems like my rage is going to come out now whether I want it to or not."

For several months, Pamela became enraged about lots of things—getting a parking ticket she felt she didn't deserve, a friend canceling going to a concert with her after she'd spent hours getting the tickets, her husband criticizing what she was wearing. "It just wasn't like me to

get so upset over such minor things," Pamela shared with me. "I'm usually so easygoing." But Pamela wasn't all that easygoing after all. After
talking about each incident, it became clear that Pamela had been stuffing her anger down for a long time in order to be seen as agreeable by
other people. After discussing each of the enraging incidents, she discovered: (1) She really was upset about the parking ticket, so she
decided to fight it—something she would have never done before. (2)
She was fed up with her friend, who often canceled on her. Even though
she recognized that she'd allowed her friend to get away with this unacceptable behavior, she vowed to never make reservations for them
again. (3) Her husband often criticized her and she usually just took it
without saying anything. She realized that she needed to confront him
on his behavior and let him know it was no longer acceptable.

Of course, the true source of Pamela's anger wasn't just an accumulation of all the times she hadn't fought for her rights or let people
know when their behavior was unacceptable—it had its origins in her
childhood. Pamela had been sexually abused as a child and was unable
at the time to express her rage at being violated. This was primarily
because she was afraid of her perpetrator. Right after the abuse, she
began to overeat, gaining quite a lot of weight in a very short amount
of time. Her overeating was mostly about stuffing down the rage she
felt but was afraid to express. Over several months, in the safe environment of my therapy offices and alone in her bedroom at home, Pamela
allowed herself to feel the rage that lay hidden inside her for years.

The relationship between food abuse and prior physical and sexual abuse is reported in many studies. Women identify eating as a way
of denying the abuse or suppressing feelings, including anger. For
example, Tice reported intense anger and low self-esteem among
obese and bulimic women, with the anger directed toward themselves,
their abuser, and projected toward other men.

Discover the Feelings underneath Your Anger

My client, Susan, had been losing weight steadily for over a month,
but she was worried because she was going on a vacation with her
mother. "I always eat too much around my mother," she told me.

"Why is that?" I asked.

"Because she makes me so irritated and angry," Susan explained.

"What does she do to make you angry?" I asked.

"Nothing really. I'm just angry when I'm around her."

I knew there was more to it. As I suspected, Susan wasn't really angry with her mother for anything she currently did—it was old anger, all the anger she had stored up for years but never allowed herself to express. Susan's mother had been very neglectful when Susan was growing up. She seldom spent time with her or took any interest in teaching her about life. Now, whenever her mother gave her advice, it made Susan very angry. "I guess I'm angry because I think to myself, 'How dare you give me advice now. I'm all grown up. Where were you when I needed you?'"

At this point, Susan started crying. This was a huge breakthrough for her because she hadn't cried in years and she had never allowed herself to cry in therapy. She wept silently for several minutes, then looked up at me and said, "I can't believe I let myself cry. I really am hurt when I think about what I missed out on as a child. It really is sad."

I was very pleased that Susan had finally let down her guard and allowed herself to feel the pain she had been avoiding for a long time. I explained to her that one of the many reasons it is important to allow yourself to feel your anger is that then you are able to access the feelings underneath it. Susan had a lot of anger to get out and a lot of grieving to do, but she had made a giant step that day in therapy.

Still concerned about gaining weight, Susan asked me what she should do in her mother's presence. "I don't want to let her know how angry I am at her," she explained. "She did the best she could and I know she's trying to make up for it now." I assured Susan that she need not involve her mother in her anger work and encouraged her to go home after her session and write down all the reasons why she was angry with her mother. Then I suggested that whenever she began to get irritated with her mother, she should find some excuse to distance herself for a few minutes, pull out her list, and remind herself why she was really angry. If she still remained angry, I suggested she take a time-out and either write about her angry feelings or go for a brisk walk before returning to her mother. Finally, I suggested she allow herself time to continue grieving for all the neglect and deprivation she experienced as a child.

When Susan came back from her vacation, she reported that she had overeaten only once. "Whenever I found myself getting irritated with my mother, I made up some excuse to get away from her for a few minutes. I read the list like you suggested and most of the time it actually worked to calm me down. One time, reading the list made me more angry, so I told my mom I needed a break and went for a long walk. By the time I got back, I felt more calm and could be with her without snapping at her."

If you find that you have a habit of stuffing down your anger with food, the following suggestions may help:

- Although smoking, eating, and drinking alcohol can bring about some tension reduction, they are certainly not considered healthy stress-reduction methods. If your stuffing comes from a need to tranquilize yourself, practice healthier methods of stress reduction such as deep breathing, yoga, punching a pillow, swimming, jogging, or getting a massage. Refer to chapter 5 for more ideas.

- When you catch yourself overeating or eating "forbidden" food, ask yourself, "What am I feeling? Angry? Sad? Afraid?"

- Tell yourself that you can eat whatever you want in a few minutes if you first commit to writing in your journal for five minutes. Write about whatever you are feeling in the moment. After five minutes, if you still feel like eating, go ahead.

- If it becomes clear that it is a particular person or place that is upsetting you, excuse yourself for a few minutes. Go for a walk or just get away to a quiet corner where you can focus on what you are feeling. This is particularly effective if you are aware that you are angry with someone but are unable at the time to express your anger.

- If you become aware that you need to release some anger energy, go for a brisk walk, hit some pillows, or put your head in a pillow and scream.

Specific Advice for Self-blamers

All those who have a passive anger style are vulnerable to self-blaming. It is a natural result of not allowing yourself to own and express your anger. But Self-blamers tend to blame themselves more than the average person with a passive anger style. All the anger that they could feel (and secretly do) toward others gets redirected toward themselves. Raymond is a good example. He is a kind and loving man who never gets angry at others. But he continually gets angry with himself. "You are so stupid," he'll say to himself out loud whenever he makes even the slightest mistake. The self-criticism is even worse inside his head. Raymond needs to learn how to stop the negative self-talk and learn to express his anger in assertive, constructive ways.

Negative self-talk is a habit. You can break this habit by using a strategy called cognitive restructuring. By being smart about the way you talk to yourself, you can avoid a buildup of negative feelings that might lead to self-defeating actions and attitudes. Here are three simple steps to rewriting your negative scripts:

1. Catch yourself in the act of negative self-talk and stop the tape.

2. Do a reality check by asking yourself a few questions to help you analyze the situation objectively. For example, when you find yourself focusing on everything you are doing wrong, ask yourself, "What am I doing right?" When you are being critical about your job performance, ask yourself, "What skills do I bring to this situation?"

3. Replace your negative message with a more accurate one. For example, perhaps you are thinking something like, "I'm so stupid. I never say what I mean. I just beat around the bush until everyone gets impatient with me." Do a reality check:

"I'm not stupid. I'm just afraid of speaking my mind." Now replace the irrational thought with: "Other people don't know I'm not saying what I want to say and they probably aren't as impatient with me as I imagine they are."

Negative self-talk is not the only way Self-blamers turn their anger against themselves. Marcie is so angry with her boyfriend that she could punch him in the mouth. Instead she goes on a food binge, eating so much that she makes her stomach hurt, then forces herself to vomit. (Unlike Pamela and Susan who overate to stuff down their anger, purging among bulimics is often interpreted as a self-punishing act.) Rachel is furious with her mother. But instead of letting her mother know how she feels, she cuts her arm over and over with a razor blade. Anger is implicated in various forms of self-harming behavior in women. Research shows that the powerlessness felt by women finds expression in unhealthy eating behaviors, substance abuse, self-mutilation, and suicidal gestures.

Often inaccurately interpreted as a suicidal gesture, self-mutilation is a response to anxiety that offers temporary relief from emotional pain. Associated with earlier childhood abuse, self-injury is an impotent rage that becomes directed at the self rather than the abuser. It becomes for some a way to anesthetize the part of their body that is being abused by distracting themselves with another type of pain. Another motivation to self-injury is providing a feeling of calm that rapidly decreases tension surrounding memories of abuse. (Herman documents the accounts of survivors who report injuring themselves to prove they exist, and thus paradoxically regards self-injury as a form of self-protection rather than a suicide attempt.)

The Causes of Self-Blame

Why are some people prone to self-blame more than others? I believe it is due to three causes: (1) fear of rejection and criticism; (2) lack of object constancy; (3) a history of childhood abuse.

Self-blamers are often terribly afraid of hurting others. They would rather beat themselves up with critical words, make themselves sick by binging on food, or physically hurt their own bodies rather than risk hurting someone else's feelings or being rejected by them. They would rather feel bad about themselves than risk having someone else see them in a bad light. Pamela, who you met earlier, is a good example. Many Self-blamers are really Self-abusers who are punishing themselves over and over with anger that is actually meant for someone else.

Children who are raised in an emotionally healthy environment are able to develop object constancy, meaning they perceive their parents as both good and bad: "Sometimes my mother can be nice and other times she can be mean." Along with object constancy, these children develop the awareness that they are indeed separate from their parents: "When my mother is mean, it may not have anything to do with me." These children become adults who aren't likely to blame themselves for their parents' problems or mistreatment or for anyone else's problems or mistreatment. But children who are abused or neglected seldom develop object constancy and never truly separate from their parents. They tend to continue blaming themselves for their parents' problems and mistreatment as well as the problems and mistreatment of those close to them. If a partner mistreats them, they blame themselves. They think that they deserve to be mistreated because they are bad people.

Justine was sexually abused by her father, yet she insisted that she was not angry with him. As a child, she tried to block out what had happened and was successful in doing so until several years ago when she began to suffer from sexual problems with her husband, which prompted her to enter therapy. But even though she came to remember her father's abuse and was able to make the connection between the abuse and her feelings of repulsion concerning certain sexual acts, she minimized the abuse and blamed herself for it: "My mother always told me that I was too old to be sitting on my dad's lap the way I always did." When her father had asked her if she wanted to see his penis, she had said yes. This was further proof to Justine that she had encouraged her father: "I must have wanted it. I could have said no. I could have told my mother, but I didn't."

Sexual abuse victims typically blame themselves. Justine did so in order to avoid facing the fact that her father had used her to satisfy his own selfish needs. If she stopped blaming herself, she'd have to face this betrayal.

Those who are sexually abused by more than one perpetrator often blame themselves because they feel they must have asked for it in some way in order for it to continue happening again and again. When Mara was six, a female baby sitter tried to get her to touch her vagina. When she was eight, a man exposed himself to her. When she was sixteen, she was date raped. "What's wrong with me?" she asked at one of our sessions. "What is it about me that makes people pick me? I feel I must be doing something to attract their attention or to encourage them in some way."

Although Mara remembered all these events and questioned why they all happened to her, she did not perceive herself as a victim of childhood sexual abuse: "None of these things really hurt me. I mean, it could have been much worse. I was drunk when the boy penetrated me when I was sixteen, so I don't remember it hurting, even though I was a virgin at the time." Nor did Mara have any anger about the fact that she'd been victimized so many times as a child. Instead Mara turned her anger on herself. This took the form of self-blame: "There really must be something wrong with me—maybe I was oversexed or something."

When I asked Mara why she wasn't angry, she explained, "I really shouldn't have been where I was when that man exposed himself. I shouldn't have been drinking, . . . " and so on. Because Mara was unable to acknowledge and express her anger at the people who had abused her, it turned to shame, causing her to blame herself.

Prescription for Self-blamers

1. The next time you find yourself being self-critical or feeling depressed, ask yourself if you are feeling angry at someone. If you are, find a safe way to express your anger so that you don't have to turn it on yourself.

2. Whenever you catch yourself being self-critical, turn the negative messages in your head into positive self-talk. Think of at least three things that you do well and remind yourself of your good qualities.

3. Don't buy into the blaming comments of others. If someone becomes critical of you, tell him that you don't appreciate being criticized and excuse yourself. Don't sit and listen as someone continues to criticize you.

4. Being victimized causes people to feel helpless and this helplessness leads them to feel humiliated and ashamed. As a protection against this feeling of helplessness and shame, they take personal responsibility for their own victimization. If you are a victim of emotional, physical, or sexual abuse, either in childhood or as an adult, it is vitally important that you come to recognize that it was not your fault and that you work on owning and releasing your anger toward your abuser.

5. In order to get to the core of your negative self-talk and self-blame, you need to learn the truth of who you really are. If you have a deep belief that you are worthless, you must discover where that belief came from and why you believe it is true. It may be that you have been unwilling to reject the negative messages given by your parents or other caretakers because you haven't been willing to feel your anger toward them and to separate from them.

CHAPTER 8

From Passive-Aggressive to Assertive

What do you mean I'm angry? I'm not angry.
—PAUL, AGE 24

Ted is an excellent example of someone with a passive-aggressive anger style. Ted came to see me because he was suffering from impotence (this was before the advent of Viagra). He had been married for over twenty years and had been impotent for five years. He blamed his wife for his problem: "She's so demanding and controlling, I just don't feel like being close to her." But Ted hadn't come to me because he was impotent with his wife; he came because he was impotent with his girlfriend.

Ted had fallen in love with a much younger woman. At first he had no problem making love to her. But after about a month, he started having problems maintaining his erection: "I'm very turned on to her, so I don't understand what the problem is. I'm afraid I'm going to lose her if I don't solve this problem soon."

After only a short time working together, it became evident that the cause of Ted's problem was his repressed and suppressed anger and his passive-aggressive style of coping with his anger. He was very happy with his girlfriend, but he confessed that it was difficult trying to juggle both relationships: "I'm exhausted most of the time.

A couple of times a week, I tell my wife I have to work late so I can see Samantha. Then I rush home to try to spend some time with my wife and kids. Annette has always complained that I don't spend enough time with them, and this, of course, doesn't make it any better. On the weekend I try to think up some excuse to get out of the house so I can see Samantha or at least call her. Of course, she's always hurt and lonely for me."

"It sounds like you've doubled your problems. Now you have two unhappy women on your hands," I offered.

"Oh no. Samantha isn't demanding like my wife is. She just misses me. And I miss her too. I wish we could be together all the time," Ted insisted.

"Then why don't you leave your wife to be with Samantha?" I asked.

Ted replied, "I can't afford it. I'd have to pay alimony and child support, and Samantha doesn't make much money, so I'd have to support her too. I just can't do it. I feel like such a failure. My wife always reminds me of all the potential I have and I know she's right. I've settled into a mediocre job just so I can support my wife and kids when I really wanted to be free to take more creative risks."

"Do you think you might resent your wife and kids for this?" I ventured.

Ted answered, "Yes, I suppose I do. If I didn't have them to worry about, I would have continued to pursue my musical career. But as you know, musicians don't make steady money."

"And now it sounds like you feel obligated to Samantha as well," I pointed out.

Ted acknowledged, "Yes, she doesn't have much, and I feel guilty about the fact that I can't be with her more often. I try to make up for it by buying her little presents or by taking her out to nice restaurants."

"Can you afford that?" I asked.

"Not really, but it seems to make her feel better. She was really beginning to make my life hell there for a while."

"What do you mean?" I inquired.

Ted responded, "Well, when I'd call on the weekend, she would start crying, telling me how much she missed me. And then she started pressuring me to leave Annette."

"How did that make you feel?" I asked.

"Guilty at first. But then I guess I started to resent her. After all, she knew I was married when we met. She knew what she was getting into."

Instead of confronting Samantha directly, Ted had begun to withdraw from her emotionally and sexually, just as he had done with his wife. And now he had one more person to blame for his unhappiness and his failures.

If you have a passive-aggressive style, like Ted, you feel others have control of your life instead of you. You may avoid conflict in the moment by going along with what someone else wants, but in the long term you actually create more conflict. Over time, you are likely to build up resentment toward those you perceive as being controlling or dominating. You often feel pressured to perform and will sometimes unconsciously try to fail as a way to defeat the person by whom you feel pressured.

In this chapter we'll focus on ways for you to modify or completely transform your passive-aggressive anger style into an anger style that is healthier and more effective. This will include the following steps:

1. Admitting you are angry

2. Confronting your issues with control

3. Discovering the roots of your passive-aggressiveness

4. Accepting your anger

5. Learning to assert yourself and express your anger directly

6. Becoming aware of your triggers

7. Letting go of your need to frustrate others

Step One: Admit You Are Angry

The first step in changing this anger style is to admit you are angry. Sure, you may not exhibit your anger in traditional ways, but you are angry nevertheless. Your anger comes out in underhanded, sly ways instead of directly. When you forget to do something or accidentally spill something, or when you play dumb so that you won't have to do something, you may be expressing your anger. Admitting this to yourself is crucial if you are to break out of this anger style. Passive-aggressive forms of anger expression also include being chronically late, pouting, sulking, whining, manipulating, backbiting, and gossiping.

As much as you are angry at others for trying to control you or pushing you around, you are equally angry with yourself for not having the courage to stand up for yourself. Every time someone gives you advice and you pretend to take it, every time you say you'll do something just to appease someone, you become angry—you get angry at the other person and at yourself for being such a wimp.

Step Two: Confront Your Issues with Control

You need to become aware of your underlying anger and resentment at being controlled. Let's face it—you just don't like being told what to do. Neither do you like to be guided, advised, or gently prodded. You want to do things your own way and in your own time. You want to be independent. Unfortunately, you don't usually express these needs out loud or directly. You don't stand up for yourself and you don't say no.

Let's return to the example I gave you at the beginning of the chapter. Even though Ted felt victimized by his wife, his girlfriend, and his circumstances, he was actually the one with major control issues. As we worked together, he became aware that he deeply resented his wife for suggesting that he take a secure job after the children were born.

He also realized that his wife had not really insisted and that he hadn't asserted himself by letting her know how important music was to him. Instead he resented her for making a suggestion he could not really argue with and labeled her controlling. Then he went along with her suggestion and blamed her for his unhappiness.

He essentially reacted the same way with his girlfriend. Everything was fine until she asked him to leave his wife. Once more, he experienced this as her telling him what to do and being controlling. Of course, he didn't tell her how he felt. Instead he punished her by becoming impotent, just as he had punished his wife this way.

In addition to recognizing your need to control, you will also need to become aware of your desire to get back at, annoy, or defeat those who you perceive as controlling or dominating. You may need to confront your need to fail in order to accomplish this. Ted got back at his wife and girlfriend by becoming impotent. What do you do when you feel someone is trying to control you? It is surprising to what lengths some people will go in order to punish others for what they experience as dominating behavior. I've had clients who failed major exams because they felt pressured by their parents to pursue a particular career, female clients who gained weight because their partner pressured them to lose weight, and male clients who sabotaged their success at work because a boss was controlling.

EXERCISE: *To What Lengths Have You Gone?*

1. Make a list of the ways you have punished others for trying to control you.

2. Include all the ways you have sabotaged your own life just to make sure others couldn't dominate you.

Step Three: Discover the Roots of Your Passive-Aggressiveness

Now that you know you are angry and realize you have control issues, it is important to discover the reason why you chose the passive-aggressive anger style in the first place. Many passive-aggressive individuals received inconsistent or mixed messages from their parents or other caretakers when they were growing up. For example, they may have been praised for being talkative and entertaining in front of guests one time and criticized for the same behavior the next. Over time, children in such homes become reluctant to do anything or risk anything, since they are never sure when they will make a mistake and anger their parents.

One client told me that his mother would ask him if he was angry with her because she'd done something to disappoint him, such as not keeping a promise. He'd be afraid to tell her the truth, but she'd assure him that it was okay. Then when he finally admitted that yes, he was angry, she'd slap him and tell him something like, "How dare you get angry with me. I'm your mother. You don't get angry with your mother."

Some people take on the passive-aggressive style because they were dominated, judged, and punished for being angry or acting aggressively when they were children. Others were led to believe that it is either not safe or not acceptable to stand up to others. This is often the case with children who are emotionally, physically, or sexually abused.

Still others take on this anger style because they are being abused as adults. Earlier I mentioned that many women (and men) who are in abusive relationships take on a passive-aggressive style of anger. If your partner constantly belittles you, criticizes you, or blames you, or if he or she frequently explodes in a rage or has unreasonable expectations, you are being emotionally abused (see my books, *The Emotionally Abusive Relationship* and *The Emotionally Abused Woman* for further information on emotional abuse and for help in stopping it). If your partner pushes, shoves, slaps, hits, or punches you, you are being physically abused.

When a partner is abusive, it begins to feel too dangerous to be direct with your anger. Instead you learn to retaliate in underhanded, secretive ways, such as stealing money from his wallet, being rough with him as you put him to bed drunk, accidentally hitting her in your sleep, or falling asleep so that you don't have to have sex with her.

Step Four: Accept Your Anger

You now know you are angry and you hopefully know why it has been difficult for you to express your anger directly. Now you need to begin working on accepting your anger. Until you can honor your angry feelings and your right to express your anger, you will not be able to shed the passive-aggressive anger style. Remind yourself daily that your anger is a normal and healthy part of life and that anger is a messenger telling you that something in your life is wrong—that some aspect of your life needs to be addressed or changed.

Your anger will help you to finally take charge of your life. It will help you to stop wasting years pretending, procrastinating, and making excuses for not completing things you didn't want to do in the first place. If you don't want to do something, say so. The other person may get angry, but the chances are great that he or she is already angry with you anyway for playing games, putting things off, and pretending.

Step Five: Learn to Assert Yourself and Express Your Anger Directly

Although the idea of asserting yourself directly no doubt frightens you, it will be the key to changing this unhealthy anger style. Instead of pretending to agree or going along with things just to keep the peace, you'll need to tell others what you really think. Instead of promising to do something you have no intention of doing, you'll need to tell the other person directly that you do not want to do it. And instead of sighing, gossiping, or getting back at people behind their back, you'll need to tell others what you really feel. This will, of course, leave you open to possible confrontations, disagreements, or even loss of support, which is why you have been reluctant to operate more openly. But the more you practice being direct and assertive, the more you'll discover that you are strong enough to handle confrontations and even attacks.

The motto of many with the passive-aggressive style is: "You'll know I'm angry by what I don't do." But this is a cop-out. By operating in this way you have been able to be angry without ever having to admit it or take responsibility for it. Instead of disappointing, upsetting, and irritating others when it is you who is really angry, you'll need to come clean about your anger. Instead of saying, "I don't understand why *you're* so angry with me. I didn't do anything," you'll need to do some soul searching to discover what you did—or more likely, didn't do. For example, did you neglect to change the oil in the car when you promised you would? Have you put off cleaning the spare room for your parents' visit? Did you conveniently forget to stop at the store to buy milk?

You never attack directly—you can never be accused of being aggressive. But this doesn't mean you don't have a great deal of rage and aggression built up inside you that needs to be acknowledged and ventilated. In the classic movie, *The Four Seasons,* Alan Alda plays a passive-aggressive man who prides himself on never getting angry. He is the picture of calmness, rationality, and congeniality. But he shows his anger by asking pointed questions and making insinuating remarks that irritate his wife and friends to no end. In the movie, his wife, played by Carol Burnett, implores, "Why don't you ever get angry? Do you know how irritating it is to be around someone who is always so rational?"

Alda looks at her like he is stricken. When she deliberately tries to start a fight with him so that he'll defend himself, he calmly tells her, "I'm getting very angry."

"You've got to be kidding," his wife says, "That's you being angry?"

"I'm furious," he says calmly.

In the movie, this scene is hilariously funny. But there is nothing funny about the fact that you have a great deal of anger and rage inside you that needs to be expressed in direct ways or that your underhanded ways of expressing anger are seriously jeopardizing your relationships with others.

Step Six: Become Aware of Your Triggers

If you have a passive-aggressive anger style, you tend to react predictably to certain types of people and situations. These common triggers include

- Situations where your performance will be judged (or you think it will be judged)
- Authority figures, powerful people
- Being told what to do
- Being threatened if you don't do something

Think about what your specific triggers are—those people and situations that create the most resistance and anger in you. Perhaps it is your wife or husband who pushes your buttons the most. Or perhaps it is the way someone asks you to do something that gets you going. Whatever it is, becoming aware of your potential triggers will help you to catch yourself in the act of passively resisting so that you can begin to react more directly and assertively.

Assignment. Identify your triggers. Make a list of all your triggers. Take your time. Although you may be aware of some of your triggers, some will be more difficult to discover.

Step Seven: Let Go of Your Need to Frustrate Others

Brian is extremely angry with his wife, Denise. Once again she has started another home improvement project—this time it is remodeling the kitchen. Of course, Brian is going to have to do most of the work. But instead of Brian telling Denise that he doesn't want to remodel the kitchen, that he's tired of working on the house every weekend, he simply goes along with the idea. He doesn't want a big argument, which he is sure Denise would win anyway. So Brian devises a plan to frustrate Denise so that she will stop all this home improvement stuff for good. He's going to make remodeling the kitchen such a nightmare for Denise that she'll never ask him to do another thing around the house.

The key to his plan is to take his time. He's going to go so slow that it will drive Denise crazy. He forgets to order materials, orders the wrong materials, and installs things improperly. All this makes the project go so slowly that Denise becomes impatient.

"When do you think you're going to be able to install the new cabinets?" she asks one Saturday when she catches him relaxing in the backyard.

"Oh, did I forget to tell you? They sent me the wrong ones," Brian replies.

"So when will the new ones get here?" Denise asks.

"I don't know," Brian answers vaguely.

"What about the new countertops? Can't you start installing those?" Denise asks.

"Wouldn't you know, I measured wrong the first time, and now I have to reorder the materials. I'll start as soon as I get them in." Brian says.

Denise is beginning to wish she'd never thought of remodeling the kitchen. She loves to cook and hates to waste money on take-out food, so as the weeks pass, she becomes more and more anxious and frustrated. "I thought you were a better carpenter than this," she tells Brian. "You're making so many mistakes and costing us so much money, we would have been better off hiring a professional."

"Bingo!" Brian thinks to himself. "Maybe she's finally getting the message and she'll leave me alone." He loves to see Denise frustrated. He smiles to himself and closes his eyes against the noonday sun.

If you are honest with yourself, you, like Brian, have no doubt received a great deal of pleasure from frustrating others. Making everyone else upset, pushing their buttons, and making them feel crazy with confusion has been your way of feeling powerful. It's been your way of giving anyone who wants you to do something the finger. It's been your way of exerting control.

If you practice assertiveness and discover the power you can feel when you stand up for yourself, you'll be less inclined to seek power in underhanded ways. The more you are clear about what you are willing and not willing to do, the less you will need to rebel in childish ways. And the more real control of yourself you maintain, the less you will need to control others.

It may be difficult to wean yourself from the feelings of power you get from seeing others frustrated and defeated by your passive-aggressive ploys. It feels good to win, even when you do it unfairly. But do you really win when you have to suffer from living with constant confusion, negativity, dishonesty, and not getting your needs met because you never tell anyone directly what they are?

You're right—no one can make you do anything. But how about you? Are you willing to make yourself do something that will change your life? Are you willing to change your anger style and gain better communication, more self-respect and respect from others, and the chance to learn what you really want?

Advice for All Those with a Passive-Aggressive Style

1. Believe that it is okay to be angry.

2. Become aware of your hidden anger.

3. Work at becoming more assertive. Refer to chapters 5 and 7 for more tips on how to be assertive.

4. Practice saying no when you do not want to do something or when you disagree instead of going along.

5. Do not confuse self-assertion with aggression.

6. Instead of trying to please others, focus more on what you want to do.

7. Work on allowing yourself to be just who you are and remind yourself that you are okay just as you are.

8. Realize that your sense of self-worth does not depend on other people's opinions.

9. Practice expressing your anger directly when you feel dominated or controlled by someone.

10. Give yourself permission to be openly defiant for a while. Just as a teenager needs to go through a period of rebellion in order to separate from his or her parents and become an autonomous adult, you may need to be defiant as a process of your growth.

11. Begin to define yourself more by what you want to do than what you don't want to do.

12. Choose people who don't pressure you to be a certain way or to perform and people who accept you just the way you are.

13. Choose people who don't need to dominate or have their way.

14. Don't allow yourself to be emotionally or physically abused.

15. Choose people who can handle confrontations and anger.

16. Choose people who will support you in becoming assertive.

Specific Advice for Anger Sneaks

More than anything, you need to start expressing your anger directly instead of getting back at others in sneaky, underhanded ways. There is obviously a risk in doing this. You're bound to make others angry, you risk rejection, and you're likely to create conflict in your relationships. But anger and conflict are a natural part of life. You've learned what happens when you try to eliminate anger and conflict from your life—it just goes underground. Why not find out what it is like to have things out in the open?

Anger expressed directly can empower you and motivate you to make needed changes in your life. This is especially important to remember if you are in an unhealthy or abusive relationship. You may tell yourself that you make things equal when you get back at a controlling or abusive person in an underhanded way, such as accidentally throwing his important papers in the trash. But even though you may feel better in the moment, he's still winning because you can't face him directly with your anger. Until you can do that, you are the child in the relationship and he is the adult; you are the slave and he is the master. If you are with someone who is so dangerous that it is impossible for you to express your anger directly, then you need to leave that relationship.

Most Anger Sneaks end up feeling guilty for the underhanded ways they have gotten revenge, which makes them feel bad about themselves. Coming clean and letting people know when you are angry instead of getting back at them behind their back will make you feel proud of yourself and help you regain your self-respect.

No more sneak attacks, no more guerrilla warfare, and no more camouflaged anger. Just honest, direct, open, and assertive communication: "I'm angry with you because____" instead of "Yes, dear (you bastard)." Tell people when you feel pushed around, when you feel controlled, and when you need them to back off instead of sitting there silently planning ways to get back at them.

Specific Advice for Escape Artists

If you don't want to do something, say so. Whether it is something your mate asks you to do or something your boss tells you to do, don't agree to do it just to get him or her off your back. You'll only end up putting it off or lying about working on it when you have no intention of doing so. You may have been raised to believe that it wasn't safe to stand up to others, but now you are an adult and you need to remind yourself that nothing horrible is going to happen to you if you say no. (If you are in an abusive relationship, this may not be completely true. You may need to get out of the relationship so that you are not in danger.)

If you don't feel like an adult or feel too inadequate to stand up for yourself, the only way you're going to feel stronger is by doing it. Start with less risky no's and work your way up. If your partner or your boss or whoever you feel intimidated by gets upset, so be it. Let him get upset. Let her rant and rave if she wants to. The more you stand up for yourself and the more you say how you honestly feel, the more the people in your life are going to respect you. Soon you'll notice that others will make fewer demands on you or that they will ask you to do something instead of telling you to do it. It will get easier and easier for you to speak up, to disagree, and to say no.

Specific Advice for Sulkers

Pouting, sulking, and giving the silent treatment is for children. It is what children do because they feel powerless in the world of adults. But you are an adult, even if you don't feel like one most of the time. The more you continue to act like a child, the more you will feel like one, and the more others will treat you like one.

It's time to grow up. No one is more powerful than you unless you give them that power. Take control of your life by speaking your truths, standing up for yourself, disagreeing with others, and stating your opinion loud and clear. If someone does something you don't like, tell him directly and clearly. Don't pout, don't sulk, and don't expect him to guess what is wrong. If someone hurt your feelings, tell her why so that she won't do it again. Don't punish her with silence and make her figure out what is wrong—how childish is that?

Begin to make your own choices and decisions. Don't just go along with someone else's, then make it abundantly clear later on that you're not happy. Others are not responsible for your happiness—you are. The only way you have a real chance at happiness is by making sure you make your own decisions and choices as opposed to always giving in to others so that they'll like you. Start with small decisions (e.g., choose a restaurant) and work your way up to bigger ones (e.g., what kind of car you want to buy). Each decision will empower you and help you to gain more confidence in yourself.

It is quite possible that you've been giving in and going along for so long that you don't know what you like and don't like. This is typical for passive-aggressors. If this is true for you, there is even more reason for you to begin making your own decisions. Each choice you make will help you find out more about your tastes, your preferences, and yourself.

Specific Advice for Pretenders

Do you remember Lexi from chapter 4? She considered herself so evolved and spiritual that she never got angry. If you are like Lexi, you may not be aware of the anger and resentment brewing under your overly pleasant facade. It may take feedback from someone else to help you see yourself as you truly are. On the other hand, my description of Lexi may have resonated with you. There may be just the slightest recognition that perhaps you have some of Lexi's qualities (i.e., a need to be seen as superior or perfect). Whichever the case may be, admitting to yourself that you have been projecting a false persona in order to be seen as nicer or more accepting than you really are is the first step to changing.

If you have adopted the pretender style of dealing with your anger, you avoid your so-called negative feelings at all costs. Many, like Lexi, even believe that in order to be truly enlightened or to be truly spiritual or religious, they must never "lower" themselves by expressing anger. But just as Lexi discovered, the more you repress or suppress your less desirable emotions, the more powerful they become. Anger then finds another way of seeping out—through facial expressions, posture, words, and unconscious behavior.

The next step to changing this unhealthy style of anger is to face these truths: We all get angry. We all want our way. We are all controlling at times. It is part of the human experience. No matter how hard we try to be perfect, it just doesn't happen. No one is enlightened to the point that they never feel dark emotions such as rage, envy, jealousy, or hatred. Own up to your anger. Take responsibility for it. Take the risk of acknowledging your grievances. Instead of harboring resentments, get them out in the open. It won't make you less of a person; in fact, it will make you a better one—and a more real one.

CHAPTER 9

Transforming a Projective-Aggressive Style

I guess all along it was my own anger I was seeing in others.

—AARON, AGE 42

If you have the projective-aggressive anger style your main task is to overcome your negative associations with anger so that you can give yourself permission to express it instead of projecting it onto others. You deny or avoid your anger because you are either afraid of it or you believe that anger is an unacceptable emotion. In this chapter we'll focus on helping you to break free from these negative beliefs and this unhealthy anger style. This will include the following steps:

1. Discovering the origins of your negative beliefs about anger

2. Challenging your old beliefs about anger

3. Taking back your projections

4. Acknowledging and accepting your anger

Step One: Discover the Origins of Your Negative Beliefs about Anger

In order to overcome your negative beliefs about anger, you'll first need to discover where you got them. It is highly likely that you either grew up in a household where the expression of anger was considered unacceptable or evil or in an environment where you witnessed someone losing control on a regular basis. For example, many with the projective-aggressive anger style grew up in strict, conservative homes where the expression of any strong emotion was considered a sign of weakness or evil. Children raised in these kinds of homes were required to blindly follow the rules of overly domineering parents and never question their authority. To question or contradict their parents may have resulted in severe punishment or rejection. Others were raised to believe that anger is evil—the work of the devil. If you had this kind of upbringing, you may have learned to repress or suppress your anger. Whenever you feel yourself getting angry, you may hear voices in your head saying, "You're not supposed to get angry," "You're going to be punished," or "You're going to hell."

If you were raised in an environment where you often witnessed someone close to you losing control of his or her anger and becoming verbally or physically violent, you may have decided that you would never get angry like that. You may have become so determined to avoid becoming like a violent or abusive father, mother, sibling, or other relative that you learned to push your anger down— out of sight and even out of your consciousness. To you, any show of anger could lead to abuse or violence, so you are afraid of your anger.

It is also possible that you got your negative beliefs about anger from being abused as an adult. If you have been in one or more relationships where you consistently witnessed or experienced a partner becoming emotionally or physically abusive, you may have come away from the experience believing that anger equals violence.

Step Two: Challenge Your Old Beliefs about Anger

The problem is that now you find it difficult to get angry even when it is justified. Your beliefs are so strong and your fears are so overwhelming that they take over as soon as you begin to feel anger. It happens so automatically that you may not be aware that you are angry in the first place. That's why you see anger in others when it isn't really there and why you continue to attract angry people who will act out your anger for you.

The way past this dilemma is for you to begin challenging your old beliefs. Hopefully you have begun to recognize how erroneous your beliefs about anger are from reading this book so far. The following exercise will also help.

EXERCISE: *Your Beliefs about Anger*

1. Make a list of all your past and present beliefs about anger (e.g., "It's never okay to get angry," "If you get angry you'll lose control," "Anger is the work of the devil").

2. Read over your list and think carefully about each item. Cross off items that no longer seem rational or true to you today.

3. Put a circle around beliefs that you still believe today.

4. Take a close look at the beliefs you have circled. Are you sure you still believe these things are true? Do they still apply to your life today?

The next time you feel yourself becoming even the slightest bit angry, pay attention to the messages you give yourself about anger. If you hear yourself saying any of the items that you crossed off your list because you no longer believe them, tell yourself, "I no longer believe that; it's not true." If you hear your inner voice saying any of the items you have circled—those you still believe today—try saying to yourself, "That may be true, but I also have a right to be angry."

Step Three: Take Back Your Projections

Once you have begun to own your anger, you can begin to take back your projections. Many of you have undoubtedly learned about projection elsewhere and I have explained it already in this book, but some of you may need a little more information to get the concept completely clear in your mind. Projection is the act of attributing to others those feelings and reactions that you are having but do not want to acknowledge, or in some cases, feelings you fear you may have or have had in the past. Just as a movie camera projects an image on a screen, you project onto others all those aspects of yourself of which you are fearful or ashamed.

Projective Identification

Projective identification refers to what occurs when one partner projects denied and disowned aspects of his or her self onto an intimate partner, then perceives these disassociated feelings as existing in the partner. This is somewhat different from getting involved with someone who actually possesses qualities that you have disowned. (For example, Ventriloquists tend to use projective identification, whereas Innocent Victims tend to primarily use projection—both in terms of who they attract and in the way they silently stand by when someone is being abusive).

With projective identification, not only are your unwanted thoughts and feelings seen as being inside your partner instead of within yourself but your partner is encouraged by means of cues and provocations to behave as if they were actually there. You can then identify vicariously with your partner's expression of the rejected thoughts, feelings, and emotions. Maggie Scarf wrote about this phenomenon in an article for the book, *Meeting the Shadow*, edited by Connie Zweig:

> One of the best and clearest examples of the way in which projective identification operates is seen in the totally nonaggressive and never angry individual. This person, who is uniquely devoid of

anger, can become aware of angry feelings only as they exist in someone else—in the intimate partner, most predictably. When something disturbing *has* happened to the never angry individual, and he *is* experiencing angry emotions, he will be consciously out of contact with them. *He will not know that he is angry, but he will be wonderfully adept at triggering an explosion of hostility and anger in his spouse.*

The mate, who may not have been feeling angry at all before the interaction, may quickly find herself completely furious; her anger, which appears to be about some completely unrelated issue, is, in fact, anger that is being acted out for her spouse. She is thus, in some sense, "protecting" him from certain aspects of his inner being which he cannot consciously own and acknowledge.

Although projection and projective identification are unconscious defense mechanisms, you can begin to notice when you are projecting your anger onto others instead of facing it yourself. The following strategies will help:

- Notice how often you are sensitive to or afraid of the anger of others. For example, if your partner blows up or puts his fist through a wall, it is reasonable for you to be afraid of him, but if he simply tells you he is angry with you, it is not reasonable to be afraid, especially if he has never become violent. If your fear does not seem warranted, it makes more sense to ask yourself whether it is your own anger you are afraid of or if your partner is reminding you of someone from your past who was violent or abusive.

- Notice how often you become critical of someone else's anger. It is quite common to be critical of the very behavior in others that we have disowned in ourselves. Although not all criticisms of others are projections, any time your response to another person seems more intense than the situation warrants, you can be certain that something unconscious within you is being activated.

- Notice how often you think that others are angry with you. Instead of assuming someone is angry, check it out. If the person tells you that she is not angry, instead of assuming she is lying, take her at her word. Because you have a history of projecting your anger onto others, the chances are good that the other person is telling the truth.

- Notice how often you are attracted to or become involved with angry people. This is not a coincidence. Often we are attracted to those who have a quality we have rejected in ourselves but would like to recapture.

- Notice how often you allow others to act out your anger for you. Do you often complain to others about someone else? Do you notice that your friends and family seem to be able to get angry at those you complain about? Has anyone close to you ever confronted another person in your life for you?

EXERCISE: *Turning It Around*

1.   Make a list of all the people you think are angry with you.

2.   Next to each person's name, write down the reason you think he or she is angry.

3.   Now challenge your thinking and ask yourself why it may actually be *you* who is angry. List all the reasons why you might be angry with each person. For example, after an entry like this—"Jason is angry with me because I got this coming holiday weekend off and he didn't"—confront your projective thinking and admit the truth: "No, that's not right. I'm the one who is angry with Jason, not the other way around. I've been upset with him ever since he got that promotion last month and I didn't. I blame him for it when the truth is it was my own fault for being late to work so often."

Step Four: Acknowledge and Accept Your Anger

Once you have confronted your negative beliefs and your fear of anger and have begun to confront your projective thinking, you will be in a better place to begin working on reclaiming your anger. The next step will be to admit to yourself how often you feel angry and how angry you are.

- Begin by making a note in your anger journal every time you become aware that you are feeling angry.

- Write about your angry feelings. State the reasons why you are angry and describe how it feels to be angry, including how it feels in your body.

- Write down what you'd like to do with your anger. Don't hold back. These are just thoughts and words, not actions. For example, you might end up writing, "I'd like to scream in his face," or "I'd like to slap that look off his face," or "I'd like to punch him out."

- Once you've written down all the things you'd like to do to this person, remind yourself that just because you have angry thoughts doesn't mean you're hurting anyone. People can't read your mind and they are not hurt by your thoughts in any way. In fact, in your case, you're more likely to hurt others by denying your anger than by admitting it to yourself.

The more you admit when you are angry and allow yourself to think angry thoughts, the less you will need to project your anger onto other people or have them act out their anger for you. Even so, be prepared to feel guilty whenever you allow yourself to feel angry. When this happens, tell yourself the following:

- "I'm only human and humans get angry."

- "I have a right to get angry."

- "Thinking angry thoughts doesn't hurt the other person."

You're in the process of changing some deep-seated beliefs, and it will take some time for you to get comfortable with your anger. But the more you practice reclaiming your anger, the less guilty and uncomfortable you will feel.

Specific Advice for Ventriloquists

Aaron began therapy with me at his wife's insistence. He had become convinced that others were out to harm him, and his wife was afraid he was becoming mentally ill, perhaps suffering from paranoia. From the way Aaron had described his problem on the phone, I was not concerned about this. I thought that perhaps he had a problem owning his anger.

Aaron had been raised in a very violent household. He frequently witnessed his father beating his mother, and he and his brother were severely punished by his father for even the smallest infraction. Aaron grew up to be a very mild-mannered, passive man who never showed his anger. He was married once before but got divorced soon afterward because his wife complained that he was too distant and aloof. He and his current wife seemed to get along very well, mostly due to the fact that she demanded very little of him in terms of interaction or affection.

Aaron had always felt victimized in his dealings with people. He felt his employers took advantage of him and didn't pay him what he deserved, and he felt his coworkers stole his ideas and competed with him for promotions, sometimes using underhanded means to win. But recently he had begun to fear that his boss and coworkers had banded together and devised a plan to force him to quit his job. His wife, Karen, who had always been supportive of him no matter how far-fetched his ideas were, put her foot down when it came to this latest idea.

"She thinks I've gone too far this time. She doesn't believe me— she thinks I've gone off the deep end," Aaron shared with me. But Aaron insisted that his perceptions were right—that there actually was a plan. I knew better than to try to convince him otherwise, so instead I focused on getting him to express his feelings about what he perceived was going on.

At first all he could talk about was his fear, but eventually he opened up and acknowledged how angry he was at his colleagues for trying to push him out. This led to his sharing with me how he had always felt that other people were angry with him. When I asked why he felt this way, he said it was because they misunderstood him and felt that he was hostile toward them.

It took several sessions before Aaron was willing to talk about the possibility that others might have been picking up on hostility in him that he himself did not recognize. Eventually he was able to make a connection between this situation and how he had been forced to hide the hostility he felt toward his father. Aaron had always been afraid that his father would kill him if he ever discovered how Aaron really felt about him.

Over time, Aaron was able to begin acknowledging and expressing his anger toward others. He found that the more he did so, the less convinced he was that other people were out to get him, including the people at work. "I guess all along it was my own anger that I was seeing in others," he shared with me (projective identification). It took even more time before he was able to address the core of his problem—his rage at his father—without fearing he would lose total control or that his father would somehow magically find out about it.

My Own Experience with Projective-Aggression

I had a similar experience to Aaron's when I was in my mid-twenties. I had begun therapy to work on feelings of depression and was focusing on my anger toward my mother. I had had a car accident and was suddenly afraid to go on the freeway. No matter how far I had to travel, I would take side streets, which was very inconvenient and time-consuming. Then I suddenly became afraid that my apartment was going to be broken into. There was no rational reason for this—I didn't live in a high-crime area, and as far as I knew, no one else's apartment had been broken into in my neighborhood.

During one session I spoke to my therapist about my fears. Without missing a beat, she said to me, "You're not afraid that someone is going to break into your apartment, you're afraid that your anger is going to break out." Her words were so true and so profound that they absolutely stopped me in my tracks. I was afraid of my own anger. I was afraid of what I would do if I acknowledged how much rage I felt toward my mother. My own anger felt so intense, so violent, that I couldn't own it. I had to project it into the world, where it manifested in my fear of another car crash or someone breaking into my apartment and murdering me.

If you identify with Aaron's story or mine, or if you recognize yourself from the previous descriptions of this anger style, there are things you can do to change.

- Every time you think someone is angry with you, assume for now that it is you who is angry with him or her. This is crucial if you are going to break your tendency to project your anger onto other people. It will be difficult at first because you will no doubt feel certain that it is the other person who is angry. But once you check in with yourself and discover it is actually you who is angry, you will gradually begin to recognize your projections. This doesn't mean that there might not be times when the other person is also angry with you. But unless he confronts you directly with his anger, it is none of your business.

- If you have begun to fear that others are out to get you, ask yourself whether you are out to get them instead. Be honest with yourself about just how angry you are at the people you fear are against you. Give yourself permission to really feel your anger. Write about it. If you can, tell someone you trust about your anger.

- If someone tells you he isn't angry, believe him. In this one area of your life, you are not the best judge of the situation. This will take a huge leap of faith on your part, but the chances are far greater that the other person is telling you the truth than that you are telling yourself the truth in this particular situation.

- Revisit any unfinished business you have with your parents or other caretakers who neglected, abandoned, or abused you and give yourself permission to become angry at them. You don't have to do it directly—in fact, they need never know about how angry you are. You can release your anger without them ever finding out.

EXERCISE: *The Anger Letter*

1. Write an anger letter to each person from your childhood toward whom you harbor angry feelings. Tell them exactly how you feel. Don't hold back anything. Remember, they need never read your letters or even learn about your anger.

2. Once you have written your letters, you can choose to keep them for future reference, tear them up, burn them in a symbolic gesture, or mail them.

3. If you choose to send a letter, make sure you are willing and able to deal with the person's reaction. You may wish to seek the advice of a professional therapist before making this important decision or to make sure you have the necessary support to help you cope with the other person's reactions to your letter.

Specific Advice for the Innocent Victim

Maria came to see me because she was terrified of her husband's anger: "He has a very bad temper—you never know what is going to set him off. Everything can be going along just fine when suddenly he explodes."

When I asked Maria why she had stayed with him for fifteen years, she explained, "Because most of the time he's a great guy. He's charming and funny, and he's a great father. The kids adore him."

"But aren't your children also afraid of him?" I asked.

"Yes, I suppose they are, but they've just learned to lay low when he's angry and to try not to provoke him."

It soon became clear to me that Maria had an investment in staying with her husband and that she was not willing to recognize that she was endangering herself and her children. As I usually do with new clients who are having marital problems, I asked her to tell me the story of their courtship and the reasons why she found her husband attractive in the first place.

She told me: "I was a very shy, quiet girl. I was raised in a very traditional Mexican home where children were expected to mind their parents no matter what and to never talk back. I met Luis right out of high school. I fell in love with him right away. He was so funny and such a talker—the opposite of me. He had so many stories to tell and he knew so much about so many things. And he wasn't afraid to stand up for himself! No one messed with Luis. They all respected him."

As we talked further, it became more and more apparent that Maria had been attracted to Luis because he was so different from her. The most significant difference was that Luis expressed his anger very openly. Maria admired this because she had never been allowed to express her anger. Even his bad temper didn't deter Maria. "When he would get mad and blow up at some waiter or store clerk for not giving him good service, I felt proud of him. I'd never have the nerve to do that," she told me.

When Maria married Luis, she began to experience his anger firsthand. "I hate it when he yells at me or the kids," she asserted once more. I knew there was a payoff for Maria, even though she might not immediately recognize it. "Is there anything positive about Luis's anger?" I asked. "Does it serve any positive function in the marriage?"

"Well, if he didn't keep the kids in line, I know I couldn't. Kids today don't respect their parents like we did. They stand up to their parents and talk back. If my kids did that with me, I don't know what I'd do. I couldn't handle it. So in that way I'm glad Luis gets on them." Because Maria was afraid to express her own anger, she allowed Luis to do it for her.

Maria didn't realize that she and her children were being emotionally abused by Luis's explosive episodes. As a consequence, their self-esteem was being damaged and their self-worth was being diminished. Maria's two sons were acting out at school, getting into fights, and bullying other children. Her daughter was so excruciatingly shy and withdrawn that she could hardly speak to adults. Maria and her children were paying a huge price so that Maria didn't have to own her own anger.

For Maria, becoming angry was perceived as something wrong, dangerous—something a woman doesn't do. Her rightful role was to obey and support her husband and be a good mother to her children. She could not acknowledge angry feelings inside herself, so she married someone who would act them out for her.

Your situation may not be as extreme as Maria's, or it may be worse. Whatever it is, if you are with an angry or abusive partner so that he or she can act out your anger for you, you are paying a huge price. If you have children, they are undoubtedly being damaged by your partner's harsh words, explosive episodes, or physical abuse. This makes you partly responsible for the harm that is coming to them. Standing by while someone else abuses your children sends them several messages: (1) that you don't care enough about them to protect them or to get them away from the abusive person; (2) you are selfishly focusing more on your own needs than on theirs; (3) it is okay to allow someone to abuse you and to not stand up for yourself.

If you identify with Maria or recognize that your partner is acting out your anger for you, you must begin to recognize the tyranny of innocence. Playing the Innocent Victim may help you to avoid your own anger, but you do so at the cost of your self-esteem, your ability to trust others, and the loss of personal power. If you have children and you put up with angry, hostile, or abusive behavior toward yourself or toward them, you are being a silent partner—a partner who stands by while his or her children are being abused.

Specific Advice for Anger Magnets

I met Julie when I first began my career as assistant director and head counselor at a shelter for battered women. Like many women who were forced to flee their abusive husbands due to repeated beatings,

Julie had been involved with several abusive men in addition to her present husband. The fact that she had a pattern of being involved with abusive men did not elude Julie, and by the time she came to the shelter, she was ready to confront the reasons for her pattern.

Like most women who are physically abused by husbands and boyfriends, Julie had come from an abusive home. Her father had beaten her mother on a regular basis, and Julie and her two sisters often witnessed this abuse. Not surprisingly, Julie didn't realize that both her mother and father had set her up to be abused when she was an adult and that she was just following their example. Although the reason for Julie's pattern may have been obvious to those of us working in the shelter, most people in her situation are unable to see this pattern on their own. Once Julie recognized her pattern and its origin, she was in a much better position to avoid repeating it.

While your pattern of being attracted to and attracting abusive people may not be as dramatic as Julie's, it is no doubt just as disconcerting to find yourself involved with the same type of person and making the same mistakes over and over again. You can break your pattern, no matter how ingrained it may seem to be. Here are some suggestions to help you:

- Face the fact that it is not a coincidence that you have a pattern of attracting angry people or being attracted to them.

- If you have doubts that you have a pattern, make a list of all the people with whom you've had an intimate relationship. Circle the people who could be characterized as angry, abusive, or violent.

- Begin to recognize that at least some of the reason for your attraction to angry people is because you have disowned your own anger.

- Recognize that your pattern probably had its origin in your childhood. It is important that you discover exactly how your pattern began and that you begin to work on your unfinished business in order to break it.

EXERCISE: *Discovering Your Pattern*

1. Make a vertical line down the center of a piece of paper. In one column, list your mother's positive and negative characteristics. Include such traits as impatient, generous, angry, critical, tolerant, loyal, quiet, and so on.

2. In the other column, list your father's characteristics.

3. On another piece of paper, draw two vertical lines dividing the page into three columns. In the first column, make a list of characteristics of your current partner.

4. In the second column, make a list of the character traits of your previous partner.

5. In the third column, make a list of the character traits of your partner before the previous one.

Take a look at your five lists and notice similarities. Circle the words that are repeated. Even though you may not use the same exact words, often the concepts may be similar.

PART THREE

Moving Ahead and Moving Beyond

CHAPTER 10

Honoring Other People's Anger

I feel good about the way I express my own anger now. But I still have problems dealing with other people's anger. I still get afraid if someone raises his voice, and I don't know how to resolve conflicts with other people.

—SALLY, AGE 48

Although our focus has been on learning how to honor your anger and change your unhealthy anger style, it is equally important that you learn how to honor other people's anger, particularly those who are close to you. In order to accomplish this I suggest you read about each anger style in this book and discover the style of each of your loved ones. The information and strategies in this chapter will also help. The first part of the chapter will focus on general information you can utilize in learning how to deal with other people's anger no matter what their anger style. In the second part of the chapter, I give you individualized advice for some of the specific anger styles.

The Importance of Listening

When we are angry, most of us have the strong and abiding need to be heard. We want the other person to understand why we are upset.

Once we feel that the other person hears us, understands us, and feels for us, we are often able to let go of our anger. But if we feel that the other person does not hear us, we are likely to remain angry or even to become angrier.

If you really want to resolve a conflict with someone, the most important thing you can do is listen carefully as she tells you why she is angry. Don't argue with her, don't cut her off, and don't become defensive or put her down for being angry. Just hear her out. The following attitudes and skills will help you to become a better listener:

1. *Listen actively.* An active listener is interested and concerned about what the other person is saying and what he or she is feeling. If you only pretend to listen, you won't fool anyone and will create feelings of anger and mistrust. In order to really hear what the other person is saying, stop all other activities and focus all your energy on the other person. Make eye contact if possible and nod occasionally to show that you hear and understand what is being said.

2. *Assume the other person has good intentions.* The effective listener assumes the other person has good intentions as opposed to viewing the other person as an enemy. He assumes the other person has a reason to be upset, and although he may not like the way the other person is acting, he does not assume she is a bad person.

3. *Listen with neutrality.* In order to fully understand the person and the reasons for the conflict, listen with a neutrality that suspends all critical judgment. Listen from a place of curiosity. Try to convey the message, "I respect you. Your thoughts and feelings are important to me, whether or not I agree with them."

4. *Put yourself in the other person's place.* It is important to be able to put yourself in the other person's place—to empathize with her. When people are angry, they want us to truly understand why they are upset; they want us to be able to see

things from their perspective. Try imagining how it feels to be in the other person's position.

5. *Listen with an open mind and an open heart.* Although it is not necessary to change your views in order to be a good listener, it is important to be open to the idea that you can learn something about yourself or your way of behaving from the feedback you are receiving or that you may be able to look at a situation from a different perspective. It is possible to learn something from everyone you meet.

Learn How to Fight Fairly

We can't avoid conflict. It is an inherent part of all relationships, especially romantic ones. The more vulnerable you feel and the more dependent you are on someone, the more power that person has to hurt you, and in turn, to anger you. The long-term success of any relationship depends greatly on discovering appropriate avenues for expressing and dealing with each other's anger.

Having the ability to freely express anger with one another is a sign of a solid, healthy relationship. Relationships in which one or both partners are unable to acknowledge their own anger or listen to the anger of their partner tend to be fragile and stilted as opposed to strong and spontaneous. Neither partner may have the confidence that the relationship can withstand the expression of anger.

Instead of fearing anger, set ground rules with which both you and the other person can live. This will help you begin on equal footing psychologically. You can create your own ground rules, but I suggest they include the following basic assumptions:

- We will take turns hearing each other out.

- We will respect each other's position.

- We understand that each person has a right to his or her own opinion, feelings, and position.

- We will do our best to find a solution to our problem and the source of our anger.

- We both agree that there will be no blaming, personal attacks, low blows, threats, or intimidation.

- There will be no manipulation, diversionary ploys, or exploitative tactics.

- There is never an excuse for hitting, pushing, or any other form of abuse.

Scheduling a Fair Fight

Make a point of talking to the person you are upset with as soon as possible. The less time that elapses, the more productive your conversation will be. Conversely, the longer the time between being hurt and expressing it to the other person, the more problematic.

On the other hand, give yourself time to cool off before confronting your partner. Schedule a time when you both will be free to talk without being distracted or interrupted.

The following tips will help you learn to fight more fairly and effectively:

1. Don't argue while using drugs or alcohol.

2. Make sure you know what you are fighting about.

3. Stick to one issue at a time.

4. Describe your feelings or how the problem affects you.

5. Don't tell the other person how he or she thinks or feels.

6. Stay in the present, do not bring up past problems.

7. Take time-outs when tension builds up.

8. Aim at working out an acceptable solution or compromise but also leave room for "agreeing to disagree."

9. Don't allow your fight to drag on and on. Try to settle things, at least temporarily, in 30 minutes.

10. Commit to follow through. Seek counseling if unable to resolve a major conflict.

The Power of Apology

In addition to being heard, what most people want when they feel offended or hurt by our actions or inaction is an apology. Apology has the power to repair harm—mending relationships, soothing wounds and hurt pride, and healing broken hearts. By apologizing, you let the other person know that you regret having hurt him or her. Amazingly, this has the power to heal even the deepest wounds. Just as important, you let the person know you respect him and care about his feelings.

Apology is also a way of showing empathy for the wronged person and a way of acknowledging an act that can't go unnoticed without compromising the relationship. It can disarm the anger of the other person, prevent further misunderstandings, and bridge the distances between people. If your apology is sincere and you are genuinely sorry for what you have done, the other person's anger may dissipate or dissolve right on the spot. This is especially true if your action was unintentional, such as inadvertently saying something that hurt the other person's feelings.

To recap, in order to resolve conflicts,

- Listen with neutrality and with an open heart and open mind
- Empathize with the other person
- Set ground rules for resolving conflicts
- Apologize to the other person

General Prescription for Dealing with Those with an Aggressive Anger Style

The following strategies will help you cope if you feel attacked by someone with an aggressive anger style:

1. *Calm down.* Take a few deep breaths and count to ten. If you start feeling like you are going to lose control, find an excuse to leave. Come back when you feel more in control.

2. *Lower your voice.* Generally speaking, when people are upset, they tend to speak in a loud voice. If you raise your voice to counter theirs, the confrontation is more likely to escalate out of control. By lowering your voice, you will deescalate the situation and help both of you to calm down. If the louder the other person speaks the softer you answer, the other person will also have to calm down in order to hear you.

3. *Don't take it personally.* Recognize that the other person is upset and it may or may not have anything to do with you. Even if he or she is upset about something you have done or left undone, you don't need to take in insults or personal attacks against you. Try to stay as detached as possible and focus on solving the problem.

4. *Don't cry.* Crying will cause the other person to lose respect for you and may invite him or her to attack you when you are down.

5. *Don't yell.* Even if the other person begins to yell, don't join in. Yelling won't resolve anything and will probably make matters worse.

6. *Don't stay.* If the other person becomes emotionally abusive or threatens physical violence, end the discussion and leave as soon as possible.

Specific Advice for Dealing with Eruptors

Eruptors may start a discussion or argument in a pleasant enough manner but will often break out into a temper tantrum as soon as you disagree with them or as a way of trying to intimidate you into giving them their way. This tactic can be quite effective, especially if your guard is down.

Eruptors are usually unable to articulate why they feel threatened, which is why their initial impulse is to become angry, to suspect others, or to blame others. By discovering what characteristics or behaviors in yourself and others make an Eruptor feel threatened, you may be able to avoid these behaviors in this person's presence. This may make you feel as if you are having to walk on eggshells around an Eruptor, and in many ways that is what it is like. This doesn't mean you shouldn't stand up for yourself if an Eruptor is mistreating you or that you have to give up important aspects of yourself or your life; it just means that if you can avoid a behavior that triggers an Eruptor's anger, you will both be happier.

Once an Eruptor does explode, she needs time to vent her fears and misgivings, even if she seems to go on and on. If she does not run down in a reasonable amount of time, however, or if you are beginning to feel beaten down or abused by her words, interrupt her and call for a time-out. Explain that you understand it is not always easy to control one's temper, but you can't hear anymore at this time. If she continues in spite of your request, simply walk away. If she follows you, go to a public place where she is more likely to feel embarrassed by her own ranting or yelling.

If an Eruptor explodes during a phone conversation, calmly say, "Please call back when you have calmed down," or "I'm more than willing to listen to you, but first I want you to calm down."

Specific Advice for Dealing with Blamers

The following information will help if you are dealing with someone who frequently blames you or makes false accusations against you. This advice also works for dealing with Ventriloquists.

- *Don't defend.* Trying to prove that you really didn't do something can make you feel foolish, childish, and guilty even when you are innocent. It also puts you in a one-down position. Besides, a Blamer or Ventriloquist isn't going to believe you no matter what you say.

- *Don't deny.* Repeated denial also puts you in a one-down position and can make you look and feel like a child ("Did not!" "Did too!").

- *Don't counterattack.* If you choose to strike back or try to win the argument with a Blamer, you'll only make him angrier. If you do it with a Ventriloquist, you'll fall into the projection and projective identification trap that the Ventriloquist has unconsciously set for you.

- *Don't withdraw.* If you remain passive and silent, you will be more likely to absorb the other person's criticism. This will cause your sense of self-esteem and personal power to deteriorate.

What should you do? Remain as neutral as you can. You may also want to restate or paraphrase the key points of what the other person is saying to show that you are actively listening and that you understand what the other person is saying. This does not mean that you have to agree with him. When you have had enough, tell him that you would like to end the conversation for now and continue it later if he needs to. Then simply walk away.

Specific Advice for Dealing with Those with a Passive Anger Style

The best thing you can do to encourage someone with a passive anger style to begin to express his or her anger in a direct and open way is to make it safe for this person to do so.

- Let her know you are open to hearing her anger. Tell her you want to encourage her direct expression of anger and want to help her.

- Don't react negatively when she does express her anger. While assuring her with words will help, your actions will speak much louder. When she does begin to express her anger directly, don't become defensive. Listen calmly to what she has to say, then give your side of the story.

- Validate her anger. Let her know it's okay to be angry by saying something like "I'm sorry you're so angry. What happened?"

- Let her know when she appears angry. A gentle nudge from you such as, "You seem angry. Is there anything wrong?" may give her the permission she needs to express her anger. This doesn't mean you should hover over her, but paying attention to her moods may be helpful.

- Be a positive role model for expressing anger assertively and directly.

- Admit when you are wrong and apologize.

- Let her know that you respect her right to voice her opinions and beliefs, even when they differ from yours.

Specific Advice for Dealing with Those with a Passive-Aggressive Anger Style

The most difficult job you will have is convincing the person with a passive-aggressive anger style that it is okay to be angry. In order for him to own up to how he feels and expose his submerged hostility, you will need to provide an atmosphere that is supportive and nonthreatening. This means you'll need to take a noncritical, accepting stance when he begins to express his anger directly—an attitude that shows you accept him for who he is, anger and all. It also means you'll need to squelch any impulse you may have to retaliate. Since he is finally able to risk speaking his anger directly, by all means don't respond with sarcasm, criticism, making fun of him, or in any other way that would indicate it is not appropriate for him to express his feelings. If you respond with hostility, you will undoubtedly shut him down.

The way you respond will have a major impact on whether he will feel comfortable enough to express his anger in the future. This will be especially difficult for you if you are uncomfortable with the open expression of anger. If this is the case, you'll need to work on giving yourself permission to express anger (see chapter 7) before you will be able to deal with someone else's anger in a positive way. Otherwise, whether it is your conscious intention or not, you'll be sending the message with your facial expression and your body language that it is not acceptable for him to get angry, you don't want to hear his anger, or you don't want to deal with his anger.

Some people have discovered that they were actually more comfortable when their partner, friend, or other loved one was dealing with his or her anger in a passive-aggressive way. When she starts to express her anger directly, they quickly try to humor her out of it ("Oh, never mind that now. It doesn't really matter. Let's just have a good time"). However irritating her passive-aggressive behavior may have been, suddenly it seems safer than dealing with her direct aggression. You may find that humoring her out of her anger is preferable in the short run, but over time it will continue to have destructive and insidious effects on the relationship.

Fighting with Someone with a Passive-Aggressive Style

Initially there is no such thing as a fair fight with a person with a passive-aggressive anger style. He will need you to help him learn that he can face conflict head on and still maintain his dignity and power. The more you assert your strength and attempt to communicate in a direct way, the more he'll feel weak and taken advantage of.

Fighting with someone with a passive-aggressive style is particularly difficult because she is likely to perceive herself as being victimized. She'll turn the tables and the subject will suddenly change from how she procrastinates to how you are too impatient and not understanding enough about how she can't take pressure.

A person with a passive-aggressive anger style will undoubtedly view compromise as a loss on her part. If she has to make the slightest compromise, she will see it as a huge concession for which you should feel grateful or guilty.

Another ploy to get you off the subject and sabotage a fair fight is the empty apology. This type of apology is clearly just a ploy to get you off his back or to stop the argument, and it is usually meaningless.

The key is for you to stay focused on the goal at hand—resolving the conflict—not in being right or making your point. If you continue to communicate openly and honestly and follow the fair fighting rules suggested earlier, the person with a passive-aggressive anger style will eventually develop a sense of trust that you won't take advantage of his vulnerability and that you are not trying to dominate and control him.

Specific Advice for Dealing with Ventriloquists

The most important thing to remember when you are dealing with a Ventriloquist is not to buy into his or her anger or accusations. If you have low self-esteem or are easily influenced, it may be especially difficult for you to not take in what a Ventriloquist is saying. You must remember that this person is projecting his anger onto you. His accusations have little or nothing to do with you. If you begin to believe his accusations, you have essentially collaborated in helping him avoid his own anger.

If you behave in such a way as to make his accusations appear to be true (such as becoming irritated, raising your voice, or engaging in a heated argument), you will likely get caught up in something you will wish you had avoided. You'll also help the Ventriloquist to feel more justified in his accusations and to feel more in control. Here are some do's and don'ts to help you:

- The best way to handle a Ventriloquist's accusations is to remain as neutral as possible.

- Don't argue and don't become defensive. If he accuses you of being angry at him, simply respond with something like, "No, I'm not at all angry with you."

- Don't ask him to explain why he thinks you are angry. This will only encourage him to continue his accusations.

CHAPTER 11

Getting Beyond Your Anger

*I feel good about allowing myself to get angry, but I don't want to
stay that way. I don't want to get stuck in my anger.*

—AMY, AGE 37

In addition to learning to handle your anger in a healthier, more balanced way, you also need to learn how to put your anger behind you. Anger is a very powerful emotion that can be used in many positive ways—to motivate us toward change, to strengthen us against our adversaries, and to protect us against pain—but sometimes we get stuck in our anger and are unable to move past it.

We all experience hurt, disappointment, betrayal, deprivation, and even violence. How do we cope with such pain? How do we avoid becoming as destructive as those who have harmed us? And how do we get past our anger so that we can move on with our lives?

Earlier in the book I introduced the two healthy anger styles: assertive and reflective. Both are positive ways of addressing the problems that anger can signal or the underlying emotions that triggered anger in the first place. Both are also positive ways of moving past your anger. Those who naturally tend to be Anger-Outs may be drawn to the assertive model, while those who are Anger-Ins may be more attracted to the reflective model.

If you adopt the assertive anger style, you communicate your distress to the person with whom you are upset in a direct way. You don't blame, you don't emotionally abuse by using sarcasm or belittling the other person, and you don't belabor the point. By being assertive in this manner, you optimize your chances of being heard—which is what we all need in order to get past our anger. You also take a stand by asserting that you will no longer tolerate a certain behavior in the future. This empowering gesture takes you out of the victim arena and helps you get past your anger.

If you take on the reflective anger style, you focus on what your anger is trying to tell you about a situation, another person, or yourself. You discover and address your underlying emotions. And, most important, you view your anger as a teacher. You focus on what you can learn from your anger and from the experience and on how you can prevent a similar situation from happening again. Much of what you have been learning about how to handle your anger in a healthy way is part of the reflective anger style. Here are the steps to follow if you choose to take on this healthy style:

1. Give yourself time to calm down. This includes taking a time-out if necessary.

2. Ask yourself, "What is my anger trying to tell me?" For example, is it telling you that you have been building up too much stress? Is it telling you that you have been triggered and that you are reacting to something that happened in the past? Or, is it telling you that there is a problem in your relationship with a certain person that needs to be addressed?

3. Ask yourself, "Is there something I need to do or change?" This could involve aspects of the assertive anger style, such as confronting another person. It may involve changing something about yourself, such as finding a constructive outlet for pent-up anger, or it may involve changing the way you behave or interact with another person.

4.   Ask yourself, "What is the underlying emotion? What feeling triggered my anger? Was I hurt by what someone said or did? Did I feel threatened (afraid) by what someone did or said? Or was I shamed by the situation? Whatever emotion was triggered by the situation, how can I best address this emotion?"

5.   Ask yourself, "What can I learn from this experience?" For example, perhaps you learned, once again, how important it is to address issues as they come up instead of letting things build up inside. Perhaps you learned that it is best for you to stay away from a particular person or to avoid a certain situation. Or perhaps you learned not to judge others as harshly and that you need to work on being more empathetic.

6.   Ask yourself, "What do I need in order to let go of my anger or to forgive the other person?"

Why Do We Remain Angry?

In spite of your best efforts to handle your anger in an assertive or reflective way, sometimes you may remain stuck in your anger, unable to move on, unable to forgive. Why does this happen? You may tend to remain angry because

- You still feel threatened by the other person. If the other person remains a threat to you, either because she continues the same behavior or because she refuses to admit that she did anything wrong, forgiveness can be extremely difficult. In these cases, remaining angry may serve as protection against further harm.

- You still feel unheard by the other person. There is nothing more frustrating than feeling like the other person did not really listen to you when you stood up for yourself and explained why his or her behavior was unacceptable to you. It is often difficult to forgive when you feel unheard, either because the other person was too busy defending himself, or because he never seemed to be able to put himself in your shoes and really understand your feelings.

- You feel the other person has not taken sufficient responsibility for his or her actions. If the other person has not acknowledged the fact that she has inconvenienced, disappointed, or harmed you, it is difficult to forgive. This is especially true if the problem has not been rectified or restitution has not been made.

- You feel you need an apology. Psychological research and anecdotal evidence show that when people apologize for something they have done, it is easier to forgive them.

Why Is It Important to Forgive?

When I was writing my book, *The Power of Apology,* I discovered several studies showing that remaining angry, obsessing about revenge thoughts, and constantly reliving a painful incident are physically and emotionally stressful, while forgiveness is healing to the body, mind, and spirit. For example, over the past decade Robert Enright, Ph.D., of the University of Wisconsin-Madison, has investigated the nature of forgiveness. He and other researchers have found that those who forgive someone who has hurt them seem to reap significant mental health benefits. And the act of forgiving appears to be one of the basic processes that keeps personal relationships functioning, according to studies of long-married couples.

Research also shows that forgiveness can be liberating. Carrying around a desire for revenge or a need to avoid someone is not healthy. Hostility and aggression are linked to a host of health problems. Research by Enright and his colleagues has consistently found that people who are able to forgive benefit through a decrease in anxiety, depression, and hostility, and an increase in hope, self-esteem, and existential well-being.

A 1998 Stanford study showed that forgiveness can substantially reduce the amount of anger a person harbors (remember, anger has been associated with an increased risk of heart attacks and it negatively influences the body's immune system). The notion that anger and an unwillingness to forgive can damage us physically has gotten a boost from new research from the University of Wisconsin in Madison. Researchers have found that the less people are able to forgive, the more diseases they have and the more medical symptoms they report. "We've been surprised at how strong forgiveness can be as a healing agent for people," says Enright, professor of educational psychology at the university.

In addition to making us more compassionate, humane beings, forgiveness brings many other personal benefits:

- Forgiveness helps relieve some of the pain you feel due to the offense and helps the wound begin to heal.

- When you forgive, you take an important step toward mending and rebuilding the relationship between yourself and the wrongdoer.

- When you forgive, you remove a burden that has been weighing you down.

- Forgiveness helps you to go on with your life instead of holding onto the past.

- Forgiveness makes you a better person and improves your overall mental and emotional health.

Forgiveness is a process that takes time, but for many, all the time in the world won't help them to forgive. Some feel that no apology can undo the damage that has been done. Others believe that the wrongdoer should make restitution of some kind before they can forgive. Still others don't trust that the other person won't hurt them again if they forgive.

In some cases, these feelings may be warranted, and the best you can do is move on, closing the door to any possibility of a continued relationship or reunion. But in other situations, these feelings may be smokescreens hiding the real reason for your inability to forgive—obstacles that not only prevent you from forgiving but from moving past the pain and going on with your life. These obstacles include pride, having unreasonable expectations of others, lack of empathy, and black and white thinking (more detailed information on these obstacles can be found in my book, *The Power of Apology*).

Forgiveness is not a self-righteous or Polyanna-like turning of the other cheek or a condoning of abhorrent behavior. Neither is it forgetting. The most important component of forgiveness is empathy. Forgiving requires you to acknowledge the other person's actions as harmful, but then to empathize with the other person. If you can understand the deep pain from which hurtful actions inflicted on you often arise, then you can be compassionate. In that act of compassion, you move from the role of the victim and see beyond the actions to the heart of the other person.

Epilogue

It takes real courage and strength to admit that you have an unhealthy anger style and to begin changing it. If you've been able to do this, you've taken the first important step in improving your life, and I want to commend you. It will take even more courage and strength to continue making the changes necessary to transform your unhealthy anger style into a healthy one, but you can do it. You wouldn't have read this book if you weren't serious about changing.

In the end, it doesn't matter whether you are an Anger-In or an Anger-Out, whether you learn to communicate your feelings and needs in a more assertive way or learn to contain your emotions and focus on what you can learn from them. What really matters is that you take responsibility for your anger and other emotions instead of blaming others, that you honor your emotions instead of allowing others to talk you out of them, and that you take control of your emotions instead of allowing them to run your life. Your anger, and all the feelings underneath, are your teachers, your guides. If you listen to what your feelings are telling you, what your body is telling you, you will have a compass to guide you through most of life's journeys. The more you connect with your feelings, the less confused you will be and the more in control of your life you will feel.

Those who have allowed others to control their lives will begin to trust that they can make their own choices, including walking away from relationships that are stifling or abusive. Those who have needed to control others in an attempt to gain some sense of control of their own lives will learn that true control comes from knowing what they are feeling at any given time and taking responsibility for that feeling instead of blaming someone else for it. Those who have been fearful of their emotions will learn that the more they risk feeling and expressing their emotions, the less dangerous these emotions become.

Anger, like all so-called negative emotions, needs to come out of the dark and into the light. Only then can you harness its power and utilize it for good instead of allowing it to fester and grow until it becomes toxic. Stop using your anger to control others, to punish others, or to punish yourself. Stop allowing others to use their anger against you to keep you quiet or keep you down. Instead, use your anger to mobilize you and strengthen your resolve. Use it to stand up for yourself and what you believe in. Use it to fight against all the inequities, abuse, and atrocities in the world.

Above all, stand up against those who try to oppress you, stand aside when it doesn't really matter who is right and who is wrong, and step down when you have risen up to dominate others.

References

Unattributed quotations are from interviews conducted by the author.

CHAPTER 1: ONE OF THE MOST IMPORTANT CHANGES YOU WILL EVER MAKE

Correctional Service of Canada, *Literature Review on Women's Anger and Other Emotions*, 2001.

De Angeles, Tori, "When Anger's a Plus," *APA Monitor,* vol. 34, no. 3, March 2003.

Kassinove, Howard, and R. Chip Tafrate, *Anger Management: The Complete Treatment Guidebook for Practice* (Atascadero, CA: Impact, 2002).

Simmons, Rachel, *Odd Girl Out: The Hidden Culture of Aggression in Girls* (New York: Harcourt Brace, 2002).

Thomas, Sandra P., Anger and its manifestations in women. In Sandra P. Thomas (Ed.), *Women and Anger,* pp. 40–67 (New York: Springer Publishing Company, Inc., 1993).

CHAPTER 2: THE FIRST STEPS TO DISCOVERING YOUR ANGER STYLE

Averill, J. R., Studies in anger and aggression: Implications for theories of emotion, *American Psychologist* 38 (1983): 1145–1160.

Dittmann, Melissa, *"Anger across the Gender Divide,"* *APA Monitor,* vol. 34, no. 3, March 2003.

Smith, Deborah, "Angry Thoughts, At-Risk Hearts," *APA Monitor,* vol. 34, no. 3, March 2003.

CHAPTER 3: DISCOVERING YOUR PRIMARY ANGER STYLE

Correctional Service of Canada, *Literature Review on Women's Anger and Other Emotions.*

CHAPTER 4: VARIATIONS ON A THEME: DISCOVERING YOUR SECONDARY ANGER STYLE

Correctional Service of Canada, *Literature Review on Women's Anger and Other Emotions.*

CHAPTER 5: THE FIRST STEPS TO CHANGE

Azar, Beth, "A New Stress Paradigm for Women," *APA Monitor,* vol. 31, no. 7, July/ August 2000.

Correctional Service of Canada, *Literature Review on Women's Anger and Other Emotions.*

Lerner, Harriet, *The Dance of Anger: A Woman's Guide to Changing the Patterns of Intimate Relationships* (New York; Harper & Row, 1985).

Nathanson, Donald, *Shame and Pride: Affect, Sex and the Birth of the Self* (New York: W. W. Norton and Company, 1992).

Thomas, Sandra P., Theoretical and empirical perspectives on anger, *Issues in Mental Health Nursing* 11 (1990): 203–216.

CHAPTER 6: MODIFYING OR TRANSFORMING AN AGGRESSIVE STYLE

Correctional Service of Canada, *Literature Review on Women's Anger and Other Emotions.*

Engel, Beverly, *The Emotionally Abusive Relationship* (New York: John Wiley and Sons, 2002).

Gentry, Doyle W., *Anger Free: Ten Basic Steps to Managing Your Anger* (New York: Harper Collins, 1999).

Kawachi, I., et al., A prospective study of anger and coronary heart disease. The Normative Aging Study, *Circulation* 94 (1996): 2090–2095.

Person, Ethel Spector, Introduction. In Robert A. Glick and Steven P. Roose (Eds.), *Rage, Power and Aggression* (New Haven, CT: Yale University Press, 1993).

Tavris, Carol, *Anger: The Misunderstood Emotion* (New York: Simon and Schuster, 1982).

Thomas, Sandra P., Introduction. In Sandra P. Thomas (Ed.), *Women and Anger,* pp. 1–19. (New York: Springer Publishing Company, Inc., 1993).

White, Jacquelyn W., and Robin M. Kowalski, Deconstructing the myth of the nonaggressive woman. *Psychology of Women Quarterly* 18 (1994): 487–508.

Williams, Redford, and Virginia Williams, *Anger Kills: 17 Strategies for Controlling The Hostility That Can Harm Your Health* (New York: Harper Paperbacks, 1993).

CHAPTER 7: FROM PASSIVE TO ASSERTIVE

Engel, Beverly, *Loving Him without Losing You* (New York: John Wiley and Sons, 2000).

Gentry, *Anger Free: Ten Basic Steps to Managing Your Anger.*

Gilligan, Carol, *In a Different Voice: Psychological Theory and Women's Development* (Cambridge, MA: Harvard University Press, 1993).

Lerner, *The Dance of Anger.*

Smith, Jane E., Michael C. Hilliard, Russell A. Walsh, Steven R. Kubacki, and C. D. Morgan, Rorschach assessment of purging and nonpurging bulimics, *Journal of Personality Assessment* 56, 2 (1991): 277–288.

Tavris, *Anger: The Misunderstood Emotion.*

Thomas, *Women and Anger.*

Valentis, Mary, and Anne Devane, *Female Rage.* (New York: Carol Southern Books, 1994).

Woodman, Marion, *The Owl Was a Baker's Daughter: Obesity, Anorexia Nervosa and the Repressed Feminine* (Ontario, Canada: Inner City, 1980).

CHAPTER 8: FROM PASSIVE-AGGRESSIVE TO ASSERTIVE

Engel, *The Emotionally Abusive Relationship.*

Engel, Beverly, *The Emotionally Abused Woman* (Los Angeles: Lowell House, 1990).

Wetzler, Scott, *Living with the Passive-Aggressive Man* (New York: Simon and Schuster, 1992).

CHAPTER 9: TRANSFORMING THE PROJECTIVE-AGGRESSIVE STYLE

Scarf, Massie, "Meeting our Opposites in Husbands and Wives" in Connie Zweig, *Meeting the Shadow* (Los Angeles: Jeremy Tarcher, 1991).

CHAPTER 10: HONORING OTHER PEOPLE'S ANGER

Engel, *The Power of Apology.*

Wetzler, *Living with the Passive-Aggressive Man.*

CHAPTER 11: GETTING BEYOND YOUR ANGER

Engel, *The Power of Apology.*

Enright, Robert D., *Exploring Forgiveness* (Wisconsin: University of Wisconsin Press, 1996).

McCullough, Michael E., Steven J. Sandage and Everett L. Worthington, *To Forgive Is Human* (Illinois: InterVarsity Press, 1997).

Recommended Reading

ANGER

Gentry, Doyle W., *Anger-Free: Ten Basic Steps to Managing Your Anger* (New York: HarperCollins, 1999).

Gottlieb, Miriam M., *The Angry Self: A Comprehensive Approach to Anger Management* (Arizona: Zeig, Tucker and Co., 1999).

Harbin, Thomas J., *Beyond Anger: A Guide for Men* (New York: Marlowe and Company, 2000).

Lerner, Harriet Goldhor, *The Dance of Anger: A Woman's Guide to Changing the Patterns of Intimate Relationships* (New York: Harper and Row, 1985).

Tavris, Carol, *Anger: The Misunderstood Emotion* (New York: Simon and Schuster, 1982).

Williams, Redford, and Virginia Williams, *Anger Kills: 17 Strategies for Controlling the Hostility That Can Harm Your Health* (New York: Harper Paperbacks, 1993).

ANGER AND CHILDREN

Fried, Suellen, *Bullies and Victims: Helping Your Child Survive the Schoolyard Battlefield* (New York: M. Evans and Co., 1998).

PASSIVE-AGGRESSIVENESS

Wetzler, Scott, *Living with the Passive-Aggressive Man* (New York: Simon and Schuster, 1992).

STRESS REDUCTION

Davis, Martha, Matthew McKay, and Elizabeth Eshelman, *The Relaxation and Stress Reduction Workbook* (Oakland: New Harbinger, 2000).

Epstein, Robert, *The Big Book of Stress Relief Games* (New York: McGraw-Hill, 2000).

Kabat-Zinn, John, *Wherever You Go, There You Are: Mindfulness Meditations for Everyday Life* (New York: Hyperion, 1995).

Miller, Fred, and Mark Bryan, *How to Calm Down* (New York: Warner Books, 2003).

Apology

Engel, Beverly, *The Power of Apology: Healing Steps to Transform All Your Relationships* (New York: John Wiley and Sons, 2001).

Tavuchis, Nicholas, *Mea Culpa: A Sociology of Apology and Reconciliation* (California: Stanford University Press, 1991).

Empathy

Ciaramicoli, Arthur, and Katherine Ketcham, *The Power of Empathy: A Practical Guide to Creating Intimacy, Self-Understanding, and Lasting Love* (New York: Dutton, 2000).

Forgiveness

Enright, Robert D., *Exploring Forgiveness* (Madison, WI: University of Wisconsin Press, 1998).

Klein, Charles, *How to Forgive When You Can't Forget: Healing Our Personal Relationships* (New York: Berkley Publishing Group, 1997).

McCullough, Michael E., Steven J. Sandage, and Everett L. Worthington, *To Forgive Is Human: How to Put Your Past in the Past* (Illinois: InterVarsity Press, 1997).

Safer, Jeanne, *Forgiving and Not Forgiving: A New Approach to Resolving Intimate Betrayal* (New York: Avon, 1999).

Smedes, Lewis B., *Forgive and Forget: Healing the Hurts We Don't Deserve* (San Francisco: Harper and Row, 1984).

Index